GRIT & GRACE

THE TRANSFORMATION OF
A SHIP & A SOUL

DEBORAH RUDELL

Helping talented writers publish exceptional books

This book is a memoir. It reflects the author's present recollections of experiences over time. Some names have been changed to protect privacy, some events have been compressed, and some dialogue has been recreated.

Grit & Grace: The Transformation of a Ship & a Soul
Copyright © 2025 Deborah Rudell. All rights reserved.

Printed in the United States of America. For information, address Acorn Publishing, LLC
3943 Irvine Blvd. Ste. 218, Irvine, CA 92602

www.acornpublishingllc.com

Interior design by Kat Ross
Cover design by Damonza

ISBN-13: 979-8-88528-110-2 (hardcover)
ISBN-13: 979-8-88528-109-6 (paperback)
Library of Congress Control Number: 2024911502

Dedicated to Tosh, Nicole & Gavin, my family,
with Love & Gratitude
for all you have taught me.

Contents

Note to Reader   vii

Gale   1

Part One
THE DREAM

1. An Old Boat   9
2. A Plan   20
3. Assessing the Mess   26
4. Not a Six-Month Project   38

Part Two
THE BONES

5. Masts, Rebirthing & Regression   51
6. Floors, Stem & Sannyas   64
7. Belize & Master   71
8. Sharkys & Leaving the Farm   82
9. Alan Watts & Bronze   93
10. Portals, Drive By & Children Arrive   103
11. Keel & Crematorium   112
12. Keel Bolts, Mast Collars & Book Orders   121
13. Celebration & Land Sailing   132
14. Swami Sangeet Gavin & Crash   139
15. Speaking Up & Sheela's House   151
16. Maha'ulepu & Krishnamurti Lake   161
17. Priming & Carving   170
18. Caulking & Missing Tosh   174
19. Lover, Coving & Press Conference   186
20. Move Along, Ma'am   193
21. Unfit   202
22. End of the Ranch   214
23. Laguna Beach & Redemption   226

24. Bhagwan Leaves His Body, Dinghy & Knees   236
25. Painting, Upholstery & Trailer   245
26. Rigging & Rejected   254
27. Stepping the Masts   260
28. Launch   266

Part Three
THE REALITY

29. Aftermath & Malcolm X   275
30. Shakedown & Lost   285
31. Abandoned, Broken Gaff & End of Shakedown   299

Part Four
THE CROSSING

32. Elixir's Last Bath & Leaving Kauai   317
33. Turn Back, Baths, Brownies & Bear Hugs   330
34. Shakya in the Head, Waffles & Fish   342
35. The Shakes, Knocked Out & Jellyfish   350
36. Man Overboard & Land Ho   364

Epilogue   378

Rajneesh Backstory   385
Afterword   389
Glossary   393
End Notes   401
Acknowledgments   403
About the Author   407

Note to Reader

This book contains information about boat building and sailing. There is a Glossary at the end of the book that explains some nautical terms, expands on some subjects, and includes additional technical information that may be of interest to some. Glossary terms and subjects are marked with an asterisk throughout the narrative. The labeled illustration of a gaff-rigged schooner before the Glossary may help readers orient themselves to the many parts of a schooner.

Gale

Pacific Ocean
June 1992

Even if I screamed no one would hear me over the sound of the waves and the fierce wind; a wind so strong my slender body couldn't stay upright unless I held onto the boat. It was pitch black, and I was alone on the helm for the predawn watch aboard a fifty-foot wooden schooner. My husband slept in the cockpit, and three more crew members were tied into their bunks below.

The compass glowed dim red in the blackness, preserving my night vision. It was the only thing my eyes discerned except the occasional foamy wave tops that glowed briefly with limey phosphorescence before being swept under the dark water of the next wave. My fingers, slick with rain and spray, encircled the spokes of the wheel as I adjusted our heading according to the pale numbers of the compass. I struggled to keep the needle on 000, our northerly heading, but the violent pitching of the vessel made it almost impossible.

The end of June was supposed to be the ideal time to cross the Pacific from Hawaii to Washington, a time when conditions were the most stable. Yet here I was in forty-five knot winds. Technically, a gale.*

Harnessed to the boat, I clung to the wheel with my hands, to the decks with my bare toes, and to the compass heading with my eyes, my mind rapidly spinning out of control. Fear. Panic. Terror. *We'll be swamped, capsize, and drown.*

The sea was immensely powerful. *Elixir* was puny, fragile like a single piece of straw in a whitewater river. *The masts will break off like toothpicks; we'll tip over and sink.* I imagined myself sliding off the boat, the cold water seeping into my foul weather gear, the waves holding my head beneath the foaming sea, breathing in the salty water, gasping. My teeth clamped tight around a paper tongue. No saliva left. I tried licking salt-water from my lips, but I couldn't swallow.

What had I been thinking over the last five years of building this boat and deciding to sail it across the Pacific? How could I have ever thought it would be fun or exciting? How did I ever dare to presume I could learn to be at sea when conditions were less than ideal? Let alone in a gale?

Unable to find any relief from the deafening noise and violent motion of the storm, I tried to search inside myself for ways to navigate extreme distress and control my panic. All I found were images of me floating face down in the dark waves, alongside the corpses of my husband and son as we drifted among bits of a broken ship. And it was only our third night at sea; we'd only just begun our long ocean journey north.

What's that? My mind alerted me. *There's something on the rail.* I strained to see through the black night. *No, nothing.* Yet I sensed something there on the rail, despite the thrashing seas and the wail-scream in the rigging. Whatever it was, the beings I intuited on the rail caught my attention, gradually pulling my focus away from my terror and thoughts of drowning. I had read books about people in life threatening situations, during which they experienced visions or heard voices that assisted them to survive untenable ordeals.

Angels? Could that be possible? Is this what is happening to me? Has my mind snapped from the intensity of my circumstances?

There seemed to be several of them, round and smushing together. A perception rather than an actual vision, they appeared to be joking with each other, laughing so hard they nearly fell off the rail. *I am definitely going off my rails.*

It was as if they were enjoying the ride, and at the same time assuring me that, despite the enormity of the sea and the ferocity of the wind, the elements were merely frolicking. This communication was through a mixture of pictures, words, and feelings conveyed in a flash. *Frolicking? Really?* Wind at this speed rips branches off trees and causes cars to veer off the road. The extremes of the Pacific Ocean proved larger, stronger, and louder than any thunder and lightning I had ever experienced on the lake where I grew up in British Columbia.

As the sky gradually lightened and the wind subsided, I was in awe of where I was and how I'd ended up at sea. I thought about the unusual twists and turns of my life. Was it really only ten years ago that I had abandoned a conventional life to live in a commune? How had I gone from sannyasin,* disciple of a spiritual teacher, and focused on the inner, energetic world to become a sailor, a disciple of the sea and focused on the outer material world? Sitting in the cockpit and absorbing the new dawn light after the terrifying blackness of the night, my mind wandered back in time to Oregon and the Big Muddy Ranch. My awareness felt drawn to the moment when I saw my guru* and master, Bhagwan Shree Rajneesh, for the first time.

"You really are new, aren't you?" The red-clad, pony-tailed sannyasin laughed kindly when I asked her what 'drive-by' was. I was eating lunch with two thousand other devotees in the cafeteria on my first day at the communal Ranch in the fall of 1982.

"Bhagwan drives by on the road every day after lunch, and we line up along the edge and sing and dance and wave to Him. It's a daily celebration," she explained.

I followed the crowd out the door and back onto and off a bus, jostled and nudged into a line along the well-maintained gravel road. People stood quietly, some talking softly. My mind and heart were in turmoil. I had just left my home, family, and career to follow a spiritual path with a living master. While I had read His books, listened to His audiotapes, and watched His videos, I had never seen Him in person. *What would it be like?*

Eventually I saw a car in the distance and then the line of disciples came alive, clapping, singing and swaying to the songs from a group of musicians half a block away. Bhagwan drove slowly, one hand moved up and down, as He celebrated with us. His dark eyes scanned the thousands of happy faces lined up to greet Him.

Standing amongst strangers, my eyes wet with tears and shining with emotion, I watched the car Bhagwan was driving follow the road lined with disciples, getting closer and closer. The last vestiges of angst, the self-doubt, the wondering what I had done by giving up my life as I knew it, all disappeared as I looked in His eyes. I felt my body dance, and my hands clapped. It was as if we were all One. Unity at last, all consumed by our love for the Master, the Enlightened One. The One who had gone before us in realizing the true nature of this world. The One who could give us glimpses of our own promise, our own abilities to transcend the density and illusion of material existence to bring peace, joy, and love from heaven above down to the Earth.

The sting of salty spray on my face disturbed my daydream, the warm tears of my past expression of love and connection to my Master transformed into the cold ocean spray of today's reality. Is this how the Kingdom of Heaven reaches the Earth? Is this how the unseen world enters the seen? Is this the purpose of the twists and turns of a life path? Why life felt so confusing and derailed? The truth seemed so elusive and hard to grasp, to find the correct words.

As a pink blush started to permeate the gray of early day, the Ranch experience slowly faded from my mind. I could make out the rail now, emerging from the dark in a rosy glow, materializing into something solid and real, absent angels or anything else. The boat parts were like apparitions emerging from a fog, once again becoming part of a whole wooden ship. It was surreal here at sea, remembering all of the hours and days and years since first meeting her. Remembering especially that first day when I could not imagine her being whole and sailing the sea ever again.

Part One

THE DREAM

Chapter 1

An Old Boat

*"If you don't believe in something bigger than yourself,
go to sea."*

Boatyard, Kauai
January 7, 1988

We'd arrived on the island of Kauai just hours before and were on our way to the boatyard, eager to meet this ship and 'lady' of our dreams. Navigating through Lihue to the harbor, the winding road opened to a grassy field littered with decrepit vessels. None of them appeared capable of ever tasting the sea again. I anxiously looked for the boat that would become the center of our lives, scanning the yard for a likeness of the photos we had received in the mail.

"There she is, over there." Tosh, my husband, pointed excitedly as he drove around the access road to the back corner.

"Yikes, she is *huge!*" I exclaimed.

At fifty feet overall, she was the biggest boat in the yard and in far worse shape than the photos we'd seen. In those images her white topsides, black waterline, and burgundy bottom paint were clear and apparent, with rig and superstructure, including rails and cabins, all intact. Today there was no rig, no rails, and her colors were barely distinguishable. I could make out the remnants of faded blue tarps, their shreds hanging off her cradle, the cabins, and over the stern. Tosh drove off the road, cut across the yard between the boats and came to a stop twenty feet from her port side. He turned off the truck. We sat in total silence for a long moment, lost in our thoughts as we looked at *Elixir*, the object of our aspirations for the last seven months.

"Whoa," my ten-year-old son Gavin said, the first to speak, "I don't think that boat will float. It's too old."

"Ahh, she just needs a little TLC and a coat of paint. She'll be shipshape in no time," Tosh countered.

I agreed with Gavin's assessment. She was enormous, at least six times as big as our newly acquired truck. She sat in a cradle of ten-by-ten-inch square beams held together with two by fours cross-structured for stability and surrounded by swathes of trash and overgrown weeds. Her dingy white topside paint was peeling down to bare wood, her bottom paint almost gone. Like a mangy dog with great furless patches, her neglect was extreme, heartbreaking.

"How do we get up there?" I pointed, unable to see the cabins from the ground.

"Climb, I guess," Tosh said. Finding foot holds on the cradle, he scrambled up and swung his leg over onto the deck twelve feet above me. I followed more cautiously, but the cradle was solid and didn't move with my weight, nor did *Elixir* as I stepped aboard for the first time.

"Watch where you put your feet," Tosh called from somewhere out of sight.

The teak decks were partially torn up, leaving holes to fall through. The two cabins had large portholes, their glass cracked, and bronze rims weathered verdigris. As I made my way aft, I gingerly picked up bits of weathered tarp to see what was hidden beneath. Behind the cabin, the deck abruptly ended, and I stared into a mess of broken beams strewn haphazardly like a pile of giant used matchsticks. They had fallen onto the old engine where it sat rusting in pools of slimy black water. I moved more of the stringy tarp and saw the companionway hatch. One of the doors was ajar, revealing a ladder descending into the dimness below.

Curious, I climbed backward down the ladder into the dark. The smell was awful; mold, damp, rot, and another scent, a creepy crawly scent I would become familiar with. There were loose boards thrown haphazardly over what I would learn were called the floors, the vertical triangles between the frames in a boat. *Where did Roy sleep?* I thought about the previous owner. *How could he have lived here?* The interior seemed to be mostly dismantled.

Stepping carefully, my eyes adjusted to the dim light, and I discerned the intact galley lockers. Golden spruce doors were decorated with small cut out anchors in the corners. *How quaint*, I thought and instinctively reached to undo a small bronze latch. The door fell open, and I was stunned for a moment as I beheld the entire inner surface of the hull inside the locker seething and squirming with cockroaches. Layered several inches thick, shiny and brown, I heard whispering accompanied by soft chitinous clicking that was coming from the frenetic movement of the insects massing together.

Reacting instantly, I closed the locker door softly but firmly. I quickly retreated up the companionway ladder to the deck where the fresh air of the harbor cleared my nostrils. After finding my way down the cradle, I noticed the skin on my entire body was crawling. I wanted to jump in the nearby ocean to wash away the entire experience.

"Did you go in there?" I asked Tosh when I got back down.

"Uh huh," he mumbled slowly.

"Is this what you thought it would be like?"

"Ahh, not quite."

"Are we still going to do this?" I wondered how on earth I could work, and eventually live, in this stinking, bug infested, decaying old boat.

"Well, we'll just clean her up, get rid of all the garbage, and see what's left, I guess."

Tosh was generally unshakable. However, in this moment, he seemed far more subdued than usual.

"I am glad you can see the possibilities here," I said, trying to find something reassuring to say, determined to stay outwardly positive. But I thought, *I can't stand the smell and the cockroaches. How could this boat ever be restored to something beautiful, clean, and wholesome?* It seemed impossible and extremely unlikely to happen. Ever. But I kept that to myself. For now.

I missed my spiritual life. I missed that place of peace and feeling that everything would be taken care of by something bigger than I was. Why did I agree to do this? Was it my love for Tosh? It looked far worse than I'd imagined, but there was nothing else left. I mean, we had no other "life," only this one. Only this boat. Only my husband and my family. That was all that mattered, wasn't it?

But let's go back a little further in time, to when I first heard about this boat, only seven months before landing in Kauai.

Silverton, British Columbia, Canada
May 1987

Tosh had cornered me in the dental office. I had seen the excited sparkle, absent for months, back in his dark eyes. That evening's conversation replayed itself, still clear in my mind.

"Karen called today." Tosh, my husband and partner of eight years, stood in the hallway of the dental clinic, an easy grace in his athletic stance.

The ex-wife. My body immediately became more alert. I paused from assembling clean instrument trays to look at him. His arm braced against the wall, he wore his coat and boots, ready to go.

"She said she hasn't been able to sell Roy's boat," he continued. His dark eyes appeared distracted as he scanned the counters in the sterilization area, automatically assessing how close I was to being done with my clean up.

Karen's second husband, Roy, had died the previous winter, and she had been saddled with disposing of his assets. One was a fifty-foot schooner, in pieces in dry dock. Roy had lived on the classic vessel, his dream to rebuild it obscured and prevented by alcoholism. He'd had a close call with the grim reaper when he fell asleep, and kerosene lamps had set the boat on fire.

"And?" I responded, a loaded pause hanging in the air between us.

"I told her I was interested."

"You what?" Diplomacy forgotten, I was instantly angry, fighting to keep my voice from rising and my mouth from spewing things I would later regret. *How could you? What a stupid idea. I don't want anything to do with her or the boat.*

"I told her I was interested," he repeated, sensing my fury.

The truth was that anything around his ex-wife pushed my

buttons and made my hackles rise. Just like after all her previous phone calls, there would certainly be an upset in our lives. "But it's all in pieces," I stammered.

"Uh huh," he responded, excitement flashing in his eyes as he thought about it.

"But ... if you were going to do a boat project, shouldn't it at least be a more modern fiberglass hull?" I was appalled.

He just continued to stand there in the doorway, his arms across his chest, watching me with those eyes lighting up. Like he knew everything I was going to say and none of it would make any difference to how intrigued he felt about this old boat.

"A fiberglass hull would be less money to restore and would have an increased resale market value, right? And wouldn't a fiberglass hull be safer? Better yet, couldn't we just charter a boat for a week somewhere? Come on, Tosh ..." I pleaded as I recognized that this project had already captivated him.

With a growing feeling of dread, I finished the tray set ups, closed the instrument sterilizers, and turned off the light. He handed me my jacket. I picked up my purse from the staff closet on the way out. As he locked the office door behind us, I admitted, "I am nervous about a project like that."

"I know you are," he answered softly. "I am, too." We walked over to our little Firefly car, and he opened the door for me.

"From what I have read, people have romantic notions about building boats, especially old, traditional, wooden ones, and the percentage of people who actually finish these projects is very low." I frantically gave voice to the cons that raced through my mind.

"Yes, that's true," he said as he started the engine. He then put the car in gear and slowly drove toward the highway and home. He continued, "But this boat appears pretty sound. Probably a six-month project, and we could do that."

"I read that most couples divorce over such a project," I persevered.

"Hey, where's your faith? This will be a piece of cake compared to what we have already been through as a couple." He chuckled.

I started to laugh, too. I mean really, hadn't we faced considerable obstacles before? Just last October, when we found the clinic in Silverton and the hilltop house to rent a block away, it had seemed ideal.

"Tosh, I love this place. Do you think it will work out here?" Peace had flooded my heart as I took in the lake and surrounding mountains capped in snow.

"Yes, it's beautiful," he had agreed but his voice still carried a hint of doubt.

"It is a very small town. Do you think people will talk about us?" I asked.

"Why? No one knows we were off living in an infamous sex cult," he joked, referring to the tabloid's provocative portrayal of the commune in the Oregon desert, a city that grew to ten thousand, all disciples of spiritual master Bhagwan Shree Rajneesh.

After living in this international community with goals for all of humanity and the world, the process of reintegrating into a nuclear family, living and working for ourselves alone, felt foreign and unappealing. Our life purpose now seemed small and shortsighted.

But I smiled, laughter emerging as I saw the humor in our situation. Like we were undercover operatives or something. There were no longer the orange clothes and identifying prayer bead necklaces to set us apart from everyone else. Our names

were normal now, too, the spiritual names left at the Ranch, as
we referred to the commune. We had married, finally, and even
shared the same last name. It felt good to laugh for a moment.
But then the underlying enormity of fitting back into society,
and professional dental roles, washed over me.

Despite my trepidation, we managed to fit into the village
life and our outwardly idyllic life carried on in Silverton.

However, by December, Tosh's unhappiness revealed itself. He
had practically thrown his instruments down on the tray at the
end of a long day in the dental clinic.

"What's the matter?" I had asked.

"I don't know, I'm just tired of doing dentistry." He'd
sounded frustrated. His salt and pepper hair was eighties long
and brushed over his tanned forehead. It dipped into his eyes in
an attractive way. At thirty-nine, he remained a handsome man.
So said my friends. I loved him now and had from the moment
we met when I was nineteen and he was twenty-seven. Such a
long time ago.

I was thirty-one now, mostly quiet and unassuming, but
with a low tolerance for any kind of conflict. I addressed
concerns head on to find resolution and peace. That night was
no exception. Not only did I want to know what was bothering
him, I wanted to be able to solve it and make it better. Immediately.

"We have only been here for three months," I reminded
him. I wanted him to feel as happy as I did. I loved our ordinary
life. Simple. Or so I thought.

"I know, but I'm sick of it. I'm tired of people complaining.
I'm tired of bending over so I can see in peoples' mouths. I'm
tired of my back hurting," he had vented.

"You're so good at what you do." Ever the optimist, I tried to smooth it over. "You are helping so many people." After a long pause, I asked, "What would you like to do?"

"I don't know. Maybe I need a change." He turned away and started to turn out the lights in the clinic.

And five months later, a new dream and adventure called. The debate about leaving Silverton, moving to Kauai, and if we should buy Roy's old boat continued into the summer.

"Tosh, I really don't want to leave here." We sat on the veranda, looking out at the lake. "We don't know how to sail, let alone know how to rebuild a boat. I honestly don't know if I can handle another 'pack everything up and start a new life' kind of move. Just the thought of it makes me anxious and afraid." I tried hard to speak calmly. "Don't you have anything to say?" I finally asked when he didn't respond.

"Not much. I have been clear with you. I don't want to stay here, and I can barely stand to keep doing dentistry through the end of the year when our lease is up."

"But you've never built a boat. You don't know anything about sailboats," I repeated.

"That's even more appealing, something new, something different than teeth and dealing with people all day."

"What about your seasickness? You get queasy swimming too far out into the lake. This is crazy ... Can't you think of another project? Like building a house or something practical?" My voice was rising, despite my best intentions to stay steady.

"I'm going inside. It's getting chilly out here." He abandoned his chair and went into the house.

I couldn't seem to effectively communicate how unreasonable this boat thing sounded to me. Getting up, I didn't notice the view anymore, just the anxiety I felt. The screen door slammed after I, too, entered the house.

"Do you understand how I feel about this?" I asked, ending our silence as we got into bed that night.

"I understand that you won't let up about it until I feel the same way you do, but that's not happening. I consider the whole thing an adventure, something fun and interesting to do."

"What about the money? We're talking about our savings."

"I don't care about the money. There will always be enough. If we run out, we will work and make some more."

"I finally have my things, my stuff, and we'll have to get rid of everything, and start over, again." I sounded pathetic, but it had been a relief to not live communally anymore. To have had a whole closet for my clothes and plates and cups and pots that were mine. Things other people didn't use and wreck and lose.

"We can put stuff in the van and park it at your sisters. Remember it's only for six months. Deb, it's not forever. And you can get all new stuff over there, it'll be fun." His voice sounded tired, tired of the argument. I could tell.

"What about your seasickness?" I asked.

"I don't care about that and will cross that bridge when I have to. Maybe I won't even get sick anymore. Who knows? In the meantime, we'll learn to sail on the lake this summer in your sister's boat. It'll be a blast, and the kids will have fun, too. You'll see." He sighed. "Can we go to sleep now? Please?"

I lay awake, trying desperately to let it go, to find a way to accept spending our savings, leaving Canada again, and giving up our work. I struggled to find a prayer, a connection to something bigger than myself to have faith in. And then I remembered my failed attempt at having a spiritual life at the Ranch. We had fled with everyone else after Bhagwan had been arrested, taken away in chains, and was deported back to India.

I'd decided this material life was all there is. Just this. This discomfort. This disagreement with the man I loved. This awful feeling of being out of control without the playpen of any spiritual beliefs to comfort me.

Chapter 2

A Plan

"You get to choose your direction in life."

Kauai
January 7, 1988

Making our way back to the guest house, we were exhausted after a long day of travel and meeting the 'crone' of our nightmares rather than the 'lady' of our dreams; the unimaginably horrid boat project. Our minds worked overtime, trying to figure out where to start, or if we should start at all.

"Well, what do you think?" I couldn't help asking, sure it would be a 'no go,' but we would get a few months' vacation in Kauai. *Perfectly fine with me,* I thought. *I was right all along. The boat was a dumb idea.*

"Remember Frodo? From Tolkien's *Lord of the Rings*?" Tosh asked.

"Uh-huh?"

"Well, like him, we'll start with one step at a time. Seems like the first step will be to tidy up, throw away the trash, and see what's underneath. You'll see, it'll fall into place."

After his initial subdued response in the boatyard, Tosh had recovered and no longer seemed particularly concerned. If anything, he appeared to be even more intrigued by the challenge.

"I don't need to freak out that we bit off more than we can chew?" I diplomatically expressed my doubt. *He would see reason, of course.*

"Not at all. It'll be great. Remember how bad the farmhouse was? And that was a whole house. This is just a fifty-foot boat."

As I got ready for bed that night, I thought about the farm and the Sproule Creek house we had renovated ten years earlier.

Sproule Creek Farm, Nelson, British Columbia
Fall 1978

"How could you have ever bought this property and wanted to live here?" I asked Tosh, exasperated. I was trying to clean the inch-thick layer of mouse droppings out of the kitchen cupboards. The 1908 farmhouse, now seventy years old, sat on the homestead he had bought some months before.

"You'll see, it will be amazing to live here. Just look at the view from this kitchen." He gestured in front of him, down at the two-acre pasture below the house and the orchard of a dozen fruit and nut trees. Beyond that, a stunning green valley opened a thousand feet below.

"It's eighty acres of exquisitely quiet and pristine property surrounded by undeveloped crown land." I repeated the line he liked to quote daily. And it was true. The land, location and view were powerfully beautiful.

I was twenty-three years old and had recently left the father of my year-old son, Gavin. Tosh and I had met four years earlier, worked in dentistry together and became lovers. Over time, I realized he was not going to divorce his wife. I left him and the practice, meeting and marrying Daryn.

When my marriage failed a few years later, I moved back to Nelson to help Tosh set up a new dental practice, grateful to have a job to support Gavin and myself. Being a single mom and wanting to be independent, I purchased a small house trailer and installed it on the farm across the field from the homestead where Tosh lived while doing the extensive renovations.

When I started working for him again, Tosh told me he was separated from his wife, and it wasn't long before we were lovers again. There was no doubt I was still madly in love with him. But I felt protective of my autonomy after a divorce, and I wanted to live on my own. I accepted my role as his assistant and lover.

Working as easily together on the farm as we did in the dental office, Tosh and I were kindred spirits who enjoyed restoring order and beauty to all things old and neglected. Today, I helped him clean out the old house while Gavin went down for his nap.

Tosh tore out the partitions in the next room. As clouds of dirt drifted into the kitchen, I investigated what could possibly cause so much dust. I found piles of what looked like dried mud all over the floor with small sticks poking out. Looking more closely, the mud on the floor appeared to be dried cow manure. I could even see the bits of hay still in it. Unreal. And he was going to live here?

In a fashion I eventually grew familiar with, Tosh quickly gutted the place, opening the walls, installing wiring and plumbing, including a waterline and septic field. Dormers were cut into the roof, creating a second floor with a stunning view and filled with light. A wide spiral staircase descended into an open living room. The outside was transformed from patchy gray asphalt shingles over tar paper, to rustic natural ship-lap cedar siding.

Kauai
January 7, 1988

We got into bed that night, now ten years since renovating the Sproule Creek farmhouse. Tosh had his yellow lined tablet and a pen in his hand as he sat beside me. He had already begun to make his list.

"What first?" I asked, shoving aside my reluctance and misgivings. He was happy and engaged. Being in Hawaii, I, too, would find ways to enjoy this impossibly crazy scheme. For starters, I experienced an automatic and easy peace in my familiar role as his assistant.

"Well, we will need tools, electricity, a place to store our stuff, a lockable place."

"Like a tool shed?"

"Yes, like those ones from Sears. Hey, that's an idea, let's just get one from Sears, already built. We can do that tomorrow. And then we can get the generator and other equipment."

And so it went.

We needed help. Tosh's identical twin brother, Kiran, and his wife, Miko, arrived from Vancouver to work on the project with us. The twins contacted Wajdo, another sannyasin friend. He was thrilled to hear of the chance to work together again after the exciting time we shared renovating kitchens in southern California right after the Ranch ended. He showed up a few days later, an attractive man, tanned, blond and nine years younger than the twins, the same age as me.

Soon after he arrived, Wajdo heard me complaining about having to shave my legs, moaning about itchy skin and ingrown hairs. He told me to make sure my razor was sharp, to use lots of lather and to shave in the direction that the hair grew.

"How do you know about such girlie things?" I asked, startled by his confidence in the subject.

"Well," he replied with a typical Wajdo grin, "I used to be a Chippendale dancer and learned all this from the other strippers."

A three-bedroom A-frame for the six of us, Miko, Kiran, Wajdo, Tosh, Gavin and I, would be available in February. The enclosed two car garage would provide ample space to gather the many boat pieces that had been scattered in various locations around the island. While I had enjoyed the last two years of nuclear family living, I hoped a return to communal living would be easy and fun.

While getting the logistics together for the house, work in the boatyard began. Amidst Kauai's warm rains, a Sears garden shed was assembled next to *Elixir*. This safe, lockable space became our tool shed after installing a plywood floor, building shelving, and reinforcing the doors.

Gavin happily opened his grade five home-school books in the shelter of the truck, and I climbed aboard *Elixir* and started taking "before" pictures of the interior and exterior to document this venture. No one would ever believe how disgusting it was if I didn't take photos. As a reader of *Wooden Boat Magazine*, I knew the benefits of thorough documentation for our own reference, as well as for insurance or resale. And maybe we would be featured in that beautiful magazine at some point in time.

Over the next few days, we donned face masks and work gloves and removed what was left of the old disintegrating tarps, piles of trash, and the residual personal effects from the previous owner. This quickly progressed to completely removing what was left of the interior and taking piles of junk to the landfill. These dump runs were accompanied by an air of melancholy: this was all that was left of a man and a dream.

While I was happy to get rid of the horrible, rotten, stinking remnants of the interior, I wondered where it would all end and if there would be anything left to restore? Would I be able to stick it out? Or would we, too, reap the same defeat as Roy?

Chapter 3

Assessing the Mess

"As uncomfortable as it is, I'd rather take messy risks than stay organized and safe."

Boatyard, Kauai
January 1988

"What is this, Tosh?"

Wajdo, shirtless and clad in long pants soaked to his thighs, was vacuuming the water out of the bilge. The three boys had spent the morning power-washing the interior of the hull to remove the dust, dirt and peeling paint down to the bare wood. He turned off the vacuum, making it quiet enough to talk despite the drone of the generator outside.

"Looks like cement to me." Tosh knelt between the frames, scratching the area around the floors with his knife. "And check this out, where the frames and the floors meet the concrete, it's filled with rot." His knife sunk easily into the spongy wood of a frame, emphasizing his observation.

Kiran, the architect, knelt next to him. "Yup, not looking too good. And who knows what the wood looks like under the cement. I'd say we need to rip it all out."

"How the heck do we do that? A chisel and hammer? I can't believe you guys. This is nuts." Wajdo emphatically shook his head.

The twins were quiet for a bit, looking down at the floors and frames, the now exposed structural components of the freshly gutted hull. They glanced up at the same moment.

"Yup, that would do it," Kiran said.

Tosh nodded, exemplifying wordless twin communication.

"What?" Wajdo was confused, "Really, a chisel and a hammer. Really? We'll be here for ten years."

"No, a jackhammer," Tosh clarified. "Waj, you stay here and finish with the wet-dry vacuuming. Kiran and I'll head over to town to rent one. Be right back."

An hour later, they unloaded a jackhammer the size of an upright vacuum from the pickup and hoisted it onto *Elixir*'s deck with ropes, blocks and tackle.* It barely fit below deck and sounded ear-splitting. Hearing protection, safety glasses, dust masks and gloves made the boys resemble sweaty, shirtless aliens.

They didn't get far as they started hammering into the cement.

"What's going on?" Kiran yelled as he struggled to get the tip of the hammer to go into the cement and break it apart.

"It looks like stuff embedded in the concrete," Tosh yelled back. "Do it a little more over here and let's see if we can get it out."

The jackhammer quickly revealed we were not just dealing

with cement but also lead bricks, two-inch steel ball bearings, and big chunks of old engine and transmission parts. "Hold it."

The three of them sat down in the cement dust. "This is way more weight than just cement," Kiran pointed out. "This is serious ballast here in the bilge. If we take it out, the waterline will be altered, the way the boat handles with the sail plan, etc., will be different. Removing this weight will have serious consequences to the overall engineering."

"Right, how about if we weigh it all as we take it out?" Tosh suggested.

"Yeah, that'll work. We also must create a plan to show exactly where the weight came from," Kiran added.

"I can't believe all the stuff you guys got out of that boat today," I commented later as I sat at the dinner table with everyone.

"Do you think we should replace the cement? Put it back in there?" Tosh asked his brother.

Kiran paused, always thinking things through a hundred different ways before answering a question. "Probably not, as the cement in the bilge is what caused the rot in the floors and frames in the first place. But ... the distribution of weight is critical for hull balance and waterline placement."

"What about all the engine parts? The lead bricks? Without the cement, how are we going to get that weight back in there?" It looked impossible. I bit my tongue, but my mind said, *I told you so! This boat was a stupid idea. Tosh will eventually see I am right.*

"From what I've read," Tosh began, "the lower the weight is in the hull, the better the balance and handling of the boat. Do you think we could melt down all that lead and form a new keel shoe to bolt up under the existing iron keel?"

"Good idea. That would free us up to repair and replace the floors and frames, as well as restore the interior without worrying about weight replacement inside the hull," Kiran added. "Do you think by lowering the weight, we won't need as much? Do you think we can toss the car parts and steel shot?"

Tosh was already out of his chair, collecting his notebook, calculator, and book on nautical engineering. After checking the tables and doing some math, he answered, "I think we can toss the car parts and steel shot. It looks like a new lead shoe will be low enough that even though the weight is reduced, it will be as effective."

Several hours later, Tosh and Kiran were still figuring things out while Miko, Kiran's wife, and I cleaned up after dinner, reminiscing about religion and our sannyasin days.

"How did you get into spirituality, Deb?" Miko asked.

"Good question." I paused briefly. "Ever since I was little, I wanted to be closer to God. People seemed mean, and I didn't like being on the planet. For all the Christians in this world, where is the 'love-one-another' part? But now, after all that went down at the Ranch, I am not so sure about anything. How about you, why did you become a disciple of Bhagwan?" I rinsed the last few dishes, piling them in the rack.

"Spirituality was not on my radar until a few years ago. I was quite happy being a talk show host on daytime TV in Japan. But a friend came back from Poona and all he could talk about was Bhagwan. Intrigued, I wrote to Bhagwan asking to be His disciple. An acceptance letter arrived from India, and it contained my new name and mala (prayer beads). And then I met Kiran. Where does this one go?" She dried the last pot, and I pointed to a cupboard. "Kiran doesn't talk about the Ranch much, but I wish I had been there. What a trip it must have been."

We both fell silent for a bit, then I responded, "I am glad

you guys are here to help us. I have a feeling there will be some interesting conversations about what happened on the Ranch and how we were all affected."

Later, when everyone had gone to bed, I sat curled up in a chair to read my book. I couldn't concentrate on the story. I thought about Miko's question, and memories from when I was very small floated into my mind.

Nelson, British Columbia
1960

"You know what I mean, don't you, Sam?" I whispered in my five-year-old voice, holding both my arms around his furry neck.

Sam is my best friend, but it's a secret. I can talk to him, you know. He talks back to me but really quiet. He's a seal, and he lives on my bed. Mommy says he isn't a real seal, just a stuffed one, but I think he's real. That's why he needs to stay a secret. "Shh."

Sam and Pandy know that Dean makes a lot of trouble. That's why Mommy is too busy, and I am not supposed to bother her. Dean is my little brother. He climbs on the counter in the kitchen. Even I know he isn't supposed to do that. But he does it a lot and then Mommy gets mad so I have to come down to my room. It is better here in my room with Sam.

Pandy has yellow eyes now. His other ones came off, so Mommy fixed them, and they are yellow now. She sewed them on. He's a bear. He's just a small bear. I can't sit on his back like I can sit on Sam. Sam is really big. That's why he stays on my bed. He is heavy. Even when I pull on his flipper, he doesn't move very far.

Pandy and I go out into the hall. Nobody is there, but I can hear Mommy. She is cross. She yells when she is angry. I don't like it when she is angry. I wish my brother would not make her mad. I am going back to my room.

"Let's go live somewhere else, Sam," I plead. "Pandy can come, too. But not Mommy or Daddy or my sister or my brothers, and no yelling allowed there. They won't be there. But I can yell there, I can make lots of noise and I won't get in trouble."

"If we go somewhere else to live, Mommy won't tell Daddy when I am bad, and it won't hurt there."

Sam knows that I cry sometimes. I am not supposed to cry. Daddy says I am the oldest so I can't cry. He says I am 'responsible,' and I have to set an 'example.' He says he spanks me because he loves me. It hurts me. And my little sister, too. The boys don't get spankings. Just my sister and me.

I stay with Sam for a long time. He knows I want to go somewhere else. My sister is braver than me. She tells Daddy to spank her so I won't get a spanking. I feel bad because I don't say that for her. I don't want him to spank me or her. I am not a good person like my sister. I don't like myself, and I don't like being here.

At Sunday school they said if you are really good you go to Heaven. Everything is good there. Jesus is there. Jesus loves me. The song says so. I want to go there. I think I would like it better than here.

———

Four years later, I am nine years old and sitting on a thick white rug in front of my grandma's big puffy chair. I love visiting with her. I feel grown up because we have grown up talks.

"You are older than you think you are," she tells me with a

twinkle in her eye, like she has a secret, and she can hardly wait for me to find out. "You have been here before, in another body, a long time ago," she continues. "That is called reincarnation. People have many lives."

"How many lives have I had, Grandma?" I ask, fascinated.

"Many, many lifetimes, dear," she responds, matter of factly. "And you will have many more."

"Grandma, this is my last one," I inform her. "I am not coming back ever again. I don't like it here."

"I know, dear, but you have many more lifetimes to live before you will be finished with the lessons on this plane."

"No, I don't," I argue passionately. "I will learn all my lessons so I don't have to come back ever again."

"Deborah Jean." She always used my full given names. "It is very arrogant of you to speak that way. Of course you will come back many more times. That's Cosmic Law. Don't ever presume you are above the Law. We all have much more evolution to go through before we will be finished here on Earth."

"What about Jesus? Does He have to come back here more?"

"No, He is a very evolved soul. He didn't have to come back here. He wanted to come here to help the rest of us to learn."

"I want to be like Jesus, then I won't have to come back here."

"Deborah Jean, you will learn, dear, that there is much to go through before you will be able to be like Jesus."

Sechelt, British Columbia
1974

"You are not Jesus; you will never be Jesus. You are you, yourself, unique. Stop trying to be somebody else," Tosh yelled at me. His words felt like gunshots into my soul.

I was nineteen years old, working in a dental office as his assistant, and was also, newly and secretly, his lover. It was the end of the day. I had locked myself in the dark room for the last hour, crying where no one would see me. Tosh coaxed me out into the waiting room, empty now of patients and other staff.

"What's wrong?" he asked with concern.

I sat in a chair, staring at the floor. My eyes stayed glued to the purple shag carpet as if it could save me from coming undone.

"I can't help it. I just can't stop crying. And I was really trying to just be loving and kind, like Jesus, but I can't stand my roommate, Georgia. Jesus wouldn't have these hateful feelings," I cried, trying to explain to him.

"Debbie, are you hearing me?" Tosh's far away voice penetrated my anxiety.

"No, I can barely hear you. I don't understand. Of course I have to do my best to be like Jesus. He was our example," I manage, my voice high and whiny. Even in my distraught state, I heard the lack of conviction in its tone.

"Yes, He was an *example*," Tosh repeats, his voice rising with compassion. "You don't have to be Him. You are *you*, no one else."

He sounded even farther away. My vision steadily diminished, like I was at one end of a tunnel, and he stood at the other.

"You need to go home, have your dinner and rest. Come on.

Grab your jacket. It's seven o'clock, and it's been a long day," he said gently.

He walked me down the stairs and hugged me a quick goodnight on the sidewalk before getting into his car, starting the motor, and driving away into the night. When Tosh and I became lovers, I knew he had a wife and a child and could not be with me as much as I wanted. Often, he couldn't be with me when I needed him, like tonight. I stood under the streetlight for a long moment before walking the one block to the old cottage where I lived with Georgia, the other dental assistant.

When I reached the corner, I turned left toward the beach instead of turning right. I couldn't face going home at that moment. I heard the sound of the ocean, and the wind tugged at my jacket, blowing my hair back from my wet face. *A storm,* I thought. *Fitting as it sure feels like one right now.*

For some reason, my eyes still ran with tears and my breath came in ragged jerks, like what happens when you cry uncontrollably. There was no one on the beach. The waves crashed against the shore, the wind blowing the tops off them, making my lips taste like salt, the same as my tears. There must have been a moon above the clouds filtering though, because it wasn't pitch black, just dark, the outlines and shapes of the sand, the rocks, the logs all well-defined despite the late hour.

Unexpectedly, I started to run as fast as I could along the water's edge, not caring if my shoes got wet. As I ran, I screamed from my soul, "What am I supposed to do? I don't understand You. I have done everything I learned from reading about You, searching for You in the Bible. I even read the Dead Sea Scrolls to find out about You. I read all the other Holy Books I could find. I read the Qur'an, I read the Bhagavad Gita, I read the Torah. I went to the Catholic Church, the Baptist Church, the Presbyterian Church and the United Church. I went to visit the Jehovah's Witnesses and the Latter-day Saints. Where are You? What am I supposed to do? Oh, where are You?" I screamed into the wind until my throat felt raw and my body became exhausted from running.

Georgia met me at the door when I eventually returned home. "Where have you been?" she demanded, sounding concerned.

Oh, my gosh, I thought, *please not now.*

I can't handle her right now. I hate her bleached hair, heavy black eye make-up, and her fake southern drawl. I hate her weird boyfriend who stays over and does drugs. I hate even more that they try to get me to do cocaine with them. But I don't say those words aloud.

"At the beach," I replied quietly, my eyes on the floor as I try to walk past her and through the kitchen to my room.

"It's ten at night. Are you crazy? You are soaking wet," she exclaimed. "It's freezing out there. What were you thinking? What's going on?"

I looked straight at her and from out of nowhere, I began to laugh uncontrollably. I couldn't stop. I was hysterical, laughing so hard I fell down and rolled around on the tiny kitchen floor trying not to hit my head on the bricks around the wood stove. At first she hesitated because my behavior was so out of character, but she quickly joined me in the frenzy. The wine and pot she used daily helped her to let go of any remaining inhibitions. I felt drunk or stoned. I am guessing, because I had never been either drunk or stoned.

The hysterical breakdown continued as my dream of being like Jesus was ripped away. The vision, inspired in Grandma's presence, had been with me since I was nine years old. *How could I make this my last lifetime and move forward without being like Him?*

At last, I managed to stumble into my room, my sides

aching from laughter, and my mind completely fried. After some time, I fell into a deep sleep.

———

I came back to my chair in Kauai, remembering the conversation over dinner and the decision to pour a new lead keel. Tosh sat at his desk across the room, working on plans. I had to admit, it was pretty exciting to be figuring all these things out each day. Things that were new and foreign, well outside of our normal dental routines. I was so busy, I hadn't missed being in Silverton or doing dentistry. And Tosh had been right. It was freeing to work on something for ourselves that didn't involve strict time schedules and fearful patients.

Working and living with other sannyasins again was mixed. Triggering, as I found it hard to coordinate who would do the grocery shopping, the cooking, who had food preferences, who didn't feel like eating so didn't want to pay for food. All the give and take in living with other individuals was also oddly sooth-ing. Even though spirituality was no longer my guiding princi-ple, I could still feel a common bond through shared past experiences. *What was so rich? Was it the connections between us? Even after all that had happened over the last few years?*

"Ready for bed yet?" I asked Tosh. I paused to rest my chin on the top of his head and wrapped my arms around his shoulders.

"I'll be in in a while," he responded as he reached up to hug me back.

———

The next morning, I watched Tosh walk back to the boat from across the yard. A mountain-sized Hawaiian man followed him.

"Deb, this is JC. He's going to sandblast the boat today."

"Great," I said, my mind reeling. *That was fast.* Just last night, after discovering so much rot during our initial clean up, we discussed the need for a more accurate assessment of the fasteners and planking. Peeling paint and rusting hardware made it difficult to see the extent of the disintegration.

As we walked around the cradle, the compressor roared to life and JC climbed up on the scaffolding. With the nozzle held under his bare armpit, he donned a helmet and gloves.

"He's not even wearing a shirt," I exclaimed as he started blasting the hull. Sand and paint came flying out in a huge dusty cloud, nearly obscuring JC's head and shoulders.

Stripping away old paint and rust revealed dark rot lesions around all of the nails holding the planks in place. It was official. The entire hull needed refastening: every single plank needed to be removed and reattached to the hull frames.

Chapter 4

Not a Six-Month Project

"I can complain, I can expect life to change, or I can change myself and my plans."

Kapaa, Kauai
February 1988

I was unpacking in the master bedroom of our new rental house, a house big enough for all the boat parts, as well as our construction crew. Despite the clutter, my heart soared with excitement. I was enjoying my new life.

Finishing up, I made my way into the kitchen where Miko had been preparing dinner. She stood on a folding stool, reaching into the overhead cupboard, her petite figure revealed in shorts and midriff baring tank top.

"How are you and Kiran doing these days?" I had known Kiran as long as I'd known Tosh, thirteen years, and I'd been close friends with his first wife, equally as beautiful.

"Pretty good. Kiran is glad to be able to work with his brother again." She turned her head as she climbed down, her long dark hair animated and shining blue-black.

I finished up the salad and set the table.

"I'll go down and get the boys," I offered when dinner was ready. As I opened the stairwell door, the fetid odor of damp, decaying wood, rusty metal, and moldy cardboard filled my nostrils.

Downstairs, Tosh, Kiran, and Wajdo had finished unloading boat parts that we had collected since our arrival. The rigging had been taken down when *Elixir* was first put in dry-dock many years earlier, countless pieces stored outside in the weather for years.

A week before, we uncovered the spars: two masts, gaffs, and four booms. They were on the ground under the trees along the property line of Karen's beach house, covered with leaves and yard debris. Alongside the spars, we found decomposed cardboard boxes of mast collars* corroded with rust and peeling paint.

"How are we supposed to move these without a semi-flatbed?" Waj had asked with his usual playful skepticism.

Sixty-five feet long and at least a foot in diameter at the base, the wooden masts were a challenge to move but needed to be rescued and protected before there was any more deterioration.

"I figure we can span them from the trailer, across the bed, and onto the roof of the truck. What do you think, Kiran?" Tosh's gaze moved doubtfully back and forth between the eight-foot U-Haul trailer, the Mazda, and the two giant columns on the ground.

"I dunno. They're bigger than telephone poles, these things," Kiran said in his thoughtful way. His eyes, too, shifted back and forth between the unlikely transport and the massively awkward load.

Amidst grunts, groans, and curses, the boys lashed them precariously into place. The narrow mast tops extended up and well beyond the small cab, out over the engine hood and front bumper.

Red flags fluttered warningly from both overhanging ends for the eleven-mile ride from Kapaa down the coast to Lihue's harbor. Twists and turns, the slightest hills up or down, were all potentials for disaster as any torquing of the load could break the fragile spars. Despite heavy island traffic, we eventually made it safely to the boatyard, and *Elixir* was reunited with her masts.

As I entered the garage a week later to get the boys up for dinner, the overwhelming smell of mold and dirt made me cough. "Hey, guys, how are things going down here?" I sputtered.

"Well, pretty good, I guess ... considering." Kiran spoke quietly, his thin lips not moving much. Never one to be dramatic, I needed to look for more subtle clues to guess what he really thought. I could tell from his eyes that he was a bit concerned at the decaying pile of lines he found himself tangled in.

Wajdo stood up in the far corner of the room, his hair wet with sweat and his slim torso naked and smeared with dirt. He was almost lost in a mountain of dirty, rusty sails, unfolded without protective bags or identifying labels. Like a giant pile of dirty laundry.

"Good? Are you crazy?" Wajdo pulled his grimy hands through his hair, leaving dark smudges on his forehead. "This is disgusting. Look at this. These boxes are falling apart because they are so wet and moldy, and all this wire is completely rusted and broken. Tosh, are you sure you want to do this?"

My sentiments exactly.

"Ah, you just don't like getting dirty." Tosh ribbed him as he piled up more broken-down cardboard boxes filled with untidy twists of frayed, old lines that ranged in size from eighth inch cord to two-inch hawse line.

"Ahh." Tosh suddenly jumped back, falling into a pile of rigging. He rolled into the collection of blocks, dozens of them from tiny one-inch blocks to huge eight-inch ones. They clattered and rattled. And he swore, "Roaches, shit."

"I hate to break up such a fun job, you guys, but supper is ready." *I'm so glad it's them down here and not me.*

"Great, I'm outta here." Wajdo climbed out from behind the sails, heading for the door. The twins slowly picked themselves up from the filthy chaos and followed him up the stairs.

The next morning with a clipboard, graph paper, and measuring tape in hand, Tosh opened the double garage doors.

"Let's drag the sails out onto the lawn," he suggested. "They look like the simplest place to begin an inventory. They're cleaner, don't smell as bad and there are only about fifteen pieces in this pile."

To be clear, we had never sailed a schooner and had no idea how any of this spaghetti went together. And there was tons of it. None of it looked appealing, and all of it was permeated with a musty smell and crawling with cockroaches and centipedes six inches long and as big around as my finger. The old photos held clues for us to reassemble the pieces, but *Wooden Boat Magazine* articles and old boat building books about rigging contributed to our information arsenal. It wasn't until much later that we located the original plans by Thomas Colvin, including rigging drawings and instructions.

As Miko and I arranged the sails on the expansive lawn,

Tosh ran upstairs to the balcony where he could see the whole layout. He kept having us move them around until they looked roughly like the schooner sails on the Canadian dime. We started with only eight of the sails and as it turned out, we didn't get it quite right. However, it was a place to start, and the errors became clearer as we worked. After measuring and identifying the sail, the head, tack, clew and throat were labeled. All ten sails* needed repair but with new sails costing three or four thousand dollars each, it was good news that none of them needed to be replaced.

Once the sails were folded, labeled, and neatly stowed back in the garage, the next challenge was unraveling the old standing rigging. As we had done with the sails, the shrouds and the stays were positioned in the driveway to figure out which ones went where.

Initially, each nasty, corroded piece was measured, and the structure analyzed to replicate them with new materials. For example: which ones had dead eyes? Which ones had loops and what size were the loops? Did they loop at the mast head or at the spreaders?* The original four-by-six color photos the previous owner had taken before he dismantled the rigging were invaluable in solving a complex puzzle that we worked on for months.

Were our solutions correct? Until the masts were stepped, and the ship was re-rigged, we wouldn't know.

Boatyard, Kauai
February 1988

"Hold it," Tosh yelled above the roar of the crane engine and motioned with a closed fist to the crane operator, who stood nonchalantly by the controls in the back of his rig. "Lower it a bit." The operator complied and Tosh quickly scrambled back up the cradle onto *Elixir*'s deck. As the slack in the cable increased, Tosh again yelled "Hold it," and gave the closed fist hand signal as he grabbed the hook and adjusted the webbing straps so the old aft cabin would hang more evenly as it was lifted off the deck. The bronze ports had been removed and the webbing was threaded through the open holes, two on each side, to make a stable sling the hook could lift from the middle of the structure.

"Okay," he yelled, "let's see if this looks better." He gave a thumbs up signal.

It was an early morning in February, the second month into the project. Due to the rotted deck around the cabins, as well as in the cabins themselves, they needed to be removed. The boys —Kiran, Waj, and Tosh—had removed all the bolts and structural fastenings the day before, in preparation for the arrival of the seventy-foot, ten-ton crane. Gavin and I had packed lunches and filled water jugs with ice, loading them efficiently into the back of the little blue Subaru before joining the boys in the yard just as the crane arrived. The sun was clinging to the horizon, forming long dewy shadows across the boatyard.

Slowly the hook rose in the air, the slack in the cable disappeared and the cabin lifted off the deck, slightly askew but much better than the initial attempt. I couldn't help myself from shuddering as I imagined the cable breaking, or the old wood of the cabin disintegrating and the heavy load crashing back onto the deck and smashing the hull, crushing Tosh. My stomach clenched, nervous sweat trickled down my sides under my T-shirt. The cable shortened until there was a four-foot clearance above the deck. Then the operator shifted positions, swung the arm around and shortened the boom so the load hovered over the chosen site. The cable lengthened until the boys could reach and guide the old cabin onto the beams specifically placed on the ground to cradle it.

"Whew." I let out my breath with relief, not realizing I had been holding it as heavy unstable objects hung high in the air. The deafening noise of the machinery contributed to the tension. I continued to walk around the periphery of the crane, snapping photos for the journal I was keeping of the project. "That's one down and two more to go," I encouraged myself.

The fore cabin was next, and with its more symmetrical shape, it was easier to balance the load. It, too, wound up resting on a cradle on the ground next to the aft cabin. Lastly, the old engine was hooked up with chains, lifted out of the cockpit and slowly lowered over the side. The little Mazda quarter ton truck was backed up next to the cradle in preparation. As the weight of the engine settled onto the truck, the springs compressed to the stops, the shocks bottomed out, and the tires started to bulge.

"Stop, stop," Tosh yelled, frantically jabbing his thumb skyward. "It's too heavy. Take it out, take it out." When the engine was back in the air, Tosh ran over and jumped in the truck, moved it out of the way, and quickly arranged a wooden pallet under the stern for the rusty old engine.

"It's pretty bad, isn't it?" I attempted to fill the heavy silence in the truck on our way home at the end of the day. "What do you think?" As usual, I was trying to get my husband, the man of few words, to talk. "Prognosis here, doctor?" My belly was in knots, filled with spider webs of anxiety about this relentlessly impossible project.

"Well ... the floors need replacing, the frames need repairing, the planks need to come off and be refastened. The stem, stern, and transom need to be removed and replaced, completely new decks and cabins ... basically build a new boat ..." He sounded tired tonight. It had been a long day, one filled with more than the usual disappointments we'd encountered up to now on the project.

"That sounds like a lot more than we planned ..." My voice trailed off, my mouth dry as I tried to cope with the awful crawling sensation in my belly.

"Yup ... it will take a lot longer than six months." He sighed, his handsome face pale and drawn in the evening light, his body slumped in the driver's seat.

"Can we stay in Kauai longer?" I asked, my mind struggling to interpret what this list of new tasks meant.

"I think so. What's our bank balance these days?"

"We are good, we have half our budget left for the next four months." I was hesitant, insecure about finances. Neither of us had an income during the project.

"And we have all of our retirement accounts."

My stomach did a flip-flop, and my breath caught in my throat. I didn't reply but my mind screamed, *No!* I took a few deep breaths, then asked, "Should we consider cutting our losses and walking away from this?"

"We could." Long pause here. "How does that feel to you?"

"Crappy, but it would be more practical, wouldn't it?" The truck was quiet except for the sound of the engine, the wind blowing in the open windows and the hum of the tires on the sunbaked asphalt. "I mean, come on, Tosh, who knows if we can even do this. Neither of us knows anything about building boats, and we only started sailing last year ... on a lake, for heaven's sake. Talk to me. How does it feel to you?"

"The thought of walking away and giving up feels pretty awful, even depressing..." Another long pause.

"And the alternative? Continuing with the project, not

even knowing if we can actually do this? Spending quite prob-ably our entire retirement savings?" I prompted, verbalizing my worst fears.

"Well, it certainly feels more exciting to me. And you know I like to make decisions without thinking about finances, I mean, if I did that, I would never do anything. I like to consider my decisions as if money wasn't an issue, because it isn't. It really isn't, you know." He looked over at me, gently, tenderly.

My throat constricted. This was not my reality. "I know you have heard me say this before, but I'm not a dentist. I can't make as much money as you can. So, yes, it's difficult for me to trust that 'money is not an issue' and it's okay to make this deci-sion based on what my heart wants to do."

Tosh put on the blinkers and turned into our driveway, parked, and turned off the engine. It was quiet except for the soft creaking of the truck as it cooled down. He patted the seat beside him, wanting me to scoot over close to him on the bench. We sat in silence for a while, as my heart pounded in my chest and my eyes ran over onto his sweaty, dirty shirt. Welcoming the feeling of his strong arms around my shoulders, I kept breathing as he started to speak. His deep voice resonated in his chest under my ear.

"I am scared, too. I mean, I don't really know if we can do this. I get seasick, so why am I even working on a boat? All I know is that I really love this project. I want to do it. I can't even imagine not doing it. We can make something beautiful of this old wreck of a boat. We can. I know we can. It doesn't make logical or financial sense. I know that, but why should we turn tail and admit defeat now?"

My being was calmer as I listened to him, letting in his enthusiasm and excitement to be going for something unknown and uncharted. And so it was, being the two souls who believed that nothing is impossible if you are tenacious enough, we decided to continue to dismantle what remained of *Elixir*. When I think about it, Tosh the dentist took on this project just like he would a badly broken-down molar. We'd committed to getting down to bare bones that were solid and rot free.

And I? I remained the faithful assistant, my job to fill in where I could, do the tasks within my capabilities, and hold a mostly unquestioning confidence that the job would be accomplished, somehow.

Could I do that? Could I keep that up indefinitely? Would there be a cost?

Part Two

THE BONES

Chapter 5

Masts, Rebirthing & Regression

"I cannot embark upon a long journey unless I leave sight of home."

Boatyard, Kauai
March 1988

As I stood against the mast,* the small blue orbital sander vibrating in my gloved hands, the repetitive motion, and the endless drone of the generator allowed my mind to wander. I pondered the path I had chosen for this life. *How did I get here, on Kauai in a boatyard, rebuilding an old boat? This was supposed to be a life dedicated to higher, more spiritual goals. Where had I gone wrong?* As my hands went through the monotonous motions, my mind traveled back through time, remembering the Sproule Creek Farm.

Our dream to build a spiritual community, and our own search for enlightenment, had started there. In those early days, rebuilding the farmhouse and working in the massive vegetable garden, we were so innocent of what would come to pass, of all we would experience, of where we would end up.

Sproule Creek Farm, Nelson, British Columbia
July 1978

"Hey, did you see the flier for the yoga retreat in the Okanagan?" I asked Tosh one day as we weeded the vegetable garden.

"No."

"Do you know that teacher, Babba Hari Dass? The one who doesn't speak?" I clarified.

"Oh, yeah, I know about him. He uses a chalk board to talk to his disciples. I went to one of his retreats. When is it?"

"Next weekend. Do you think we can take the kids?"

"They love kids there, and Nicole had a good time the year we went."

I paused in my thirty-foot row of carrots. Gypsy, Nicole's three-year-old horse, was trying to eat the shirt off my shoulder, her way of reminding me that she loved the carrot thinnings. The thought of being around other people doing yoga and meditation was appealing. And familiar. My grandmother had taught yoga, and I'd practiced as a teenager. "I'd like to go and check it out. Can we?"

Tosh leaned on his hoe for a moment, the corn coming up past his waist already. "Sounds like a fun thing to do. We could take the van and the tent, and swim in the lake. Good idea."

We left for the yoga retreat the following weekend. The meals were communal and vegan, and there were lectures on Ayurveda, a system of herbal medicine originating in ancient

India. Mornings were spent in meditation and yoga practice. In the afternoons, a hundred or so of us gathered and sat with the teacher, Babba Hari Dass.

While I didn't have a profound spiritual experience sitting with him, there was an unexplained familiarity that brought me peace. Revati, the "Shining Light" showing the path to others, was the Sanskrit name he gave me. I was happy to change my name from Deborah because I had read it meant Queen Bee and I was often accused of being bossy. I hoped, with a new name, I wouldn't be perceived that way anymore.

We met another couple, Tree and Jeffrey, at the retreat who talked about a man called Leonard Orr. He lived in Campbell Hot Springs in California and was doing work called 'rebirthing,' a breathing practice and affirmation system that helped to heal negative old patterns. Somehow, the breathing helped you to relive your actual birth process. This enabled you to become aware of what conclusions you came to at the moment of birth and reprogram these to more positive patterns of thinking.

Both Tosh and I were fascinated and agreed to host the couple to come up to Ainsworth Hot Springs, twenty-five miles from our farm in Sproule Creek, to do a workshop for us and our like-minded friends.

The sputtering noise of the generator running out of gas quickly brought me back to the boatyard, and the endless sanding.

"Four more feet of this mast to sand, and I will be ready for the first coat of varnish," I say aloud to myself.

It's exciting to think that these masts will once again be doing their job, supporting a huge sailing rig. I open the gas can and the funnel is ready to insert into the generator's fuel tank. The slosh of the gasoline and the familiar petrol fumes accompany the task as I fill it to the top, screw the cap back on and return the gas can and funnel to the shed.

Back to the sanding, I pause for a moment, savoring the feel of the trade winds blowing across my face and through my hair. The very breath of the islands, it never ceases. As I deeply inhale the tropical air, I savor the balminess of it, detecting its saltiness on my tongue. My body automatically connects each breath, reminding me of past meditations and years of focused breath work.

Ainsworth, British Columbia
November 1978

"Okay, Debbie, just start breathing, nice deep breaths, in ... and out ... all the way in ... and all the way out ... feel your stomach and your chest rise as the breath fills you all the way in ... and no pause, all the way out ... good, that's it."

As Tree spoke, her hand was lightly in the middle of my chest, a physical reminder to help me pull the air from my belly into my upper body. She lay close beside me on the bed, her head propped up on one elbow, her full attention focused intently on me for my first rebirthing session.

I was participating in the Ainsworth Retreat, the beginning of our rebirthing community. About fifteen friends and colleagues attended, going through the process for three days. We worked in pairs and did a session a day, one as a practitioner and one as a participant, learning the techniques to go deeply into our psyche following our breath, as well as how to guide one another into these previously unexplored areas of our souls. The hot springs location allowed us to work 'dry' and 'wet,' where you were immersed in a bathtub or a hot tub for the entire three-hour session. The warm water facilitated more profound releases and revelations.

"Are you warm enough?" Tree had asked me in preparation for my first dry session. She was a small, slightly voluptuous woman, middle-aged, with brown shoulder length hair and deep dark eyes. Her lively bubbly energy was muted in preparation for this inner journey. I trusted. Not her so much, but the fact that I was guided to this process and clung to my faith that this was something I needed to do.

Nodding, I closed my eyes. *What would it be like?* I was lying on a bed in the tiny motel room, nervous to attempt a journey into such an unknown frontier; my own subconscious memory. Beyond my mind. *Would I be able to go there?* My friends were all paired up and doing the same thing in the six other available rooms of this quaint old cliffside resort. We had shared our orientations as a group. Tree and her partner Jeffrey explained the process of keeping the awareness on the breath. If the mind wandered, just bring it back to the breath. There were no pauses, no holding of the breath, even for a second at the beginning of the breath nor at the end. Just one continuous circle. I hoped I would be able to do it.

"Good, Debbie, keep breathing, nice deep breaths, in ... and out ..."

I kept breathing, Tree's guidance helping to keep my mind focused. *Oh, no. My hands and feet are tingling. Never mind, just keep breathing, you can do this.*

"What's happening?"

I tell her about the tingling.

"It's all good, let's slow down the breathing a little, that's it. Keep going."

My eyes are running. What is this?

"Good, this is good." Tree's voice in my ear helped me to keep following the circle of breaths, despite the tears flowing from the corners of my eyes.

She guides me with her soft words, as well as her gentle fingertips, the breathing rhythm changing from short and quick to long and slow.

A prayer fills my mind, *only you, Jesus, please let this be the truth, help me to find what is real. Keep me safe and in the Light.* Suddenly my breath became jerky, and my body stiff, straining.

"That's right," Tree's voice was in my ear, "just keep trusting. You are on your way."

And I kept feeling my way through what was happening. *My body was stiff and pushing and pushing. It felt so, so tight. What was this? Only you, dear Lord. Only you. Please keep me safe.* I could feel, observe and hear myself, crying out, sobbing.

Tree's voice continued to guide me. "Yes, Debbie, this is where you want to go, keep going, straight through it."

My feet hurt.

"Your feet? What's happening to your feet?" Gentle, encouraging, calm.

"I'm upside down ... he flicked my heels with his fingers. Ow!" I felt such a sharp pain up my legs and back and into my neck, it literally took my breath away for some moments.

"I think it is my birth, the walls are green, a hospital. People are talking so loudly, it hurts my ears. Something is crashing, scissors landing in a metal dish. The doctor, he held me up ..."

"Yes, that's right and what are you feeling?"

"I hurt my mother ..." I'm crying, feeling terribly guilty.

"Yes, and what is your mother feeling right now?"

I paused, looking inside. "She is happy. She doesn't think I hurt her ..." Awe and amazement wash over me. My mind reels. "I thought I hurt her. I have been feeling so guilty. And she didn't feel that way at all."

Crying, the thoughts flying by in my mind, seeing all the ways I had behaved in my life, trying to make it up to her, trying to fix things. All based on the false assumption I had made when I emerged out of the birth canal and into this world. The breathing kept going, like a river, carrying me, emotions running over, the thoughts flying past. No need to stop and focus on any of them, just keep going, breathing in and out.

I was on a journey and following where I was being led. Not getting stuck in anything, not holding onto anything, like on a highway. Looking out the window there are interesting sights, but you watch and then pass by.

And so began a daily meditation practice that continued for several years. Three hours every morning and three hours every evening, immersed in the bathtub with just my nose above the water, following my breath, breathing through sensations, thoughts, memories, and emotions. Learning to recognize what I was thinking and feeling. Learning to be brutally honest about all of it. It also began an extensive practice of journaling, filling notebooks with struggles, inspirations, and affirmations.

We returned home to the farm, enthused about our spiritual community, and committed to working together regularly to continue our self-discovery processes.

The barn was renovated and transformed into a meditation and retreat space: hay loft floors were repaired, a wide staircase installed, and 1,800 square feet of orange commercial grade carpet laid down. Over the five years we lived at the farm, throughout the summer months, we held three-day rebirthing and meditation retreats for dozens of people.

Boatyard, Kauai
March 1988

"Yay!" I yell as loud as I can. "I finished sanding the mast. Yippee!" I holler over the noise of the generator. The boys are busy working on the hull, but they dutifully stop what they are doing and bang their tools together to make a celebratory noise. They know I have been at the repair and sanding of just one mast for five straight days. Sixty-five feet are a lot of feet. I thoroughly wipe down the entire length with clean dry cloths.

I make my way back over to the shed with renewed energy, eager to mix varnish and turpentine in the yogurt container, ready to apply the first coat with a new foam brush that won't leave streaks. There is nothing like that first coat of varnish after all the preparation of the wood. It is a surprise. How will the wood appear under its new finish? Will it be blond or dark? Will it have a dark grain or one that is barely visible? Will there be a holographic-like shimmer that draws you into the depth of the grain? What hidden patterns will be revealed as the finish is applied? This is spruce wood with a straight grain, and it becomes a deep honey-blond under the varnish.

After the initial excitement of the new task, the repetitious monotony of painting frees my mind to wander back once again into introspection. I am filled with a yearning to understand my spiritual journey.

Why am I in Kauai working in a boatyard with no apparent spiritual purpose?

Sproule Creek Farm, Nelson, British Columbia
December 1978

"Are you comfortable?" Tosh asked in his quiet, calm voice, ready to regress me for the first time.

Even dentistry was not exempt from the radical experimentation of the seventies. Many of our patients did not want to use traditional sedatives or anesthetics and were requesting hypnosis for anxiety and pain management. Tosh attended hypnotherapy training to be professionally proficient at meeting his patient's demands. Interestingly, hypnotherapy training includes various induction techniques, including those for age and past life regressions. This, too, became an active tool for exploring our inner world. How had my past life affected this one? What could I heal in my past, to improve the quality of my life now?

Tosh sat in a kitchen chair placed beside the bed in our newly renovated farmhouse. A friend sat on another one placed on the other side of the bed. She held a notebook, her pen ready. I lay atop the bed, a single candle burning on the bedside table, its golden light filtering reddish through my closed eyelids.

"Yes," I whispered, answering Tosh's question, feeling very relaxed in my body, but anxious in my mind. *Maybe nothing would happen. Maybe it wouldn't work for me.* Slowly, I focused on my breathing, following it in and out, feeling my stomach moving up and down.

"You ... are ... feeling ... very ... relaxed," Tosh continued slowly in a reassuring voice. "Feel ... your ... breath ... moving ... in ... and out ... notice your toes, and how relaxed they are ... feel your legs ... so heavy, sinking into the bed ..." and on he went, through my whole body until everything was relaxed and very, very heavy, sinking deeper and deeper into the bed.

"When you are ready, move out of your body and float a foot above the bed ..." he continued, "and notice the room, the tables, the chairs ..." He continued his induction through noticing the room floating six feet above the bed, noticing the roof and fields floating above the house, noticing the town in the distance floating above the valley, noticing the moon and stars floating above the earth.

"When you are ready, tune in to a time and a place that is of the most significance to you ... and when you are ready look down at your feet and describe what you see ..."

"I see black sticks ..." I manage to croak out, my voice soft, too lazy to engage my vocal cord muscles. "I am confused, I don't see my feet ... I just see these black sticks ... oh, those are my legs."

"Describe them."

"They are .... incredibly old and black and ... withered ... laying on stone ..." I am aware that I am detached from the experience somehow, like an observer, answering the questions in a flat emotionless way.

"Good, very good," Tosh's voice guides me, reassuring, "and what do you see around you?"

"Just blackness, it is very dark ... there is no light here."

"Where are you?"

"In a pyramid," I say without hesitation, shocking myself as I hear the words.

"And what are you doing in a pyramid?"

"I am waiting."

"What are you waiting for?"

"I am waiting for my body to come back."

"Your body to come back?"

"Yes, they said I needed to wait here until I could use the body again." Just answers arriving in my mind without any background. Letting the unknown to be there, watching, observing, listening to what I say out loud. Allowing the pieces to coalesce into a deeper perspective of what was going on, allowing understanding to find its way into my perception.

"Who said this?"

"The priests ... and me ... I said I had to wait here. I am a blue light, but I am very pale now. I am almost gone. I have been waiting so long."

"How long have you been waiting?"

"I don't know ... thousands of years, so very, very long. A Man came, a Man of White Light and He wanted me to go with Him, but I told Him I had to wait here. He came again another time when I was almost all gone, there was barely any blue light left, and He lifted me up and carried me out of here."

"Where did He take you?"

"I don't know where it is ... there are rainbows all around. The people are all colors of the rainbow. Even the air is filled with swirling rainbows. I am healing and restoring my soul here. I am being filled with more light and all the colors and am not so weak now."

"Why were you so weak?"

"I ... I ..." the realizations hit my mind like explosions, shocking me. "I believed something, and it wasn't true. But I believed it and stayed there. Even when the Light Man came to get me, I wouldn't go. I was ... loyal ... stubborn. I believed what I had learned and had to stay with my physical body. My soul was almost gone, there was hardly any energy left in it from being in the dark, alone, for so long. The Light Man came again and took me to a place to help my soul get light back in it ..."

"Go back to a time before you were in the pyramid," Tosh paused before continuing, "Look at your feet ... describe what you are seeing."

"I have sandals on."

Tosh guiding me with questions, I recognize I am a woman

wearing a long sleeveless white dress. I describe the warm climate of Egypt, the large room with huge floor to ceiling windows, like being outside. I am alone on a high patio, feeding raw meat to black cats as large as dogs. My name is Helena with a silent H and I tell the future to kings.

"Is there anything else you want to say?" Tosh asks.

"No."

"I am going to start to count backward from ten ... As I count, you will slowly come back to the present time, ten ... gently and slowly ... nine ... you are coming back ..."

And I came back to the present. My friend had taken notes and the three of us debriefed the session. I had believed my soul had to stay with my dead physical body so wholeheartedly that I remained loyal to that belief for two thousand years. My soul was affected for that long. And I also had the experience of feeling the light of my soul, and when it was full and bright and when it was faded and depleted to almost nothing.

The time at the Sproule Creek Farm was an idyllic life in many ways, working in a conventional profession at the same time as experimenting with radical lifestyle changes and searching for a deeper meaning to life than what was apparent on the surface. In keeping with that same flavor of radical change, even more was in store for us and our tiny Shangri-La on the Sproule Creek Farm.

Boatyard, Kauai
March 1988

I was nearing the end of the second mast. Wow. First coat all done. The wood was beautifully golden, but the texture was rough. Part of the process of finishing wood is applying many coats. The varnish fills small voids, the surface getting smoother and smoother until you can see yourself in the reflection, like a mirror. I cleaned up the paint containers and put all my supplies back in the shed. The generator was still going strong, the boys working in the hull. I collected Gavin from the table rock under the ironwood trees where he was doing his schoolwork and loaded the lunch coolers into the back of the Subaru before heading for home and the beach.

The swim across Nawiliwili harbor after work every day cleared my mind of the sawdust and noise of the yard, stretching out my body after the demanding physicality of the job. Parking in a shady spot, we grabbed our swim gear and walked through the lovely grounds of the Westin Kauai toward the shore.

"Race ya, Mom." Gavin dropped his towel, kicked off his flip flops, and ran across the hot sand into the wild embrace of the crashing waves.

Chapter 6

Floors, Stem & Sannyas

"Staying home is safe, but that isn't what our souls are built for."

Boatyard, Kauai
May 1988

"What's next?" Wajdo asked after I completed the masts, which were carefully wrapped and stored on the sawhorses alongside the hull. Who knew when we would step them, dropping them through carefully constructed holes in new cabin roofs, seating their square peg bottoms in special timbers bolted to the keel.

"Probably the smaller gaffs and booms. No shortage of things to sand and varnish," I quipped as I retrieved the coolers and drink buckets from the car and set up lunch for everyone beneath the stern. Kiran turned off the generator and joined us for a welcome break. "How are the floors coming along?" I asked him.

"I'm on number fourteen of thirty-five," he said with a wry grin, "Almost half-way there."

The floors are roughly triangular shaped pieces of wood that are mounted across the V-shaped bottom in a wooden boat and hold the opposing frames and keel together. He could only complete two or three of them in a day as the angled cuts were so complex.

Tosh came up from the other side of the hull, "Almost done with getting the new stem in place." The stem is the main foremost timber of a wooden boat and goes from the keel all the way up to the deck. He was excited. "It is like a sculpture, with precise, compound shapes. I have gone through two saw blades because that rosewood is so dense. Such a shame no one will ever see this gorgeous piece of wood. Now I understand why the wood guy didn't want to sell me this stuff. Hey, remind me again why we are doing this project?"

I knew he was joking in a way, referring to how much rot we kept finding as we started taking the old boat apart, but this exact question screamed daily in my own head. When the large timbers of the stem were unsound and needed to be replaced, this presented a dilemma of finding hardwood in big enough chunks for structural use. Luckily, we had found an exotic wood supplier on Kauai. There was also one in Washington State who shipped us slabs of Honduras mahogany.

Even on the outside, it became clear that a coat of paint was not all this lady needed. The original hull had been built in Taiwan in the 1960s of solid teak and fastened with iron nails. Beginning in the 1980s, dwindling forests and available teak created logging and importing restrictions. Our restoration project was a tiny contribution to conserving and recycling a valuable and irreplaceable resource, a small rationalization for my involvement with such a crazy project.

Back to the hull, our research showed that refastening her

with silicon bronze screws would be a better solution than replacing the corroded iron nails. While none of our suppliers could come up with the 3.5-inch fasteners we needed for re-planking, our sandblasting neighbor discovered three boxes of the coveted screws hiding in a corner of his junk yard.

I couldn't imagine taking planks off the hull. I mean, wouldn't the whole thing collapse and fold in on itself like those Popsicle stick houses you tried to build as a kid in summer camp? To prevent this and preserve the integrity of the shape and strength of the ship, the planks were removed from only a third of the hull at a time. Teasing with a crowbar and pounding with a hammer from the inside, the planks separated easily from the dried-out frames without damaging the precious wood. Each piece was then labeled, laid out on sawhorses, sanded to sound wood, and soaked in reconditioning linseed oil. While the bottom third of the planks were off, the floors and frames were accessible for repair and replacement.

Tosh shook his head as he finished wiping his hands on a clean rag after using the lava soap, an industrial waterless hand cleaner. "Ah, but rot and the challenges to find materials aside, we are having so much fun," he jested as he pulled up a chair. And he was having fun, while to me, it appeared to be a contin-uous exercise in frustration.

"Is this easier than working on the Ranch?" Wajdo asked, always curious about our time in Oregon because he hadn't been there.

"No, it's about the same," Tosh responded with his mouth full of sandwich. "Well maybe a little dirtier here, I mean the epoxy and sawdust and all. I built the electrical substation with another guy. That was cool. An electrical substation for a city of ten thousand people. Can you believe that? It was like a jigsaw puzzle in a box. All the parts arrived, and we had to figure out how to put it together."

"Don't you ever decide that you just can't do something?" Wajdo asked.

"Where's the fun in that?" Tosh laughed.

"What about you, Kiran? What did you do there?"

"I was one of the architects. I designed the eight-bedroom town houses in such a way as they could be built in a factory and then assembled on site, like prefab homes. It was rewarding to be able to do cutting edge design for massive building projects and see the whole thing completed in months. In the real world, these projects take years. Like this boat." He reached for the water jug, the ice cubes rattling inside.

"How did you ever get involved with Rajneesh, Debbie?"

"It was Kiran's fault," I scoffed, but it was the truth. I remembered that day in 1980 when the phone rang in the old farmhouse in Sproule Creek.

Sproule Creek Farm, British Columbia
January 1980

"Who was that?" I asked Tosh, trying to sound casual. It was difficult as my stomach had instantly sprouted butterflies upon overhearing his side of the conversation. The wintry scene below the Sproule Creek farmhouse picture windows made me grateful for the wood stove burning beside me.

"Kiran," he replied, as if that were enough information, which it wasn't. Tosh's brother lived five-hundred miles away.

"So, what's up?" I asked.

I always knew when something was about to happen, when my world would be turned upside down. Like when Gavin's father came home from a trip, before he told me we were done. The clammy hands, the pounding heart, and the dread in my belly, all speaking to me in the body language of fear. A long pause before he answered me. Not a good sign.

"Well," another long pause, "he's going to India."

"And?" I persevered, my mouth all dry and feeling like cotton wool. Another long pause. *What is it about this man that he can't just answer a question?*

He definitely didn't want to finish the sentence, but I waited for the rest of it without interrupting, "Ah, he wants me to go with him." There. He said it. And he was waiting for the inescapable argument that was going to follow any discussion about Rajneesh.

I prolonged the unavoidable a bit longer by asking, "And what did you say?" Maybe he didn't want to go, although I knew he did. He had spoken of going to India at least once a week for a year.

"I want to go with him." Tosh fell quiet, his gaze on the floor.

There it was. Out in the open. The thing I had been dreading for the last year was going to happen. Dreading since Tosh had taken sannyas, the word used when a person becomes a disciple of a spiritual master. He had dyed all his shirts orange, the traditional color of clothing for a devotee, and changed his name from Bob (Robert) to Tosh (Anutosh meant contentment). "How long is he going for?"

"Three months."

"I don't want you to go," I blurted out, I couldn't help it. I wanted to scream it as loud as I could, my voice alone preventing him from leaving. But I didn't yell. I said the words in a quiet, desperate way, knowing already that his departure was inevitable. "What about the practice? What about the farm? You can't leave everything for three months." I rushed into logic to save me from panic. *Surely he would see the impracticality of such a journey?*

"Do you want to come?"

His question surprised me.

"No," I replied vehemently. Tosh knew I didn't agree with the teachings of Bhagwan. Bhagwan believed in free love and that it was okay to have multiple partners. He didn't believe in marriage or having children. While not entirely traditional, I still felt far more old-fashioned than Tosh did. I was good with our weekend retreats and rebirthing workshops. Sannyas was too extreme for me.

At that moment, my mind went to the root of my fear. He would meet other women in Poona. Sexual freedom was part of the culture of sannyas. The farm, the children, the dental practice, and the spiritual community we had nurtured were already falling apart. I would lose my world and my place in it. Upset, struggling to maintain some inner equilibrium, I determined that if Tosh had found his spiritual teacher, and a new way of life, then so would I. And it was not Rajneesh, I knew that for certain.

A few days later, I spun the globe. Wherever my finger landed; I would go there and find my teacher. My finger landed in Belize, in San Pedro on Ambergris Caye. Determined not to stay at home pining and despite my fear, I would take two-and-a-half-year-old Gavin, my backpack, and my paints and fly to Miami, then Belize. My eleven-year-old stepdaughter Nicole would stay in school and at the farm with her aunt. From Belize I would figure out how to get to the Cays. That night I saw my teacher in a dream. He had thick black hair and compassionate dark eyes, twinkling with a wry sense of humor.

Boatyard, Kauai
May 1988

"No, you didn't really just spin the globe?" Wajdo was incredulous. "That's crazy. You are just as bad as these guys," he gestured toward the twins with his second sandwich.

"Well, you must be crazy, too, Waj, with a name like that. How did you get involved with sannyas?" I asked him.

"Mail order, like Miko, after doing meditations with a small group in Portland."

"What? You wrote away to get involved with a wild teacher guy you never even met? You are even crazier than us," Kiran ribbed him.

"So, did you get to Belize? Did you meet your teacher?" Wajdo probed, curious.

Chapter 7

Belize & Master

"Leave your safe harbor. Explore, dream and discover."

Belize
April 1980

"Señora," the radio man said after glancing briefly at my note, "no planes flying."

I'd been in San Pedro, a cay (island) off the coast of Belize for a month, and my return flight to the United States was scheduled for the following day. There were no telephones on the cay. To confirm my return airline tickets, Gavin and I searched for the ham radio man. In a blue basement room surrounded by tables of electronic equipment, we found him with his face in front of a microphone and his ears covered with puffy black headphones. I handed him a note with my travel information so he could patch a radio call to the phone system on the mainland.

"Excuse me," I said. "There are no planes?"

"Señora," he began, "aeropuerto cerrado."

"San Pedro Airport is closed?"

"No, airport in Belize City closed." As if sensing my rising panic, he explained further, "War bad now, all airports closed."

"For how long?" I tried to stay calm enough to think of the right questions to ask.

"No se." He shrugged in a helpless gesture that conveyed his lack of knowledge.

"What should I do?" I asked, trying not to break down in front of him. I was completely out of money.

"Come each day. I tell you if flying or not," he said kindly.

My mind reeled, silently screaming, *what am I going to do now?* I thanked him as calmly as I could, switched Gavin over to my other hip, reclaimed my paper with its now obsolete travel arrangements and walked out into the intense sunlight.

Overwhelmed by emotion, tears flooded my cheeks, pooling inside the rims of my sunglasses, making them steamy and hard to see through. Why had I ever believed in that dream of finding my master? It was all a hallucination. A pipe dream. Wishful thinking. How could I have possibly thought I could spin the globe and travel to this remote place with my toddler and it would work out? Self-doubt enveloped me, the flap sealed tight, and I felt like I would suffocate.

"Mommy, look ..." Gavin took his thumb out of his mouth and pointed a wet finger at the beach, "'phins."

While I struggled to take another breath, keep hold of him on my hip, and maintain my balance in the soft sand of the walkway, I looked up through the smear of tears in my glasses and followed his small finger.

"You are right. Look at them jumping and splashing. They're dolphins, honey, dolphins." While we had seen them a few times over the month, they had never been so close.

Following our morning habit, we made our way to the beach and Gavin ran to the water's edge, plopping down in the warm water and clapping his hands. I sat close by and watched the gray sea dancers as they made their way along the shoreline. Their joyful magnificence splashed away at my fear, lessening it enough to help my breathing come more easily.

"Castle, Mommy?" Gavin asked as he started digging.

"Sure, honey." I automatically scooped up a handful of wet sand and let it drip onto the small pile he had started.

With the warm wind caressing us, the dolphins cavorting and the handfuls of sand repetitively dripping onto the pile, the castle of the day slowly emerged. The tears stopped, and I washed my sunglasses off in the sea.

What had happened in the month since I arrived? Had I missed some sign of my master to assure me I was in the right place?

Belize
March 1980 (A month prior)

After landing in Belize at the international airport outside of Belize City, extreme heat and humidity struck me as I emerged from the plane. And the noise. The British Air Force in their Harrier jump jets, with vertical take-off and landing capabilities, were practicing maneuvers just a few plane lengths away. Their screaming engines were deafening.

"Pretty impressive, aren't they?" yelled a fellow traveler who paused beside me on the jet way as we headed for the terminal.

"Like science fiction," I yelled back, nodding.

"The British are here because of the war that is going on next door in Guatemala," the man continued.

"A war?" No wonder I'd felt so anxious. *I should never have come.*

The man looked more closely at me, holding a toddler on my hip, and continued an easy conversation. It turned out that he and his friends were on their annual fishing trip to San Pedro but one of their party had canceled. I was welcome to take his place in the Cessna and fill his room when we arrived. Surprisingly, when I look back now, concerns about these men causing harm or taking advantage of me never crossed my mind (nor were they warranted).

The small plane landed on the cay on the narrow dusty airstrip edged on both sides by azure blue water. There were no roads or cars, only white sandy walkways and fierce sunlight even though it was late in the day. I followed the men with a heavy pack on my back while carrying Gavin in my arms. Sweat stung my eyes as I labored to keep my footing in the loose beach sand. Thankfully, Gavin sleepily sucked his thumb, his eyes taking in a new world.

The six-room lodging house was the nicest accommodation on the island and our room at the end of a second-floor veranda, extended over the beach. Sighing with relief, I set down Gavin and the heavy bags. Opening the wooden slats covering the screened windows on three sides of the room, the tropical winds rushed in and chased out damp, moldy air. I had a room with a bathroom, and a bed to fall into after two very long days and several time changes away from British Columbia.

"Wow, Gavin, we did it. We're finally here," I said as he ate snacks from my bag.

He looked up at me with bits of cracker on his chin and hands. "More, please, Mommy?"

As I got more food and refilled his cup with bottled water, a tsunami of fear and homesickness washed through me. I had thought that making the journey, not knowing how or if I would arrive, was the root of my anxiety. But it was still here. Everything sounded, smelled, and felt unfamiliar. And I was alone, without Tosh. I kept myself from giving in to tears as I washed Gavin and put him into bed.

"I love you, Mommy," he said, reaching up to touch my cheek.

I tucked him in, enviously watching him fall asleep. After washing off the grime of travel, I collapsed into bed. The tears finally escaped and soaked into the pillow. But we'd done it. We were here, despite two-year old temper tantrums, thousands of miles, and walking through foreign airports. I drifted into sleep on wisps of gratitude for the businessmen from Texas and especially for the one who hadn't shown up.

I awoke to the sounds of fishermen below my window, pulling their worn wooden boats up on the sand and calling to each other in Spanish. Sunbeams danced through the slats over the windows, but within moments, the apprehension I had felt before falling asleep returned. What was I doing here? Before the fear engulfed me, I reminded myself I had been guided to this journey, to this place. It took immense willpower to stay focused on faith that all would be provided for, just as it had been the day before.

A sweltering sun blazed high in the morning sky while we made our way to the water's edge after breakfast in the bare concrete basement of the rooming house. Putting a foot in the Caribbean Sea for the first time, I was astonished by how warm and clear the water was, like a bath, and Gavin relished it. The village children immediately crowded around to play with him touching his blond head, unique amongst all their dark ones. It became our routine in the mornings to be at the shore reading CS Lewis's *Narnia* books aloud. Even in a foreign language and without pictures, the children loved story time.

During Gavin's afternoon naps, I would paint on the veranda overlooking the ocean. There was just enough shade and ocean breeze to comfortably enjoy several precious hours on my own. Sometimes, I used this time of the day for meditation and the breath work that Tosh and I practiced at the farm.

The tropical days passed; each one similar to the one before. Routine was helpful with a small child, and it helped to calm the ever-present anxiety about being alone in a foreign country. The days became familiar and easier as I relaxed into a vacation lifestyle in the tropics, my being slowly unraveling the tensions and worry of the last year of changes at the farm and in my life. Still, I saw no sign of my master, despite being out every day. As the weeks floated serenely by, I even became relaxed about that. Maybe this idyllic lifestyle itself was the master, the teacher, the answer for my soul.

Eventually, my departure date arrived. I found the ham radio man in the blue basement room and heard his pronouncement that the planes were not flying, and the airports were closed indefinitely. The Guatemalan Civil War (1960-1996) had escalated, and we were officially trapped in a war zone. While I had heard rumors about the war over the last month, it hadn't crossed my mind that it could affect me or my travel plans.

Journaling that night, I tried to organize my thoughts by planning how to get through the next few days, hoping to quiet myself before sleep. But I awoke in the night, drenched in sweat. I dreamed Gavin and I were in a war and couldn't escape. We could never return to Canada. What kind of a mother was I that I had not even considered such a thing? That I was so unprepared?

Our daily routine remained the same with the added visit to the radio man each morning. On the third day, Gavin and I returned to our room after being told there were no flights. My stomach was in knots and despite trying to remember to breathe and keep calm, it wasn't working. I had eighteen dollars left for food. The room rent was paid for four more days. Everyone took cash only, so my credit card was useless. What if we were stuck here for weeks? Or forever like in my dream?

My hands shook as I got Gavin set up to play with Lego's on his bed before laying down on mine to begin a breathing meditation. I was determined to stay positive and not let the fear and panic overtake me. Despite wearing only my swimsuit, and opening the louvers in the window, it was humidly hot. Outside, I could hear the distinctive tropical rustling of stiff palm fronds as they danced, unconcerned, in gusty warm drafts of Caribbean air.

After some time, my heart rate slowed down, and my hands stopped shaking. A familiar blanket of peace enveloped my being, and I noticed the tickling of curiosity as the watcher inside began to emerge in my awareness: like a delicate feather inside my skull, right in the very middle. My jaw relaxed and I felt my mouth bend in a tiny smile, happy that I could steal some moments of tranquility despite the war, closed airports, and no money.

I took another long, connected breath, tuning into the space I was so familiar with from my daily meditations. Exhaling slowly, I noticed images appearing behind my closed eyes even though I was awake. It was dark and there were many people around me dressed in long dresses and baggy trousers. I was still in my swimsuit. The sultry air was laden with the scents of unfamiliar flowers and spices. I could hear darshan music, devotional tones of sitars and tablas.

And there was Tosh, dressed in an orange shirt I had never seen before and yoga pants of the same color. He had a burgundy blanket draped around his shoulders as he snuggled up closely with a woman I didn't know. The name Ana appeared in my mind. Her shoulder length blond hair swept across her pretty face as she spoke with a heavy German accent. They were both excited and happy, like new lovers, glowing. I was detached, beyond jealousy, observing and knowing. Peaceful. Her long dress was dark pink and fell softly around her petite frame as they rose and walked toward the music and an open meeting hall. Rajneesh Mandir. Even though I had never been there before, the knowing flooded me. I was in the Rajneesh Ashram in Poona, India.

I followed them into the hall but soon lost them as my eyes traveled to the front of the space, past hundreds of orange clad disciples seated cross legged on the floor, to my first glimpse of Him.

Bhagwan, in a simple white robe, sat in a wing chair on a small dais, his legs crossed at the knee, one tabi clad foot suspended effortlessly in the air. His waist length beard was wispy and almost white. His head was shining, bald, a fringe of long white hair flowing in the air from the fans overhead, mingling into his beard. Large, luminously dark eyes had traveled across the hall meeting mine, holding them infinitely beyond all space and time. My breath stopped. My eyes ran with tears. Tears of joy, of love, of immense gratitude. Tears spilling every emotion simultaneously down my cheeks. I breathed in. Very slowly. And still the emotions poured out my eyes from my soul. I experienced a connection with Bhagwan, fell in love with Him, and knew beyond any doubt that He was my teacher despite how much I had railed against Him over the last year. Even though he didn't appear the same as the teacher in my dream, the energetic signature was identical, a joyous, mischievous love and acceptance beyond anything I had ever felt.

I continued following my breath, watching the pictures go by behind my eyelids, feeling the feelings as they washed through me, breathing until I was done. It was an odd thing that morning in Belize, visiting Poona where it was night, and meeting my Master at last. Clad only in my bathing suit.

Boatyard, Kauai
March 1988

"Hey, whoa, hold it hold it, you lost me," Wajdo interrupted me. "How is that possible? I don't understand. This is way too woo-woo for me."

"I don't really understand, either," I responded, challenged by how to articulate such an experience. "The only thing I have read about that comes close is something called astral traveling, where the energy body leaves the physical body and is not inhibited by time or distance."

"Tosh, help me out here. What's she talking about?"

Tosh had finished up his sandwich and was leaning back in his beach chair, his hands clasped behind his head, a bemused expression on his face.

"Well, Waj, I don't know either. But what I do know is she showed me her diary when she came home, and she had described everything perfectly. And yes, my girlfriend's name was Ana. And she was German. And the meditation building was as she described it. It was weird. But then again, she pretty much knows stuff even when I don't tell her. I sure learned that over the years. Women are like that. You might find out someday if you ever get serious about a girl."

"Never. But really, how can she be in two places at once?" he persevered.

"It was very odd. Later, when I was looking at a globe of the earth, I realized that San Pedro was geographically opposite Poona. If I had a long needle and pushed it exactly through the center of the globe, it would exit the globe in the spot that was Poona. Jules Verne anyone," I joked about the 1864 science fiction novel *Journey to the Center of the Earth*.

"But wait, you guys were together again at the farm? What about Tosh having a girlfriend in Poona?" Wajdo asked, not understanding.

"Yes, we were reunited at the farm." I admitted. "I had a choice to leave him or to stay. Despite what I had seen, our connection was so strong, I decided to stay."

Wajdo was quiet for a moment before he continued. "How did you get out of Belize?"

Belize
April 1980

On the fifth day, the radio man told me that the airports were open. I could fly to Belize the next morning and my international flight was confirmed to Miami. After a day of saying goodbye to the friends Gavin and I had made over the past six weeks, I packed up our bags and climbed aboard the small Cessna on the beach sand runway of the cay.

At the International Airport in Belize, I was struck with culture shock once again. Following the quiet of the cays, the airport was a mass of intense activity. Many people were trying to leave, as this was the first day in more than a week that the airport was open. As I stepped through the gate and onto the tarmac toward the plane bound for the United States, a man leaned in front of me and gave me fifty dollars in cash to hold Gavin on my lap, thus freeing up one more seat out of the war-torn country.

Following the instructions from a dream, I had spun the globe and launched into an adventure of a lifetime. I had personally met my spiritual master from across the world, defying physical laws of time and distance. And now I even had some cash.

Chapter 8

Sharkys & Leaving the Farm

"Adventures won't come to you; venture forth to greet them."

Lihue, Kauai
April 1988

"Did you guys know the Ranch would end?" Wajdo asked as he played with the ice cubes in his drink. The six of us were at dinner at the new Sharkys' Restaurant. The eatery featured an enormous indoor aquarium with live sharks swimming around in at least five hundred square feet of seawater.

"No, we actually thought it would go on forever," Tosh answered. He paused and the table fell silent. Forever is a long time.

It was April of 1988 and after two months in the A-frame, we had rented the last cliff house on the grounds of what was then the Westin Kauai, of Robin Leach's *Lifestyles of the Rich and Famous* fame; Kiran, Miko, and Waj in the upstairs apartment and Tosh, Gavin, and I downstairs.

We ordered dinner and the conversation somehow got onto the subject of sannyas, a topic that came up regularly as we'd all been commune members and disciples of Rajneesh. He had been arrested and deported back to India. During and in the aftermath of His demise, intense national and international media coverage ensued about the controversial guru and his community in the desert. Three years later, as part of that dispersed community, we were still pondering and digesting what had happened and how such an amazing experiment could fail so dramatically, and on such a worldwide stage.

"No, we thought it would go on forever," Tosh repeated. "This was our life. I mean, we had left everything behind when we went there in 1981." He sounded reflective as he recalled those idealistic times.

"Seriously, everything?" Wajdo was skeptical.

"Yup, clothes, furniture, house, practice, cars, even my favorite van ... all left behind. Nothing to go back to. Total commitment. Right, Deb? Tell them about how we left the farm."

I hesitated. "Really, you guys want to know about that?"

"Actually, I am quite curious, you had it made at the farm by the sounds of it. How could you ever leave?" Miko commented.

"I know, it was crazy, and thinking about it now, it seems really insane ..." I began.

The year after our trips to Belize and India resulted in constant change. The meditation gatherings at the farm were bigger and more frequent than ever, yet Tosh and I knew that our time with our small local community would end soon. We wanted to take our spiritual journey further than we could on our own, and we were exploring the possibility of living communally with other sannyasins.

Soon after Tosh's visit to Poona, Rajneesh left India and came to the United States, settling in Oregon on the ranch known as the Big Muddy. It wasn't long before the Ranch community contacted Tosh and invited him to come to Oregon to be their dentist. Tosh said yes, but only if he could bring me with him. They agreed to his condition.

Sproule Creek Farm
November 1981

After one last walk around the farm, I made my way to the red van in the driveway. The engine was running, Tosh was waiting. With an aching heart I climbed up into the passenger seat and slowly pulled the door shut. It was all I could do to keep from crying.

"Is that it?" Tosh asked, wanting a verbal confirmation that we were indeed all packed up and ready to go, ready to embark on the next chapter of our lives.

"Yes," I managed to get a sound out of my constricted throat. I was practicing my breath work to stay calm and focused, trying to tap into my practical side to keep my emotions from taking over and sinking into a complete, screaming meltdown.

I must keep it together. If I let these feelings come up now, they will never stop.

Tosh put the van in drive and released the brake. Slowly, we coasted down the hill and away from my life, my family, my things, my home. The children, Gavin and Nicole, were safely with their natural father and mother respectively. The tightening in my throat was getting more and more intense. Finally, my whole body convulsed as the sobs escaped my mouth. All the self-discipline of the last months of preparation for leaving the farm disintegrated, and the raw reality of what I was embarking upon was fully expressed.

Tosh didn't say much, but then he usually didn't. My friends and family were always asking me if he was okay or if he liked them as they could never tell. He seemed quiet and reserved. Of course, I knew another side, the side I loved and the side that was real to me. Thoughtful, I called it. Spiritual. Deep. Always figuring out ways to see situations, life, people, from an alternative perspective. Sometimes he would talk and share these insights with me, broadening my thinking and how I viewed my place in the world.

Today, he knew there was absolutely nothing to be said that would comfort me or change the emotions that were releasing as I willingly closed the door on our life at the farm, on my life as a dental assistant, my life as a mother and homemaker, my life as Tosh's partner. I knew all of it was done, and I would go through the next phase, however long it took, to find whatever was waiting under these old ideas of who I thought I was.

After all the work to make the farm so very special and beautiful, we had decided to go to the commune in Oregon for a month and see how it went.

We put all our things in the barn, rented the farmhouse, got a locum for the dental practice and drove away in our red van with only one suitcase each. Just like that, my idyllic life at the Sproule Creek farm ended.

Leaving was traumatic. The sobs wracked my body for hours as we drove. I would have a few moments of respite, and then another wave would wash over me. Waves of fear, waves of regret, waves of sorrow, as I mourned a way of life I had achieved and cherished and now was leaving, probably forever.

"We're doing the right thing, aren't we, Tosh?" I eventually managed to ask.

"I don't know," he answered slowly. "But what I do know is that we could have just stayed at the farm for the next twenty years until we retired, but that would be so boring. And think about it, we are on our way to a spiritual commune, a community with an Enlightened Master. There are thousands of people there. Other sannyasins that want to live together in peace, other people that want to be self-sufficient and live off the land, other people that know the old, traditional way of living is a lie."

His words spoke to my soul. Would this be the love really? My radical, unabashed idealism was sure it was possible. It had to be. Hadn't I been guided to Belize, guided to my Master, Bhagwan, and now guided to leave the Sproule Creek Farm? Slowly my body relaxed into the motion of the van as it drove south and west, six hundred miles toward Oregon.

"What's wrong?" I asked eight hours later. It was just past dinner time, and the engine sounded different, hesitating and sputtering. We were slowing down.

"Not sure," Tosh responded, "but something sure is."

It was dark and we were about forty miles from the Big Muddy Ranch. Tosh steered the van onto the shoulder and let it coast. Except for the crunching of the gravel under the tires, the van silently rolled to a stop.

"Well, that's it," he said, "the end of the road for this old van."

"What?"

"Yup, I think she's done."

"Can't you fix it?" I was not sure if he was kidding. His cars and vans were always breaking down, and he always jumped out, lifted the hood, and fixed it.

"Not this time," he said, "unfortunately, I think we just blew the engine."

"Really? Now, when we are almost there?"

"Yup, 'fraid so." He paused for a while and then continued seemingly unconcerned, "Looks like we will have to hitch hike the rest of the way."

"But what about the van?"

"Well, we can leave her here, I guess. We won't need it at the Ranch."

Oh no, I thought, *here we go.*

We each had a large suitcase, trunk sized, that we maneuvered awkwardly out of the van. Tosh took all the important papers out of the glove box and the license plates off the bumpers. And then we hitched.

It wasn't long before a pickup truck stopped. It was the middle of gun carrying cowboy country Oregon, and I was nervous about who would stop for hitchhikers. And glad I wasn't alone. When the cab's dome light went on, the driver had red clothes and was wearing a mala, the necklace of prayer beads around his neck identifying him as a sannyasin. This is the spiritual equivalent of 'family.' Tosh and I needed no further scrutiny of his reputation or intention, our relief palpable at finding "one of our own" and a ride into the Big Muddy.

"Name's Swami Pradu," he introduced himself across the long bench seat of the burgundy-colored Ford. "I assume you are headed into the Ranch?"

After loading the trunks in the back, we climbed up into the cab.

"You two are certainly lucky tonight," he began after we had settled into the seat. "I just happened to have gone into Bend today to get parts, but generally there isn't much traffic along here and pretty much none into the Ranch after dark. The road's a bit tricky in parts. Hang on." He slowed down to navigate a switch back corner before he asked, "What brings you two up here?"

Tosh told him, then asked, "How long have you been here?"

"Only a couple of months," he laughed, "but it feels like years. Don't get me wrong, it's amazing to be here. I am so immersed, I don't even think about my past or of doing anything else. Everything is moving so fast, it's a rush to be part of it."

He continued talking about how new people arrived every day, but not usually hitchhiking in the dark, and everyone had a job to do, and everyone met up at night at the cafeteria. He was part of the heavy equipment department and repaired the huge earth movers being used to build the dam.

"A dam?" Tosh asked, incredulous.

"Oh, yeah. They say if we back up the river, then we'll have a reservoir and there's enough water to make this desert green again. The city planners are all over it." He laughed as he again downshifted into another tight turn. The road was very dark. No ambient light out here in the desert. Just a million stars, awaiting the arrival of the moon.

It was an hour of navigating the long dirt road into the Ranch before we arrived in front of a double wide trailer, the extensive, well-lit driveway filled with work trucks and vans, all covered in mud.

"Sheela's place. We call it Jesus Grove," Pradu informed us. "You can check in here."

"Thanks. I guess we'll see you around?" Tosh asked uncertainly after he unloaded our trunks from the back of the truck.

"No doubt," he said with a smile, waving as he drove off.

Even though it was past seven in the evening, there seemed to be a lot of activity with people coming and going, their red clothes conspicuous as they walked through the pools of light illuminating the driveway. They laughed and joked with easy familiarity.

So far, so good. I wonder what's next?

A woman welcomed us enthusiastically, guiding us toward the wide veranda where the entrance appeared to be.

"Your stuff 'll be okay here," she said, indicating a spot to the side of the veranda. "Come on in and meet Sheela."

The door opened to a long hallway, neatly lined with dirty boots and shoes on both sides.

"Oh, yeah," our guide grinned, "boots off here." Turning away from us, she yelled down the hall into what appeared to be a living room, "Sheela, got some new ones here for you."

I stepped out of my boots, hoping I would be able to find them again amidst all the other footwear. My heart raced, and I felt numb at the same time, an experience of going through the motions when my nervous system could not process any more input. Tosh was ahead of me, saying "hi" to people as he passed down the hall. I followed, trying not to trip on the discarded shoes or bump into the people leaving. *Gosh, it was busy. Holy smokes.*

"Who the hell are you?" I heard a strident woman's voice above all the others, it had an Indian accent.

"Anutosh," Tosh was answering, an unsure chuckle in his speech. "I'm the new dentist from Canada?"

"Well, about bloody time!" she exclaimed. "Ready to go to work?"

"Ah, yeah, sure ..." he stammered, shocked at the crudeness of the exchange.

"Did you bring your girlfriend?"

"Yup, she's here," he quickly stepped aside, exposing me to the roomful of wild looking strangers all dressed in red and orange. The men with bushy beards, the women all looking like cowboys, like the men, no makeup, hair falling out of messy ponytails. They were all sitting around a trim Indian woman with short raven black hair. Her strong voice, tough manner, and large dark eyes flashing fire were at odds with her petite frame and delicate hands that moved gracefully as she spoke.

"Well, speak up," she prompted me. "I'm Sheela, by the way, in case you didn't guess," she continued without pausing for me to respond. The room giggled as one. "I run this place. Anything going on here you don't like, you come an' see me. It'll get straightened out in no time, is that clear?" the Indian accent with an English one on top continued.

"Yes," I managed to get out. "My name's Gandharvo." This was the name I had received in the mail from Bhagwan when I wrote to him, asking to take sannyas after my trip to Belize the year before.

"Oh no, another one," she moaned affectedly, "but the other one is an old man. Well, where are we going to put you? How about a bus driver? Sue was just telling us that she needs bus drivers. Here you go, Sue."

I was in shock. I disliked driving, and I had never driven a bus. Sheela had walked closer to me, noticing the panic on my face. "What's the matter? You don't like your new job already? You just got here." People were laughing at her comments.

"I am not a good driver," I managed to get out and with my

heart pounding I risked a request, "Can I work in the dental office, too?"

"Absolutely not. No one does their old job here at the Ranch. Everyone's doing something completely and utterly new."

I didn't argue with her although it was obviously not true as Tosh was going to work in the dental office. But she softened slightly, looking more closely at me. As she did so, my eyes locked into hers and there were some moments where time stood still, the periphery of my vision darkened. I fell into her eyes, overwhelmed with the sensation of dropping through a long black tunnel obliterating the sound of her voice and the awareness of the other people in the room. Gradually, the feeling of falling lessened and the room grew lighter, the sounds returning to my ears, to hear her continuing.

"So that should do it then. You don't have to be a bus driver; you'll be in the publishing house. Check in with Rama in Buddhagosha in the morning. Geetam, take her to Alan Watts, the A-frames."

Kauai
April 1988

"And look at where you guys are now." Wajdo expansively waved his arm, taking in the torchlit avenue outside Sharkies after our dinner on the terrace. To one side there was a wedding gazebo built on stilts over the water of the lagoon with spectacular lighting in and around it: fountains sending golden shards of shimmering spray in myriad directions.

"Do you folks need a ride back to the hotel?" A horse drawn carriage driver asked as we walked by his magnificent

Percheron horse, a breed of draft horse from France. They were waiting patiently outside the restaurant, part of a fleet of a hundred that carried guests around the lagoons and along the cliffs to the hotel.

"No, we live in the cliff cottages and are happy to walk tonight. It is so lovely out," Tosh answered.

Walking home together to the cottage, I felt like we were all in a dream—it was beautiful, magical, and timeless. During my time on the Ranch, I would never have imagined living the lifestyle I now found myself in, completely self-employed, self-motivated, and living in a tropical paradise. Why would God have placed me here? What was I to learn? How was any of this worldly beauty and luxury 'spiritual?'

Later, home and ready for bed, the moon shone through the floor to ceiling glass sliders that were open onto the lanai off the bedroom. The trade winds gently ventured into the room, accompanied by the rhythmic sounds of the ocean crashing into the rocks directly below the cottage. Getting into bed, I snuggled up to Tosh, reveling in his warmth and the feeling of his strong arms around me in our new cliff house. Yet another luxury and one I didn't take for granted. Unbidden, hazy memories surfaced of my first night at the Ranch.

Chapter 9

Alan Watts & Bronze

"When a sailor arrives, he is already a local, but a tourist is always an outsider."

That first night at the Ranch was one of those life transitions that are incredibly painful yet necessary. You do them out of bravery or insanity, the line between these two rationales mostly fuzzy and gray.

Rajneeshpuram, Oregon
Fall 1981

"You're coming with me." A petite woman with dark hair addressed me in a business-like way. "Which suitcases are yours?"

The roar in my head was making it difficult to focus. *Tosh*

*and I did everything together. Why was my case going some-
where his wasn't?* Numbly, I pointed out which of the two
identical trunks was mine and watched as it was picked up and
thrown easily into the bed of a truck. It was obvious I was to
climb in the cab with this woman, but my body was frozen. I
stared as Tosh climbed into another van, his blue trunk already
aboard. *Could I run over and hug him goodbye? Would I see
him again? When?* The panic was unbearable. *You can do this.
You knew this was the lifestyle. You can do this. Just get in the
truck.* I ran over to the van and grabbed onto Tosh, awkwardly
hugging him as he was climbing into the van.

"Goodnight, Tosh," I managed to get out of my dry mouth.

"Oh, yeah, night, Gandi." Seeing my stricken facial expression, he added, "You'll be okay, I will see you in the morning at
the cafeteria."

It all seemed so matter of fact. *This is how things are done
here.* Woodenly, I walked over to the waiting truck, pulled open
the door and climbed into the cab.

"So, where'd you come from?" My driver's voice sounded
far away.

"From B.C.," I answered after a pause.

"D.C? Wow, that's really far away."

"No. B.C. British Columbia." I clarified, the act helping to
get my mind back in gear. "Just a day's drive away." *Had it just
been this morning that we had driven away from the farm? And
was I even on the same planet?* "How 'bout you? Where'd you
come from?" I figured if she talked, I wouldn't have to.

"From Germany."

"Now that's far. How long have you been here?"

"Only three months, but it feels like forever. Here's the
turn up to Alan Watts, the A-frames. They're cute, I live in this
one." She pointed out into the darkness, spottily illuminated
with knee high electric lanterns along the roads and paths.

"Here's the shower trailer, and I think this cabin's yours, right up here." We were at the end of the road and there were six or seven paths diverging away from the clearing and the double-wide, verandaed trailer she had indicated.

"There is no water in the A-frames, you come down here for the toilets and showers. Here I'll help you get this trunk up there." As I tried to wrap my head around this new information, she had managed to walk up the path and deposit the big suitcase on the small porch. There was a light on. Opening the door without knocking, she exclaimed, "Oh, hi, Sunit. You have a new roommate, Gandharvo." A tiny woman with a halo of large brown curls around her face smiled and dragged the trunk in and across the carpeted floor of the cabin.

"Hi, Gandharvo. This is your bed, obviously, no place to get lost in here. Thanks, Geetam. See you later." And my driver quickly disappeared out the door. "Here's your closet where you can unpack your things." And she went back to sit on her bed. The whole room was twelve-by-twelve feet with the classic steep roof of the A-frame that doubled as walls. There was a window at one end and the door with a window at the other. Closets at the end of the beds and a built-in shelf cupboard under the window between the beds completed the room.

"Thanks," I managed to mutter under my breath before emotions engulfed me and overran my eyes. I could barely see as I started to open the trunk. *Just forget the trunk tonight. You have your day pack all set with your toiletries and pajamas ... remember?*

"It's okay, I know how you feel. It's overwhelming when you first arrive." Sunit's voice was soft and reassuring. "Here's a towel for you to take down to the trailer to wash up if you like. Save you having to unpack tonight."

"Thanks," I said again as I took it, picked up my pack and reached for the door.

Outside, in the cool dark, I gulped a huge breath of air. *You got this. You can do this.* Smelling the small conifers helped me feel at home, just a little. And before I knew it, I was in the shower trailer, empty, the bright lights on. Everything was white and cream and spotlessly clean. The high narrow windows were open, the air fresh, moving and crisp on my face. Without thinking about it I stripped down, hung my clothes on the pegs and got into a warm shower.

Back up in the A-frame, Sunit was asleep when I returned. I fell into the single futon bed on the floor, emotionally and physically exhausted. My eyes started running again. I must have set a record for the number of tears cried this day. It's so unreal to be here without Tosh. I mean, I never sleep without him. *What have I done?*

Cliff House, Kauai
Spring 1988

Perched precariously on the edge of the cliff, I stood on the overhanging lanai of the cottage, peering over the railing. A hundred feet below me, the ocean crashed loudly onto the rocks. It was the morning following the dinner at Sharkys and Nawiliwili Harbor spread out before me, complete with a thick rainbow extending from the boatyard on my left to the Westin on my right. Creating an unlikely workshop with an enviable view, Tosh had set up a worktable and bench grinder on the lanai.

So many pieces of bronze, it will take me forever, I thought, staring at the seven boxes overflowing with boat hardware lined up along the wall. Donning a dust mask, safety glasses, and soft cotton work gloves, I started with the pile of dorades, the bronze cowlings that allowed air to circulate into the cabin without allowing sea water to enter. Like golden periscopes, wide and squat, there were six of them, ranging from one to two feet tall and six-to-twelve inches in diameter. Under the assault of two-hundred grit sandpaper, the peeling paint and thick layer of oxidized bronze disappeared in clouds of green dust. Like a pirate's treasure, these boat pieces looked as distressed and improbable as an old trunk, until the lid is lifted and the gold shines bright.

Stationed at the workbench sanding bronze, my mind returned to my recollections of the previous night, reflecting on how I had lived such a different lifestyle than the one I currently found myself in. How had I ever coped with the insecurity of not being with Tosh? What had I learned?

<hr />

Rajneeshpuram, Oregon
Fall 1981

"Are you listening to me?"

Oh my gosh, what am I doing here? An Australian accent was talking to me, but I couldn't actually hear the words. They seemed jumbled and distant. I heard my voice emerge from my throat, also sounding far away. "Yes," I lied. *The gist of the situation. Focus, what is the gist of the scene here.*

It was the first morning after our arrival in Rajneeshpuram. Catching the bus to Magdalena, the cafeteria, eating and then catching another bus to Zarathustra, the book warehouse, were a blur. I had not been able to find Tosh in the cafeteria, amongst the thousands of people there. Sunit had been kind and stayed with me, pointing me in the direction of buses, food lines, and more buses.

And now I was at my new job as the personal assistant for Rama, the publisher for the Rajneesh International Publishing House. Geeta, the manager of this huge warehouse, was explaining how things worked: shipping books, posters, photos, audiotapes, and videos worldwide.

"Oh, here is Rama now. I'll introduce you."

A very big man had just walked into the mail order office where we were sitting at Geeta's desk. Dressed head to toe in burgundy, he wore corduroy dress shirt and pants, even his cowboy boots were maroon. His dark hair curled over his ears, and a full beard covered most of his face. Dark brown eyes met mine as the introductions were made.

"Come 'ere," he said, beckoning with his arm as he walked over to his desk.

My anxiety increased even more and the pent-up emotions from the morning pushed their way out my eyes, the tears pouring down my face. Panic stricken, I looked at Geeta.

Taking my hand, she dragged me over to Rama's desk. "No worries, we've all been there."

Rama took my other hand and pulled me onto his immense lap, his arms enfolding me and letting me cry all over his shirt. *What is happening to me? I don't even know this person. What on earth have I done, giving up my life and for what?* I don't know how long I sobbed but he didn't seem to mind, and his solid reassuring embrace gradually calmed me.

"Rough landing?" he asked in a soft voice after a while.

"I guess so. I'm not usually like this. I don't know what's happening to me." My voice didn't sound quite so far away.

"Yeah, well, you just jumped into a huge new reality, dear. It'll take a while to adjust. Trust me on that one." He chuckled, completely unperturbed at my out-of-control emotional state. "I've been part of the commune for years, India and now here, and I still wonder when I'll be done with this 'adjustment.' So, where'd you come from? Let's start with the easy questions."

Still on his knee, I started talking, telling him where I was from, and that our van had broken down and that I was supposed to be working in dentistry with my partner, but Sheela had said no, and I couldn't even find him at breakfast, and where was he, anyway? And I missed my kids, and why was I even here? Rama listened and nodded and agreed with me.

Gradually, as we were talking, I began to notice the room around me. There were many desks and red-clad people sitting at every one of them. While they were all aware of me and the situation at the boss's desk, they didn't seem particularly concerned or interested. Somehow, they were acting as if it was a normal occurrence. Later, I realized that it was kind of normal. When new people arrived, sometimes they experienced culture shock, and it was often expressed emotionally. The residents took it in their stride and comforted and reassured the new ones.

The desk facing Rama's was empty, "Waiting for your arrival," he gestured toward it, "but it's teatime. Let's go get some."

Boatyard, Kauai
May 1988

Well, so much for a quick fix and launch, we were so naive, I thought to myself and laughed out loud as I looked right through *Elixir* where the bottom third of her planking was removed, exposing her frames.* They looked like ribs in a huge, landlocked whale skeleton.

It was early morning. I had just parked by the big rocks alongside *Elixir*, Gavin dozing in the backseat with his schoolbooks. Almost summer, the air was still and quiet but for the cooing of doves in the ironwood trees. We had been at the project for six months and time had flown. *And not even close to a launch date.* As I walked the forty-foot length of the hull to the tool shed, I appreciated the sculpture of the floors,* weeks of Kiran's intricate work. Once the planks were back on, they would be part of the bilge, forever hidden from view.

Reaching the bow, the new stem* was now in place, fitting perfectly where the old one, seriously damaged from marine borers and dry rot, had been replaced. It was like a three-dimensional jigsaw puzzle, the angles of cuts and interlocking pieces adding to the strength of the hull. *I can't believe I am learning this nautical language.*

Sun's rays created shafts of light filtering through the trees, creating long shadows in the grass. My arms reached up to the sky, reveling in the feeling of health, vitality, and strength that came from the daily physical labor and my two-mile swims across Nawiliwili Bay. Forgotten were the challenges of being with a man who was totally absorbed in his project. I had made myself part of the project, actively participating however I could, every day. And I loved it, too. Restoring neglected boat parts to their original luster and brilliance felt oddly nourishing to my soul.

Unlocking the shed, I dragged out the generator and ran the extension cord aft to the sawhorses where I would work on the spreaders, the wooden cross pieces that sit at the top of the masts and support the standing rigging. Tosh had repaired them. Today, I would start to sand the golden spruce that matched the masts, booms, and gaffs.

The boys arrived, like triplets, similar in build and size, only Wajdo's wispy blond hair setting him apart from the dark-haired twins. Wearing grimy T-shirts with the sleeves ripped off and baggy epoxy-stained work pants, they unloaded a rented oxy-acetylene torch.

"What's up?" I asked.

"We're ready to start on the new lead shoe to be added below the old iron keel. It'll be easier when the bottom planks are still off," Tosh explained.

"Yeah, remember all that lead we jackhammered out of the hull a few months ago?" Wajdo joked, as if any of us would forget.

"Yesterday I tried to get the old keel bolts off but after being immersed in wet cement for forty years, they were too badly corroded. We'll have to cut them off with a torch," Kiran explained in his quiet, concise way.

"But how will you get them out?" I asked, puzzled.

"The plan is to drive the remainder of the bolts down through the keel with an iron rod and a sledgehammer. But ..." Kiran paused and added with a chuckle, "we'll find out soon enough if that'll work."

As Kiran and Wajdo got ready to cut the tops off the keel bolts, Tosh looked intently at the stern,* a sharp awl in his hand to poke into the wood. Like a dentist with a sharp explorer looking for sticky, decaying areas in teeth, he tested all the original wood. If the wood was soft, it got cut out and replaced, just like a filling.

"Dang, it looks like the stern will have to be replaced as well as the stem. This supports the rudder." He swore good naturedly, accustomed by now to the extent of rot in the old structures.

"How do you do this?" I asked. "I'm freaking out. Oh, no, another big chunk of fancy wood. Oh, no, how do I do this?

How much more time is this going to take? But you just seem so relaxed with it all. Don't you ever want to be done with this boat?"

He started laughing. His shaggy salt and pepper hair couldn't cover up his shining green eyes, lustrous in his tanned face. He was happy. I could feel it.

"Deb," he began, "this is heaven to me. Problems to figure out, complex structures to build. I love that I don't know how. Figuring it out is the best part. I don't care how long it takes. Look, we're in paradise. The longer it takes, the better, right?"

"But what if the money runs out?"

"Don't worry about the money. We will always have enough. You'll see. I promise." He sounded so certain, so sure I couldn't help but relax and agree with him. And it was true about our life so far. Money had never been an issue. If Tosh wanted to do something, he did it. And it would be the same here in Hawaii. We still had savings and were enjoying an amazing lifestyle, building something beautiful, living in the tropics, swimming every day. His strong brown arms encircled me, reinforcing the wave of assurance, certainty and joy emanating from him.

"Hey, knock it off, you two. We're ready to go with these bolts." Kiran was inside the hull, donning welders' goggles and leather gloves, and anxious to wield a modern-day flamethrower to destroy the last of the left-over corrosion in the keel, corruption in the very foundation.

Chapter 10

Portals, Drive By & Children Arrive

"The success of the journey is determined by how you navigate the storms rather than by who you are."

Boatyard, Kauai
September 1989

The sun glinted off the golden rim of the fourteen-inch porthole. Solid bronze, it weighed at least eight pounds without the glass. I held it up against the industrial grinder, leaning into the rouge impregnated rag wheel. Rouge is the deep red wax that jewelers and dentists use to polish metals. I was accustomed to polishing crowns and bridges in the dental office with a bar the size of a stick of butter. This rouge bar was the two-pound variety and had a deep round trough worn out of it already where it rubbed on the cloth of the rag wheel before I pressed the bronze against it.

We had removed fourteen bronze ports from the original

cabins when we dismantled them earlier. Rectangular and round, small and large, the gaskets and cracked panes were replaced with new rubber and quarter-inch safety glass, rendering them like new.

My mind had finished sorting out the logistics for the day, the lunches were made and in the cooler under the stern of the hull. Gavin was set up with his schoolwork on the flat rock under the ironwood trees a hundred feet away. Tosh, Kiran, and Wajdo worked on the big timbers that made up the stern. The hum of the generator bled into the background, isolating me from other sounds, any other distraction.

I was grateful for the mindlessness of the task, a task that revealed shining beauty as I sanded away the verdigris and old paint. The orbital sander had begun the restoration with coarse two-hundred grit paper up to the fine black six-hundred grit Emery sheets, a giant version of an emery board for your fingernails. Polishing with rouge was the final step, plus the most rewarding. *A ring for a giant*, I thought, *or a bracelet? How can a window be such a beautiful thing?* And without the glass, it was easy to imagine stepping through them, into another world. Unlike me, *Elixir* had traveled the seas, voyaged to places I had never seen. But then, *Elixir* had not experienced the Oregon desert.

Rajneeshpuram, Oregon
Fall 1981

"It's teatime, let's go get some." Rama had announced.

The whole office was suddenly filing out the door and into the warehouse where tables of hot coffee, tea, and hot chocolate were dispensed from huge electric urns. Massive trays of home-made muffins and bread were accompanied by restaurant-sized jars of peanut butter and jam. Bowls of powdered sugar and cinnamon with squeeze bottles of honey completed the menu. The cafeteria prepared and delivered tea mid-morning and again mid-afternoon to all the work sites on the expansive Ranch.

There must have been a hundred people all grabbing big melamine mugs in assorted colors and fixing bread to their preference. Finding seats on warehouse boxes, forklifts, and the polished concrete floor, people sat in small groups all talking at once.

Thirty minutes later, I was back at my desk, going through my desk drawers with Geeta and learning about our phone system. The phone on my desk was for Ranch calls only, and I had a Rolodex of hundreds of numbers for the different departments and their worshippers (workers). Rama had a red phone on his desk to make off Ranch calls for the mail order and publishing business. The only outside lines for personal use (and shared by thousands of residents) were four pay phones by the side of the county road.

Suddenly it was noon. Once again, all the workers pushed back their chairs, grabbed their orange puffy vests and jackets, and filed out the office door. Following Geeta's lead, we headed for the stop where three yellow buses waited to take us up to Magdalena for the midday meal. *Maybe I will see Tosh there, maybe I will have better luck than I did at breakfast.* But the lines of people were longer than at breakfast, the dining hall even more crowded.

Queues moved quickly with sannyasins on both sides of long serving tables. Huge bowls of fresh salad greens, sprouts and full-sized pitchers of salad dressing preceded the steam tables with hot vegetarian entrées. Baskets of bread and buns, fresh from the ovens, smelled remarkable. Stainless steel tubs of butter pats were floating in buckets of ice. I learned later that even the butter and yogurt were made on the Ranch with milk from our dairy cows.

The sounds were deafening with people shouting hellos and clanging the huge metal serving spoons back into the stain-less-steel bowls. Hair netted cafeteria worshippers (workers) pushed tall carts packed with trays of food to refill the tables promptly.

"See ya, Gandi," Geeta called as she carried her food tray off toward friends waving at her. "We are back at Zarathustra at two-thirty."

Another girl beside me piped up, "Are you new here?"

"Yeah, first day, actually," I responded.

"Wow, isn't the food amazing? Hey, come sit with us if you like."

I gratefully followed her bouncing dark ponytail through the rows of white melamine tables and stools to some empty places at a table by the windows, windows that looked out at a vast display of brown hills across the valley and blue cloudless skies. While the strangers around me talked together, I played with the vegetables on my plate. I had no appetite despite the appealing, fresh food. Struggling to keep above waves of panic, my eyes scanned the huge room looking for Tosh's silver hair, unsuccessfully.

"Hurry up and finish," the ponytail girl encouraged. "You don't want to miss drive-by."

"What's that?" I asked, confused.

"You really are new, aren't you?" She laughed kindly. "Bhagwan drives by on the road every day after lunch and we line up along the edge and sing and dance and wave to Him. It's a daily celebration."

I followed the crowd out the door and back onto and off a bus, jostled and nudged into a line along the well-maintained gravel road. People stood quietly, some talking softly. My mind spun in turmoil, like batter in a mixing bowl, the beaters on high. While I had read His books, listened to His audiotapes, and watched His videos, I had never seen Him in person. *What would it be like?*

I saw a car in the distance and then the line of disciples came alive, clapping, singing, and swaying to the songs from a group of musicians half a block away. Bhagwan drove slowly, one hand moved up and down, as He celebrated with us. His dark eyes scanned the thousands of happy faces lined up to greet Him. Ensconced in the silver of the car, his face surrounded by the white of His beard, it was as if He rode on a wave of light that glowed and washed over us all as He passed.

Standing amongst strangers, I found my eyes growing wet with tears and shining with emotion. Bhagwan got closer and closer. Gone were the last vestiges of angst, the self-doubt, the wondering what I had done by giving up my life as I knew it. All uncertainties disappeared as I looked in His eyes, felt my body dancing, and my hands clapping. It was as if we were all One. Unity at last, all consumed by our love for the Master, the Enlightened One. The One who had gone before us in realizing the true nature of this world. The One who could give us glimpses of our own promise, our own abilities to transcend the density and illusion of material existence to bring the peace, joy, and love from heaven above down to the Earth.

Gone was the worry of giving up my relationship and my children. The benefits of transcending this world would make it all worthwhile, would be well worth the sacrifice. I could feel it in the cells of my body and soul.

The beautiful silver Rolls Royce slowly passed by and continued its journey across the Ranch. And drive-by was over. Groups of people slowly made their way back to the bus stops and work.

I found myself walking back to Zarathustra, well in time for the resumption of worship (work). As my tall leather boots crunched on the gravel road, my mind slowly came back and with it, anxiety, as the reality of the foreignness of my surroundings engulfed me. But I had had a taste of something beautiful and transforming; a joy and ecstasy that moved me beyond my mind.

Boatyard, Kauai
September 1989 (same day)

Had I really tasted that unity? That joy and ecstasy beyond my mind? Yes, I had, but it went away. Was I deceived? Was I naive? I pushed the thoughts away and focused instead on what I could see in front of me. What I could touch and feel with my hands. The finished ports were resting on their rims along the back of the workbench, leaning on the shed wall. Gleaming and gold, heavy, solid, beautiful, new.

Rajneeshpuram, Oregon
Fall 1981

"Tosh," I yelled. It was the second night, and I spotted his silver hair in the crowd. I made my way forward into the cafeteria line. He was having an animated discussion with several women from his work. After briefly looking up, he went back to his conversation.

Wasn't he as anxious to find me as I was to find him? "Hi," I said breathlessly when I caught up to him, feeling unsure when he didn't stop talking and welcome me with a bear hug.

"Oh, hi, Gandi," he responded as if I were a passing acquaintance and not his partner of the last eight years. He introduced me to his colleagues and continued his conversation.

I wasn't sure how to respond. My jaw quivered, my eyes threatened to overflow, and I willed myself to keep it together. Trying to hide my feelings of shame, my need for him, I stammered something and kept walking. *It was all a new way of relating, much more autonomous*, I rationalized, blinking away the flood in my eyes.

With so many people here, there was no reason to rely on him alone as I had in my old life. I didn't need him to help with the children as they weren't here, and we were no longer managing a dental practice together, either. I swallowed hard and clamped my jaw tighter. He had made new friends and so had I.

We grew apart from the physical circumstances of having roommates and no privacy to be together, as well as the attention of others in our more accessible surroundings. At mealtimes, we would hug and say hi but somehow, even my need to be with him receded, obscured by the obstacles of a new lifestyle. Too painful to feel, it was easier to pay attention to all the other things going on, gradually allowing my old life to blur away from my immediate focus.

I settled into a new routine of going to the cafeteria, work, lunch, drive by and dinner. Looking back now, every waking moment was full, leaving no opportunity to think or question, no opportunity for reflection.

And at the end of a long day? Yes, the nights were challenging. Where was Tosh?

And then our month-long trial period was up. Each day had been filled with working, learning new skills, and collaborating together to accomplish huge goals. In Publications, we got the contract with Waldenbooks and Barnes & Noble, two of the biggest booksellers in America. This meant processing and shipping orders to every one of their stores in the country.

We worked all night to get boxes packaged and mailed in our three-day guaranteed processing time. Today with computers and automation, this is accomplished within hours at Amazon. But at that time, big software managing systems had yet to be developed. Thrilled with our leading-edge word processors for typing invoices and labels, we were proud to utilize first generation computers for inventory and accounting.

Ranch-wide, we worked to build a solid infrastructure, but we encountered opposition from the Oregon Land Management Bureau when applying for building permits. After consulting with attorneys, everyone was excited and optimistic about our plans to incorporate as a city so we could dispense our own permits and continue to grow.

Tosh and I had been accepted into the burgeoning commune, relieved and elated to secure permission to bring our children. It felt like the restoration of missing body parts.

Nicole, eleven, and Gavin, five, quickly became immersed in their new lives with their caregivers and the other children. All the kids, from the youngest kindergartner to the oldest teen, had areas where they apprenticed. Gavin worked at the chicken farm, helping to feed thousands of birds and collecting the eggs. Nicole worked in the repair shop upstairs in the same warehouse I worked. Older, she was unhappy to have left her life and friends. In her lunchtimes, she visited the horses in their corral across from the publishing house, a small, inadequate comfort after leaving her own pony behind in Canada.

I saw them daily, but our encounters were brief, usually at mealtimes in the cafeteria. While I was consumed with my job and Ranch life, and relieved to have them closer, my heart continued to ache, longing to be with them and Tosh more. It was an emotional place I had no time to explore or question.

I had consciously chosen a new and radically different lifestyle, one I continued to gladly participate in. The excitement of our accomplishments as a community, the trust that this lifestyle would be a positive one for all of us, remained strong. After all, I'd had many lifetimes of ordinary lives, this lifetime would be an extraordinary one. Any pain and doubt were a price I continued to be willing to pay.

Chapter 11

Keel & Crematorium

"Deep in the wooden heart of a ship is the soul song laid by the dream of the ship builder."

Boatyard, Kauai
June 1988

"What's on fire? What's burning?" I could hear Wajdo's panicked voice, but I couldn't see anything or anyone. The smoke appeared suddenly, completely filling the air around the boat. There was no moon to help orient my eyes in the clouded darkness. Chosen purposefully for obscurity, this moonless night was the perfect time to melt down the original 3,500 pounds of lead pigs (ingots) that were jackhammered out of the cement in the bilge and to pour a new keel. *But now what? What's burning?* My stomach tightened, concern growing.

"Gavin," I yelled.

"I'm right here, Mom," he answered from close by. Momentary relief before my mind rushed on. *Is the boat on fire, part of the cradle? Would the tanks of propane and acetylene explode?*

"There are no flames, just smoke." I heard Tosh's disembodied voice from over near the mold that was sunken into the ground. "Damn, the wooden form is burning because the lead is so hot, burning without flames, literally going up in smoke." Tosh turned flood lights into the smoke, trying to see. Kiran, Wajdo, Gavin, and I stood back to escape breathing the acrid air, all of us on edge. What had gone wrong?

The night began innocently enough as Gavin and I drove over to the harbor from our cliff house.

"Mom, are we going to stay at the yard all night?" he asked with excitement.

"I hope not." I laughed. "But you never know. We've never done this before. Just like everything else on this boat, it'll be an adventure."

"How come we have to do this at night, Mom?"

"Well, no doubt there are rules about melting down almost two tons of lead, not to mention having open fires in the boatyard. It's probably good to do it when all the Coast Guard guys and the Harbor Police aren't around." *What was I teaching this almost eleven-year-old?*

"How hot will it get? Like red hot, Mom?" He seemed fascinated.

"Pretty hot, honey, six- or seven-hundred degrees Fahrenheit, according to the book Tosh was reading." I was nervous. Pouring a keel. Such a simple sentence, but such a big deal. The keel is the very bottom of a boat, the part that keeps a boat from capsizing. Pouring a foundation: it felt like pouring the foundation for the rest of our lives. *No, I corrected myself. Calm down, and don't exaggerate.* So extreme. Unwieldy weight. Immense temperatures. The boys had prepared for months, talking through countless scenarios.

Tosh and Kiran had done all the engineering back in January when we cleared out the old hull. The lower the weight is placed in the hull, the more stable the boat, so it was decided to pour a new lead keel and fasten it below the existing iron one. The safety of the vessel would depend on this foundation, and we were changing it from the original plans. *Who were we to mess with professional nautical engineers?* I wondered. *We better get this right.* Last night was their first attempt to melt the soft dense metal bricks, but the fire hadn't been hot enough. Tonight, the rented propane and acetylene torches remedied that problem.

"Will the boat catch on fire?" Gavin had asked just hours ago.

"I hope not," I had answered quietly, even more nervous as I thought about what we were doing.

"There aren't any fire hydrants in the boatyard, Mom," he persisted, a keen observer.

"Uh-huh," I responded, trying not to think about it. The fire hazard was real. *Elixir* was in a big grassy field and surrounded by dozens of tall ironwood trees and derelict old wooden boats that had been drying out since the last tropical storm, ten years before. The trade winds never stop. Just one spark and ...

Shuddering, I kept driving, my eyes on the dark road winding down to the harbor. My mind would not stop. Lead is toxic and causes brain damage, especially from the fumes when it's melted. It's toxic on the skin, as well as through inhalation, even when outside.

Arriving at the yard, I parked the Subaru and unloaded the water jugs and cooler on our flat 'table rock' behind the boat.

Gavin ran over to where the four-foot square container had been built of cinder blocks around an old stainless-steel tank.

"Hey, Gavin, are you ready for the show?" Wajdo greeted him, tousling his hair as he walked by.

"What's the vacuum doing out here?" Gavin asked, wondering why the shop vac was next to the 'furnace.'

"We have charcoal briquettes under the cinder block furnace and to make the fire hotter, we'll use the vacuum to blow air on them, like this, see?" Waj turned the vacuum on blowing mode and aimed it toward the briquettes. They instantly glowed red, burning brighter and hotter.

"That's a lot of charcoal you have there," I commented.

"Yup, eighteen twenty-five-pound bags. The boys did the calculations and figured that's what it'll take. A lotta steaks could get barbecued with that much charcoal," he joked.

"Hey, Tosh, everything ready?" I called over to him as he inspected the wooden form they had built in the ground. Ten feet long, twelve inches wide and deep, it was lined with tin and had bar clamps every two feet to support the weight of the lead. There was a tap and three-inch steel pipe to drain the liquid metal from the vat into the form. He turned the tap open and closed to make sure it would run smoothly.

"Yup, looks like we are all set. Hey, Kiran, it's a go!" He shouted to his brother over the noise of the generator, signaling him to start up the torch.

Donning heavy leather welders' gloves, safety goggles and a respirator, they again looked like extraterrestrials, the firelight illuminating their oddly masked faces in the flickering light of the torch. The first of about a hundred ingots of lead was laid on the inclined tray inside the cinder block container. Imagine a regular brick. These were gray and weighed about thirty-five pounds. I needed two hands to lift one. Turning the torch on full, it took a long time for the metal to start melting down the tray and into the bottom of the tank. Checking my watch, I realized if each ingot took forty-five minutes to melt, the night would not be nearly long enough. It would take three days.

As usual, I snapped photos, documenting the equipment, the people, and the scene, pretty sure this would be another 'no-go' tonight. So disappointing for Tosh. *Hey, what's that?* From my vantage point on the table rock, I could see that Wajdo was more excited and had loaded another heavy pig onto the melting tray. *Really? Was it going to work tonight?*

Making my way back over to the makeshift forge, sure enough, another ingot was already half melted and slowly running down the tray, like an ice cube on a hot summer day. Unreal.

"Hey, Gavin, you wanna do this?" Tosh yelled over the noise from the generator, the shop vac and the hiss from the torch. As Gavin eagerly approached him, he continued, "Get some goggles and a respirator."

Kiran handed over his gear, cinching up the straps around Gavin's smaller head. "Time for me to take a break."

Walking over to where I stood, Kiran looked excited, a wide grin exposing his even teeth, identical to my husband's. "This is awesome. I've never melted metal before. What a rush. I think it may actually work tonight. As the lead in the bin gets hotter, the ingots melt more easily. It's going to start going fast now."

And he was right. It got down to less than five minutes per ingot. Amazing. It was so hot, well past the liquefying point of the lead, the brick would just lay on the inclined piece of I-beam and start to melt. The stainless-steel tray had a much higher melting temperature than the lead and was not even glowing red.

Less than two hours later, the last pig made its final journey down the ramp of the makeshift crucible.

"Heat up the tap and drainpipe with the torch," Tosh

directed Kiran as he checked out the form one last time and ensured we had full five-gallon pails of water moved from around the forge to all along the mold. There was a water tap in the yard, but it was a block away, so we had filled buckets in preparation for fire. I wished we had a hose.

"Just a sec. Check this out, Deb. You need a picture of this." Kiran pointed into the crucible.

Approaching the forge, I was amazed. The twenty-five-pound sledgehammer and massive crowbar were floating in the vat of molten lead, the silver pool rippling like primordial water. It could support the iron tools because they had less density than the lead.

Using a shovel, Kiran fished the heavy tools out of the lead before the wooden handle started to burn. Directing the torch to the tap, Kiran looked like the stereotype of an aboriginal shaman in the dark, dancing in step with the flames moving along the four-foot length of the drainpipe. It had to be hot, so the lead didn't cool down and solidify on the way to the form. I noticed I was chewing my fingernails. This was a crucial part in the process. Such a huge amount of hot metal, I prayed it wouldn't go anywhere except in the form. No splashes, no accidents.

The big moment arrived and Tosh and Wajdo, on two sides of the extended tap handles, pushed and pulled when the tap opened. The silver spout of lead came out of the pipe with more than a ton of force behind it, as liquid as mercury. It crashed into the mold and slammed into the far end of the form with such force it splashed up in a spray of molten lead that ended up leaving a three-hundred-pound puddle on the ground.

But we were oblivious of this because the air was suddenly filled with smoke.

"The boat's okay? The cradle? The tanks?" Kiran asked, reading my mind.

"Yeah, all seem to be okay, just the form," Tosh responded out of the dark.

Relieved, I started noticing the swirling smoke with the light dancing on it. The hellish scene made my shutter finger itch, and I started to take photos. My mind lightened up, and I couldn't help but envision a medieval alchemist with his wand, "abracardabra" and "poof" with heaps of sudden gray smoke from which something appears out of nowhere.

It was difficult to see anything, but the vat was empty and that was as much as we knew until the trade winds blew the smoke away. Only then could we see that there was a new keel waiting in the ground for us.

"I can't believe we did it," I breathed a huge sigh of relief. "And no accidents, thank goodness."

"Yeah, well, check out these pants, Deb," Wajdo was inspecting his trousers. There were perfect quarter inch holes burned into them where sparks had landed "Hey, guys, you got holes in your pants?"

And they all three did, with only a couple of spots that left a blister, but they had all been so focused they never felt a thing.

After dismantling the vat, fire pit, tap, sluice pipes, torch, acetylene, and propane canisters, we headed home. It wasn't even midnight.

"Deb, you're gonna laugh when you hear what I was thinking about tonight with all that smoke."

"Well, I could do with a laugh. Are you gonna share it?" I asked.

"The crematorium at the Ranch."

Looking up at the dark sky, the stars quietly introduced themselves to my sight, slowly filling my vision, and reminding me of a similar darkened sky with the same stars, four years earlier.

Rajneeshpuram, Oregon
September 1985

"It's like fireworks, millions of tiny sparks, all winding their way to heaven." Tosh held my hand. We had met after our long workday, a rarity. I snuggled closer. It was cold. I could see my breath as we stood in a crowd of thousands of sannyasins. There was live music, and people danced, swaying gently. Many of us were lost in similar thoughts as we contemplated death and the soul at this cremation and celebration of life of a fellow disciple.

"Did you know him?" I asked Tosh.

"No, not really," he answered, quiet, somber. "I just came from Pythagorus." This was the medical center for the Ranch and included a dental clinic and a hospital, all staffed with fully licensed medical professionals and state of the art equipment. "Indivar and I prepared the body."

"What? Holy crap, I didn't know you knew how to do that?" I was aghast.

"Yeah, well, I never did it before. It was quite something."

"Are you okay? I mean, was it upsetting for you?"

"Yeah, but I'm okay, I mean, I feel privileged that I was able to be with Lazarus during his time of transition. It was quite powerful."

We were quiet, each thinking about the seriousness of life, and that life actually ends sometime. Hard to imagine during our regular days of constantly doing our jobs and running here and there. But here we were. Bhagwan lectured that death is a time to celebrate, the soul freed from the confines of this earth, this material existence. Unlike traditional Christian beliefs, belief in reincarnation was a given, following the tradition of many Eastern religions.

"I can't help but remember the story of Jesus and Lazarus. So interesting that Bhagwan gave him that name." I said aloud. "Do you know why he died?"

"He'd been sick for some time. They think he had AIDS*. He passed away from lymphoma, a complication from the disease."

The world was just learning about AIDS in the 1980s, and there was much we didn't know. I didn't want to think about it. It was too much more unknown in a world that I already felt lost in. Focusing instead on what was in front of me, I peered through the crowds of dancers. *Would I see a body?*

There was a wide copper roof that appeared to be suspended from the sky, hovering weightless above the bright, flickering, flames of an open fire. While I could see a platform through the orange blaze, there was no body to be seen. Grateful, my eyes looked up into the sky, the stars visible despite the glow from the crematorium. I was fascinated by the countless sparks escaping the top of the copper chimney that jutted thirty feet into the air. Particles alight, infinitesimal bits of the body of a man, or was it the light of his spirit, escaping? Stony canyon walls on two sides of the narrow valley seemed to add their embrace to the ascent of his soul as it made its way home, into the heavens, into the infinite.

Chapter 12

Keel Bolts, Mast Collars & Book Orders

"Sadness and regret make up the ballast that keeps us stable and lets us sail in all kinds of weather in any direction we choose."

Boatyard, Kauai
June 1988

"How are the math problems coming along?" I asked Gavin, trying to keep a positive tone in my voice as we drove to the boatyard a few days after pouring the keel.

"I don't want to talk about it." His ten-year-old voice sounded sullen.

Glancing in the rear-view mirror, I was discouraged. I had hoped he would enjoy homeschooling after all the teasing he received in his previous school as the 'new kid.' It didn't help that he wore thick eyeglasses and was a know-it-all kind of kid. Homeschooling presented its own issues, mainly that he didn't want to do the homework even though he voraciously read all his lessons and textbooks in a month. When I asked him why he wouldn't do the exercises and send them to his distance teacher, he informed me in a quiet, matter-of-fact way, "I don't need to prove to anyone that I read the stuff."

The days after pouring the keel brought new challenges, but nothing that didn't possess some kind of solution. The wooden form in the ground had mostly smoldered away, and the bar clamps came off uneventfully. However, the tin that lined the form never did get unstuck from the lead. Overall it was not an issue, except as one of only a handful of problems in the whole project that Tosh was not able to solve.

Arriving in the boat yard, Gavin and I walked together over to where the boys grappled to get the new lead shoe moved into position under the boat.

"What's that?" Gavin asked, indicating the chains and ratchet handles attached to the nearly four-thousand-pound beam of metal.

"A 'come-a-long,'" Kiran answered, straightening and wiping sweat off his forehead.

"A horizontal jack," Tosh elaborated between panting breaths of exertion, "to move heavy objects."

"Yeah, like come-along little two-ton log." Wajdo couldn't refrain from joking as he strained on the ratchet handle, his t-shirt soaked with perspiration.

They had jacked up *Elixir*, adding more supports under her cradle, and dug a trench underneath to accommodate the new keel.

"Do you think there is enough room under there?" Gavin bent over, taking a closer look, like peering under his bed for a lost sock.

"Damn well better be," came the grunted response as they wrestled the cumbersome length over the grassy ground inch by inch.

Finally in position, we all took a break.

"So how are you going to get that keel attached to the old one?" Gavin asked, still eyeballing the cramped space under the boat.

Tosh indicated the six giant bolts scattered on the ground to one side. Like tacks for the sole of a giant's shoe, they were nearly two feet long and two inches in diameter.

"We'll drill through nearly two feet of metal, and jack that puppy right up into place," Wajdo explained.

"Just like that," Tosh said, snapping his fingers. A sarcastic expression escaped around his smile as he took a long drag from the water bottle.

"Well, there are a few more issues," Kiran began slowly. "Like electrolysis, for example."

"What's that?" Gavin asked.

"It's what happens between metals in salt water; an electric current is generated, and it makes metal actually dissolve. Here we have lead, iron, and stainless steel bolts, all different metals. To prevent this, a 'sacrificial' zinc, a softer metal, is placed on the keel to stop the breakdown of the actual keel," Kiran continued.

"Do you think the tar and roofing paper between the keels will be enough of a barrier for this?" Tosh asked Kiran.

"Let's hope so," he responded wryly, thoughtfully scratching his head, "and hopefully, coating the bolts with boat-yard bedding compound before installing them will act as a gap sealer to prevent sea water from getting up inside the keel," he finished.

Break and science lesson over, I handed Gavin his back-pack and followed him over to his desk, the table rock under the ironwood trees. Already opening his book, he kicked off his flip flops and rested bare feet on the rock. His face was open and relaxed, content to let his mind wander off into another adventure between pages that didn't include math problems.

A month later...

The boys were already hard at work when we arrived in the yard, the generator whirring and the power tools screeching. They were reattaching the top third of the hull. The planks, numbered when they were removed, went back into place, each one smoothed with the belt sander, fitted into position, and refastened with the new silicon bronze screws.

"Wow, she is almost back together again," I joked with Wajdo after settling Gavin in with his lessons. "All except the garboard," I yelled over all the noise.

The garboard, the first plank above the keel, was massive: thirty feet long, eighteen inches deep and one and a half inches thick. I felt reverential when I looked at it laying there along-side the boat: it was just a part of what must have been a giant teak tree. This plank would stay off for another two years, thus allowing the sawdust from construction to fall out of the bottom of the boat. When it was all bunged, faired, primed, and caulked, our nautical friends called the process 'paying the devil.' No wonder it was left until last.

"Are you ready for the mast collars today?" Waj asked. The boys had rented a sand blaster earlier, and they had set up a table for me off to one side, well downwind from the hull.

"Yup, sure thing," I affirmed, giving him a thumbs up.

Grabbing a long-sleeved shirt and pants off the hook in the shed, I pulled them on over my shorts and tied a bandanna around my head to protect my hair. The ear protector muffs went around my neck, I got a new face mask out of the box, put big clear safety glasses over my own, and slid my slender fingers into thick cotton work gloves. This would be a filthy job. Good thing it was early and not too hot.

"I need a picture of this," Tosh joked as he came over. "You look like a Martian or something."

I laughed, trying to stay positive and cheerful, while I pulled out the messy boxes of unlabeled metal mast, boom, and gaff collars. I had already made a detailed inventory, including a description of each piece and compared it to the list Tosh had made from his perusals of the old photographs of *Elixir* before her rig was dismantled. It was quite a puzzle to sort through as each piece was unique and included eyes (loops) for attaching blocks. Each piece also had a unique diameter, depending on where they were on the tapered masts. Most of the collars were in two pieces separated from their other half. When I think about it now, it is a wonder we were able to correctly piece it together and that it worked when the rig was raised.

Back to the sorry pile of metal collars. Like the rest of the ship had been, the pieces looked hopelessly weathered. I picked up the first one, laid it out on the table and picked up the rented sandblaster nozzle.

"Here's your reservoir to refill with sand when you get low." Tosh pointed it out to me, undoing the top and checking the level of sand inside. "Here's your 'on' switch. If you let go of the trigger, it will automatically stop. Give it a go."

Knowing the blaster generated sixty to one hundred pounds per square inch, and could blow the flesh off my fingers, I placed the collar in the bench vice and cinched it down tight. "Is that tight enough do you think?" I asked Tosh.

He nodded.

I aimed the nozzle, depressed the trigger and the sand hissed out, smashing into the metal, old paint, and rust, which flew off in all directions. Releasing the trigger, the sand stopped immediately.

"This is amazing!" I exclaimed, smiling behind my mask. "It's so much easier than using sandpaper." I pulled up the ear protectors and continued.

Tosh watched me for a bit, nodded and gave me a thumbs up. Going back to the hull, he left me in my own world of dusty noise and dozens of metal pieces, all waiting to be restored. *Such a production line,* I thought to myself. *A hundred planks to finish and attach, dozens of spars and rigging pieces, bronze parts, and now the collars. Just like the publishing house at the Ranch.*

Inside my cocoon of protective clothing and the unnatural silence of the earmuffs, my mind followed its calming review of the book order production line. But angst returned as soon as it was done. Whenever my mind had a moment to drift, not actively engaged in figuring out something new, it fell into a hopeless loop of questions and longing from my heart, a heart that didn't want to accept I was wrong, and the Ranch had been a mistake. A heart that longed for some kind of comfort in knowing why I was here working on a boat. A heart that couldn't tolerate the emptiness of a world without Spirit, without an experience of the Unseen, without God.

The metal pieces went more smoothly. I knew how to fasten them in the vice to get the most surface area blasted clean before I had to re-clamp it. Forcing my mind to relax from its torturous questioning, I remembered being in Buddhagosha before the First Annual World celebration in 1982 and the mountains of orders that seemed impossible to finish. Just like these piles of boat pieces that seemed endless and unlikely to ever be part of an actual floating vessel.

Rajneeshpuram, Oregon
July 1982

"Is that the last one?" Rama asked me, fatigue clearly showing through his bearded face.

"I think so," I responded, hoping I was right.

It was the day before the First Annual World Celebration in Oregon's city of Rajneeshpuram. After months of preparation the visitors had arrived. Around five thousand people added to our two thousand residents were going to meet every morning to sit together in silence with Bhagwan Shree Rajneesh, an enlightened spiritual master. Rama and I were set up in the bookstore, taking book and video orders for sannyas centers located around the world. Rama would guide them to titles most appropriate for their communities. And of course the photos. There were hundreds of images of our beloved Bhagwan in every size, framed and unframed. I would fill out the order forms, collect the money and send the information to Buddhagosha for the warehouse staff to package items for people to carry back to their countries.

"How many orders so far?" I asked

"Five hundred or so? I think we have seen all the major centers except California, although I saw the folks from the California center this morning at breakfast." *Five hundred orders of more than a thousand dollars apiece?* The numbers were beyond my narrow imagination. Rama was busy packing up his papers, filling his burgundy briefcase, a present he had received from Bhagwan.

It was seven at night, not quite dark yet, as we trudged down the wooden walkway outside the bookstore to catch a bus back to Zarathustra.

"What will it be like, Rama? You had all those years sitting for hours in lectures and satsang in India, I've never sat with

Him before." Satsang is a Sanskrit word meaning "to associate with true people" or people "gathering for the truth." After months of preparation for all the visitors and in the presence of thousands of sannyasins, the anticipation and excitement had built up phenomenally. After all, this was the whole reason I was here, right? To sit with and learn all I could from an enlightened master?

"Well, it's different for everyone," he began, stroking his narrow goatee with his left hand as he thought about what to say to me, this 'mail order' sannyasin who had never been in the actual presence of Bhagwan. "And I guess I have to say that it can be the highest ecstatic experience to the most mundane, the whole spectrum."

"I'll find out tomorrow," I laughed, giddy with anticipation as we got off the bus and walked into the warehouse.

"Watcha got for us?" Geeta jumped up from her desk, looking excited. "Your team has expanded to thirty for the next week. We're ready to pack hundreds of books and videos."

Opening his briefcase, Rama was dramatic, slowly withdrawing a two-inch pile of order forms. The team would work overnight to invoice and pack each order and ensure they were ready for the next day's stack of sales.

After delegating all the paperwork we had generated, Rama beckoned me over to his desk. As I approached, his boots came down off the desk and he sat up straighter. Happily, I climbed into his lap, platonically supportive, for our debrief from the day.

"How are you holding up, Gandi? Really, you have been through so many changes these last few months. I'm proud of you, it's been a lot."

"Well, yes, my kids are here now and that is easier in some ways, but hard because I rarely see them. It's so different, not living with them. They really do have their own lives here, even at age five and twelve."

"How are they doing with the lifestyle changes?" He was genuinely interested, yet in a detached kind of way, like everything was okay.

"Nicole misses her horse, so while she works upstairs here in the repair shop, she spends her breaks and lunch hours across the field with the horses." Climbing off his knee, I pulled a wheeled chair up close, resting my booted feet up on the opened bottom drawer of Rama's desk. His returned to the top of the desk, his hands clasped behind his head, lost in the mass of dark curls that covered his ears. He was an interesting man. He had a girlfriend, but I had never met her. At least fifteen years older than I, in his forties, maybe, I respected his insight and experience with the communal lifestyle.

"She seems to be friends with the other girls her age," Rama remarked. "I see all three girls over there on the corral fence, feeding carrots to the horses."

"The three of them share an A-frame. How amazing it must be to have their own place at twelve years old."

"What about Gavin?" Rama continued with his questioning.

Geeta, walking past with a stack of invoices, stopped and asked, "Are those new videos ready upstairs, Rama? We have a lot of orders for them here, by the way."

"Yes, they're on Rabyia's desk." He pointed to them.

"Gavin and my son are mates, you know," Geeta volunteered, her Australian heritage audible.

"Really?" I asked, surprised. "Which one is your son?"

"Govind, the smallest one." She laughed. "Takes after me."

"That's crazy, I had no idea he was your son. Those two, along with Forest, get into trouble pretty much daily." I heard about the escapades from Gavin, though I'm sure I only heard about half of all the adventures they entertained themselves with.

Geeta laughed as she collected the requested video tapes from the desk. "Well, they certainly won't have anything to rebel against when they grow up."

"What do you think, Rama?" I asked.

"Seems to me, only time will tell. They have a lot of freedom here, that's for sure. So back to business. Can you write up a memo for Buddhagosha about our hours during celebration days?"

"Sure, go ahead, I am ready." I was never near his desk without my steno pad and pen.

Boatyard, Kauai
July 1988

And these mast collars are ready, too, I thought as I released the heavy metal half circle of the last piece from the vise and placed it atop the finished pile.

The trade winds caressed my sweaty face as I peeled off ear protectors, safety glasses and mask. Shrugging off the protective layer of clothes, I took deep breaths, relieved to be free from the stifling gear.

"Ready for the foundry," I yelled up to Tosh where he stood on the scaffolding, refastening planks for the final top section of the hull.

"Great, Deb, let's take a look." He jumped down and switched off the generator. He laughed and took a long drink from his giant insulated water jug as he walked over to the pile of bright steel semi circles. He picked up the pieces, examining them.

"Good news. It looks like they all have enough thickness and strength to be reused. I wasn't sure how much metal would be left after all the paint and rust came off. Thank goodness we don't have to make any new ones." He started piling the pieces back into the wooden crate he had built for them. "I can take these over to the shipping yard tomorrow. They'll go in a container ship to the foundry where they'll be re-galvanized before we paint them, make them less likely to rust, at least for a while." He grinned, the irony not lost on him that these collars had been galvanized when they were new. They eventually rusted, like everything at sea.

Later that afternoon after my swim across the bay, I relaxed on the sand, drying in the late afternoon sun. The swim had washed the rest of the dust and dirt off me, clearing my head. Rama came to mind again, and all the people and work that went into the annual celebrations at the Ranch. It felt so peaceful here on the sand. And solitary. Such a contrast to the thousands of people and intense excitement of that First Annual World Celebration.

Chapter 13

Celebration & Land Sailing

"How we relate to our challenges determines their influence in our lives. We can either drown or fly."

Rajneeshpuram, Oregon
July 1982

"Over here, Gandi." Tosh waved to me from his position in a long line of brilliantly colored devotees. Thankfully, we spent a little more time together now.

The big day was here, and I would be sitting in Rajneesh Mandir with my beloved Master for the first time. I hurried over to where Tosh had saved a place in line for me. After a brief hug, he asked, "How are you doing today?"

"I'm nervous. Isn't that insane?" I responded, noticing the butterflies in my stomach. *What would it be like to sit with Him? Would I get enlightened just by being with Him? Would I be able to sit still for three straight hours? Would I have to cough? Would my legs go to sleep?* I had been told to take a large shawl to sit on to help with that. *Would it work?*

Our line arrived at the shoe check pavilion. Removing my shoes, I handed them over to the attendant, amazed that seven thousand pairs of shoes could be organized and retrieved after the meditation. I pinned the number tag on my waistband and waited a moment for Tosh.

Walking together into the huge, covered building, I felt awed by the immensity of the place. It appeared to be the size of two football fields, under one roof with clear plastic for the walls, protecting the interior from the weather but not the light. The floor was hard packed sand, entirely covered with white linoleum. This made a clean firm surface that was not as hard as concrete, easier to dance and sit on.

"You need to walk past these two at the door," Tosh whispered in my ear. "The sniffers." Bhagwan had severe allergies to perfumes so all personal products on the Ranch were fragrance free. Visitors were well informed but just in case someone arrived wearing perfume, or any scent from laundry soap or lotion, the sniffers would ask them to leave.

Music drifted out of the auditorium, live musicians playing peaceful, calming melodies. The floor was cold and smooth under my bare feet as I walked up toward the white podium with the lone chair where He would sit. I barely noticed more than a dozen burgundy clad bodyguards standing around the periphery. They stood completely still, apart from their heads slowly scanning the entire space. The inner circle of Bhagwan's oldest disciples and His personal caregivers all sat in the front rows. There were no chairs or even markings on the floor. The space filled quickly as disciples silently sat down in an orderly way, side by side and row by row. There were no bags, or personal items with us. Thankfully I had remembered the shawl. Rolling it neatly, I placed it beneath me as I sat. Tucking my legs into a cross-legged position, my knees almost touched Tosh's on my right and someone else's on my left.

I took a deep breath, letting the music calm me after all the busy days and late nights we had put into preparing for these special few days with our Master. Tosh took my hand and smiled reassuringly. He had sat with Bhagwan in Poona and was familiar with the protocols.

Looking forward, I focused on the empty white wingback chair on the dais twenty feet in front of me. Closing my eyes, I let the music carry me inside, into meditation, into my longing for the Light, the Love, another way of being in this world.

Then the music changed, from soft, almost silent, to celebratory; alive and joyous. Music that made the whole hall vibrate and dance with life. But everyone stayed seated, softly swaying where they sat, heads and arms reaching skyward. All eyes were open now, focused on the back of the dais where Bhagwan would walk through the archway after disembarking from His Rolls Royce.

And suddenly there He was, gracefully gliding out onto the dais, dressed magnificently in one of His beautiful handmade robes with a matching crocheted hat. His arms were raised, gently conducting the music and all of us into our ecstasy, our love of being with each other and with Him. After walking along the front of the dais and spending moments connecting with His eyes to everyone in the massive room, He made His way to the chair and slowly sat down. Removing one sandal, He carefully crossed His legs, His white tabi-clad foot extended. The music stopped. He clasped his beautifully manicured hands in his lap and closed his eyes. Everyone stopped moving, closed their eyes, and fell into silence. The entire place, all seven thousand disciples, sat perfectly still. There was no coughing, sneezing or sound of any kind except the birds we could hear outside the open walls and doorways.

He was beautiful. His huge eyes were dark, full of laughter and compassion, emitting immense joy in being with all of us. Everything disappeared from my mind. It felt swept free from my earlier anxiety, melting into the energy of the room, into what Bhagwan called the Buddha-field, that space where thousands of like-minded souls are united in their desire for peace, and love for God, and each other. Briefly, my mind was distracted by my body, hoping I had arranged my legs properly so they wouldn't fall asleep. And so we all sat. For three hours. Barely moving.

Time stood still or passed in an instant. For several hours, my awareness was only of the peace of another world filling my being, until my legs drew me back into my body. They were completely numb and felt like wood. *Oh no, they're asleep,* I silently panicked. Shifting slightly, I was brought back to reality with the stabbing sensations of pins and needles from my toes to my hips.

The person next to me moved slightly and her leg bumped into mine, sending cascades of sharp pain through my legs. I breathed, willing myself to tolerate the discomfort and not stir or make a sound. As my legs returned to normal, I drew in a deep breath of relief. *Oh no,* the deep breath had tickled my throat. *Don't cough,* I said to myself, trying to suck more saliva out of my already dry mouth, in order to swallow and stop the itch. My forehead started to sweat, and my face flushed. *Please don't let me cough.*

And then the time was up. The music started and Bhagwan smoothly arose from his chair and stood on the dais, gracefully waving his arms. We were joined in ecstasy, our arms, our heads, and our hearts, together in a dance with the Divine.

Bhagwan slowly made his way to the back of the stage and exited to His car. As soon as he drove off, we all stood and danced together; masses of swirling red and orange. The music was ecstatic and carried us beyond this material world. Our souls merged as one, flooding us with knowing that love is the answer and the most important thing; the thing that transcends all chaos and separation. The thing that bonds whole worlds together beyond age, or gender or race or religion or body, just the dance, just the being, totally present.

This was why I was here. This was why I could give up my traditional life and live a different one. It was all worth it. This was the direction, the way this world would learn to live in love. This was the experiment that would teach us the way of the future, would prepare us for the time to come, to show us alternatives to the current status quo that seemed so inauthentic and unsustainable.

Gliding across the vast expanse of white floor, I found Tosh, and we made our way out the doors to the shoe check pavilion. And yes, quickly and efficiently, I had my shoes back on my feet, and my feet back on the ground. But my mind and heart were filled with bliss. *How would I ever be able to think straight after this?* I wondered. It was like nothing I had ever experienced.

Little did I know then, how that moment would stay with me for a lifetime.

Was there angst amid my idealist fervor? Of course, loads of it. I missed being with my children and while I saw them each day, it was so little compared to my previous life. I missed Tosh. I missed doing dentistry and sharing my profession with him. I missed my family in Canada.

Working in the publications department as a personal assistant to the publisher was all encompassing. Someone else did my laundry and cleaned the bedroom I shared with another mother of three. I ate my meals in a communal dining room that fed thousands, so I never cooked or shopped. I didn't have any money, so never bought anything. I didn't have a car, so I didn't drive anywhere. Every day was similar as there were no weekends off. We all worked every day, all year long, every year. All things associated with our modern culture were altered.

There was a tremendous sacrifice of personal desire that I willingly made to find out more about who I really was, stripped of my conditioned lifestyle and identities of wife, mother, and dental assistant. The constant activity, the excitement about our overall community accomplishments of living on the land, supporting our own city, even having our own electric plant, airport, roads, and transportation system was inspiring. Even more inspiring was our meditation time together in Rajneesh Mandir, a powerful experience of doing an active meditation known as 'dynamic' with thousands of others in the same space at the same time.

This meditation had been started with Rajneesh in the 1970s and had five parts: deep chaotic breathing, catharsis, using the mantra 'Hoo,' silence, and dancing. He had noticed that Westerners were unable to sit still and meditate in silence without first physically exhausting themselves, hence the physically active, five-part structure.

Tosh and I had started doing dynamic meditation at the farm several years before and had incorporated it into our community retreats. Now I was here in Rajneeshpuram with thousands of others, part of a much larger community, just as I had hoped and envisioned when we left our northern Shangri La.

Boatyard, Kauai
Fall 1988

"How fast was I going, Mom?" Gavin rolled up to me in his go-cart, Illusion. It was fashioned out of scrap wood from the yard with wheels from the hardware store.

"Twenty miles-per-hour," I answered, impressed.

The constant trade winds filled the recycled blue tarp sail and drove him back across the expansive tarmac in the launch ramp area of the boatyard. He was taking a break from carving small figurines and pipes out of exotic hardwood.

Gavin and I would pack up from the boatyard around three or four every afternoon and head for the beach. I would swim across the bay to wash the sawdust and generator noise out of my being. While I swam, Gavin visited his bartender friend at Duke's and drank sodas for free. He would come home with stories of the interesting characters he had met at the bar that day. It seems amazing to think about this now, as he was only eleven years old. Back then, it seemed perfectly natural that he would be independently hanging out in an open air, everyone welcome, beach bar. Years later, he told me the rest of the story. The bartender had a hash habit, and Gavin carved hardwood pipes to sell to him and all his hash smoking friends.

A flash of blue sail zoomed by me as he took another tack* around the pavement. Sitting on the rocks near the ramp, I relished this time with him, enjoying his delight and pride in his accomplishment. He was so grown-up at eleven. I suddenly remembered him when he was half that age—at the Ranch, his legs too short for a grown-up chair, but his independence and sense of adventure strong even then.

Chapter 14

Swami Sangeet Gavin & Crash

"To anyone wanting to go to sea, I say go."

Rajneeshpuram, Oregon
August 1982

"Gandharvo," Yashen, my new boss, yelled up at me on the conveyor where I was nail gunning plywood onto floor sections.

After the Celebration, I had been transferred out of Buddhagosha and the publishing house and into the factory, building prefab sections for the new townhouses. I missed Rama and the books, but it was exhilarating to be in a more physical job for a while. And it didn't really matter to me where I worked now. There were heartfelt connections everywhere, every day. I straightened up from my task and lifted my safety goggles to see Yashen better. He motioned the universal signal of a hand across his throat, indicating I was to stop my work. I untangled myself from the compressed air hose, carefully lowering the heavy metal gun to the platform before I lightly jumped the four feet to the factory floor.

"Hey, Vidsy wants to see you in Socrates," he continued, yelling to be heard over the compressors and forklift engines.

"Right now?" I asked

"Yup, right now," he repeated.

Socrates was the main administration building for the city, all our buildings and departments were named for saints, seers, and holy men. Ma Anand Vidya, or 'Vidsy', was the 'mom' or head of personnel.

"Am I getting transferred again?"

"No clue, I just work here." He chuckled as he gave the typical answer to that question. "Better get going."

I left my safety glasses and work gloves in my cubby, collected my backpack, and walked through the factory to the entrance. There was a well-graveled driveway up to the road and the bus stop. In less than five minutes, a yellow school bus came down the dusty dirt road. I hopped aboard.

The commune had purchased school buses from school districts, getting them for bottom line prices at state auctions. The roads were well graded and graveled, none of them paved. While there were no personal vehicles, there were many work vehicles and trucks for the various departments.

As I rode toward my meeting, my eyes focused on my surroundings, definitely barren and brown, except for the areas that were irrigated along the river, where grass and fruit trees had been planted to stop the erosion along the banks. As we got closer to Socrates and the middle of the city, I could see the many buildings we had put up. There were buildings for construction, buildings for vehicle maintenance, the Fire Department, the Peace (Police) Department, the airplane hangars and the airstrip easy to spot in the distance. Hanging flower baskets and large planted barrels, colorful against the backdrop of the high desert, had been planted around all the structures. Ten minutes later, I stepped off the bus at Socrates.

I crunched across another gravel walkway into the two-story warehouse with windows, and up the stairs to Vidsy's office, apprehensive about what change was coming next. I was surprised to see my five-year-old sitting on a chair, his feet dangling.

"Hey, Gavin, what are you doing here?"

Vidsy interjected before Gavin could answer me, "He's been running away from the chicken farm again, along with Forest and Govind. Found them in the culvert under the road this morning." Vidsy was a tall blonde lady from South Africa known for her no-nonsense way of dealing with people.

"Ah ..." Gavin was looking at the floor, not saying anything, his light brown hair falling into his eyes.

"Well, go on, tell your mom what you told me," Vidsy prompted him curtly.

"I wanna go live with Daryn Dad."

My stomach lurched; I was not expecting that one. "Are you sure, Gavin?" I was pleading as much as was possible in those four words for him to say no.

"Yeah, I don't wanna be here anymore. I miss my dad." His legs swung back and forth a whole foot above the carpet, emphasizing his small frame.

"We can't have these kids running away all the time," Vidsy continued, looking at me. "They are playing in the culvert where it's not safe and who knows where else they run off to. We found Govind stuck in the excavator bucket a few days ago. Deepak fished the three of them out of the river mud last week, and yesterday they were on the cliffs above the road, throwing rocks at the cars when they drove by."

"I understand," I said, as controlled as possible with a mouth that had quickly gone dry. I didn't. The scenarios she'd itemized were news to me. I was dismayed that they were running so wild and free. While I saw him each day at mealtimes, the thirty or so children between the ages of three and sixteen were under the supervision of assigned caretakers, I assumed the caretakers always knew where the children were. "I will have a talk with him and get back to you in a few weeks," I bluffed in desperation.

"Nope, not possible. He is going to his dad's. Make the arrangements. We're done here." She grabbed a new file, motioning to her assistant to bring in the next person.

My heart stopped beating; my breath caught in my throat. Her words stabbed me, making my brain stop working. I knew the rules. Any dissent or disagreement was easily dealt with here. If you didn't like what direction one of the 'moms' gave you, you could leave. Period. No discussion. I knew I had agreed to these unspoken rules when I arrived, and I wanted to stay but really? Did I have to give up my son? Was this really happening? In the moments following her pronouncement, my mind and my heart battled, exhausting me. Taking in a ragged breath, I knew I had to get out of her office as quickly as possible.

I lifted Gavin off the chair to the floor and held his hand as we walked out of the office and down the stairs. Outside, we sat on a bench for a bit, my heart continuing to pound in my chest, hurting. My soul screamed, *No, this can't be happening. How can I possibly be separated from my son? How can I make such a choice?* Out loud, my voice sounded normal, calm, "Wow, Gavin, what was that all about?"

"Me and Govind like to play in the tunnel. It's fun in there. We yell, and it echoes."

"Uh huh, and why was Govind in the excavator bucket?"

"Well, he couldn't get out, his legs were too short," he said, as if that explained it.

"And you left him there?"

"Me and Forest tried to get him out, but we couldn't reach him."

Oh, my gosh, I thought. "And what about the river?" I continued aloud, curious about his side of the story. "What were you guys doing down there?"

"We were on the fence." When I looked puzzled, he continued, "You know, Mom, the fence to keep the cows out of the river, we kept our boots in the wire squares to stay out of the mud, but we fell off. We had our snow pants on, we didn't get very wet."

"Yes, but I bet you were pretty muddy. What did Izza say?" Izza was one of the caretakers in charge of the children.

He looked down. "She wasn't very happy to see us."

"I guess it was a bit messy." I paused. "Gavin, is it true you want to go back to Canada to live with Daryn Dad?"

"Yeah, I miss him."

I snuggled with him on the bench as my eyes filled with tears. I knew there was no use pretending to think about this. Vidsy had made her command, and I would obey. At least if I wanted to remain here.

But Gavin had made his request, too, and even though he was only five, I did listen to and consider his wishes. I always had, even though at the time, children were considered incapable of knowing anything for themselves. I knew differently, especially about Gavin. I respected his voice at the same time as I guided him toward his best interests as was my parental duty.

Gavin had two parents. Maybe it would be good for him to have some time with his dad. Daryn and I had an agreement about Gavin's living arrangements: if or when he asked to live with a certain parent, we would honor that request. I'd asked him, and he had given me his answer.

"Shall we go give him a call?"

"Can I talk to him?" he asked.

"Of course, let's go see if he's home," I responded, still outwardly calm, yet every word piercing me to the core.

Boatyard, Kauai
Fall 1988

"Mom, did you see that?" Gavin yelled, bringing me back to the yard in an instant.

I jumped up off the rocks and ran across the tarmac where he was untangling himself from the wreckage of his go cart.

"The wheel fell off. What a cool wipe out," he said, breathless as he pulled the pieces back close to their original positions and rolled the sail up a bit.

"Are you hurt?" I frantically scanned his bare arms and legs for blood or road rash.

"No, I'm good. Hey, can you hold this for a minute?" He gestured to the axle that was missing a wheel on one end.

I did as directed while he confidently snapped the wheel back into the bracket and uprighted the cart. It was suddenly all in one piece again. He climbed back in, excited to be off in the wind one more time.

I made my way back to the edge of the ramp to the rocky breakwater and climbed back into my racetrack grandstand and shook my head. *Boys. They really are a different species.* It felt like he loved the crash as much as the racing.

Rajneeshpuram
August 1982

After the meeting with Vidsy, the next hours and days blurred past. My heart was broken, my head so conflicted I could only function by going through the motions of getting up, eating, working, and sleeping. I felt alone and cut off from Tosh. He was on a project with a deadline and didn't share the same mealtimes. As far as discussing it with others, most of the other residents didn't have children at all and didn't understand what my angst was about. "He'll be fine with his dad, and less for you to worry about," they all seemed to agree.

Gavin appeared happy to be going to see his dad, and that was a consolation. He would spend some months with Daryn and then I expected to get a call that he missed me and wanted to come back. This was how these things worked, right? Parents shared children between families all the time. It was just that the two residences were six-hundred miles apart: one of them a traditional family setting with a stepmom, two older stepsiblings, and practicing a born-again Christian religion. And the other was set up like a kibbutz with men, women, and children all housed separately, eating communally, and under the spiritual direction of an East Indian mystic. And it didn't help that the commune was constantly in the media as controversies erupted weekly about building permits, taking over the county, and the big one: society's disapproval over our so-called "free love."

Daryn and his mother, Gail, took two days to drive down from British Columbia. Gavin and I met them at the Ranch's Welcome Center around midday of the second day. Daryn gave me the obligatory hug and mumbled something about "nice to see you" under his breath. Gail did the same and added that "it was a long drive into this place."

"Would you like some tea or coffee?" I asked, awkward in this public building and without a home of my own to play hostess in, completely estranged from anything socially familiar.

"Oh, no, we're good, thanks. We'd better be getting back on the road," Daryn replied, equally as awkward. Gail acted upbeat, her voice loud and cheerful with a forced undertone, like they drove six hundred miles and visited a commune every day.

"What do you think of the Ranch?" I asked, trying to cut through the fake and into something real.

"It's amazing," Gail answered me, not missing a beat, and even though she had not done a tour. "You have all done so much here, quite an accomplishment." She had given Gavin a hug and directed her attention toward him. "What do you think, Gavin? Time for a car ride with your granny and your dad?"

I put my hand on Daryn's arm, trying to have a moment to speak, but his eyes were wide and preoccupied. "I let you know as soon as he wanted to be with you, as we discussed last year. I trust you will do the same for me, as part of this agreement," I blurted out, determined to say what was on my mind despite the lack of privacy or time.

"Yeah, sure, Deb, we're good," he said as he picked up Gavin's small duffel bag and started to walk toward the door and the car waiting by the curb.

Outside, I knelt in the road beside the car to give Gavin one last hug goodbye.

"Love you lots, Gavinooski. We'll talk on the phone, okay?" It was almost impossible to get the words past the constriction in my throat and my eyes were blurring with tears as I helped him up into the car where Daryn took over and fastened a seatbelt around him. Gail was already in the passenger seat in the front, waving and smiling. Daryn closed the car door, Gavin's head barely visible above the windowsill as he waved at me with a big smile, excited to be off on an adventure with his dad.

"Take good care of our little guy," I managed to whisper in Daryn's ear as I gave him a rushed hug before he got in the driver's seat. I stepped back and he closed the door, giving a small, distracted wave, fastening his own seat belt while driving away.

I sat down on the curb, watching the car until it was lost behind the curves of the muddy road winding out of the Ranch. My tears fell onto my red jacket, leaving wet trails down the front and over my heart. *He'll be okay. He will have a regular life for a little while.* I prayed I had done the right thing, although it simply felt like it was the only choice at that moment in time.

Tosh's ex-wife came to visit a few weeks later and took her daughter, Nicole, back to Ontario with her. This decision and hand off was Tosh's, and I was not there when Nicole drove away with her mom. Despite this, I again went through emotional upheaval, episodic crying over a period of months. I missed both children.

Still, I stayed and participated in this huge experiment of communal living. I was being guided to continue by a conscious inner knowing that some lifetimes are just supposed to be used for living outside the norms, to break down perceived reality into a new, more authentic way of being. Aware of the uniqueness of my path, and how crazy it must appear to my family and friends, I remained at Rajneeshpuram.

Six months sped by, and it was February 1983, seven thirty, the end of the day. Gauchami's, our evening prayers, were finished, and I walked outside the Buddhagosha warehouse along with everyone else. After finishing construction on the townhouses, I had returned to working with Rama in the publishing house.

I was missing Tosh. He was working late with the electricians and off Ranch electrical contractors, installing the new substation for the city. They were still in a 'crunch' to get it done before the permit expired. I zipped my red down jacket up over my chin and pulled my crocheted hat down low over my ears and forehead. The wind was cold, the light from the streetlights illuminating my breath, clouds of white in the dark.

Stamping my feet in my boots as I waited for the bus, I thought about how different my life had become. I barely remembered my past life, as a wife, mother, farmer, dental assistant, daughter, sister. This life was so full of activity every day, and all day shared with many new friends from all over the world; friends who had also left full and successful lives. Lives that they, too, didn't have the time or the inclination to speak or think about now. Or, after our long days, was it simply because we were just too tired?

I missed the children, too. They had both returned to Canada with their other parents last summer. Along with many other parents whose children were out in the world with ex-spouses, I sent letters and called them from the pay phone once a week. I remembered the last call a few nights before.

"Collect call for Gavin from Gandharvo. Do you accept the charges?"

I heard the operator's voice in my ear, sounding foreign and far away. It was after dinner, past eight o'clock, the only free time I had. It was cold that night. A light skiff of snow covered the ground. A single streetlight cast a lonely circle of light around the four payphones standing by the side of the country road near the entrance to the city. There were no enclosures around them, just a small box around the phone itself, to protect it from the weather. Every one of them was in use. I had waited half an hour before one was free.

A long pause, and then "Yes" came the sound of Gavin's stepmother, Gina, on the other end. "Gavin, your mother is on the phone," I heard her call him. *What was he doing? How was his life? Did he like living with his dad? More than living here?*

It's so cold. My hands inside my gloves were freezing. And so were my feet. I tramped them down, the tiny bit of snow making a small crunch under my boots. White against the black of the starless sky, my breath was shallow, constricted.

"Hi, Mom." Finally hearing his young, six-year-old voice, I fought back tears. Struggling to make my voice sound normal, I asked him about his life, and he answered with yes or no answers.

All too soon, I heard Gina's voice, "You have to get off the phone now, Gav. It's bedtime. Say goodbye."

"Bye, Mom."

"Bye, Gavinooski. I love you bunches," I managed to get the familiar words out of my mouth, praying he couldn't hear my voice breaking over the scratchy long-distance phone line. "Click." I held the phone to my ear for a while, not wanting the connection to be over, tears running down my cold cheeks into my collar.

But there were others waiting to make their calls. I put the receiver back into its cradle, turned, and slowly made my way back through the dark to the bus stop. *It feels so strange and unnatural to be separated from him.*

I could barely acknowledge the judgment I felt from Gina and Daryn about my lifestyle choices. *Do they say mean things about me to him?* Still crying, I snugged my chin into my zipped-up jacket, tugged my knitted cap down lower and pushed my gloved hands into my pockets, wishing I could also push the feelings away.

The bus finally arrived. I barely noticed the warm air on my face as I climbed inside. Walking back to an empty seat, I kept my eyes down, feeling painfully conflicted.

Am I still willing to be part of this massive experiment in communal, spiritual living? Will I regret this? Is the price too high?

Chapter 15

Speaking Up & Sheela's House

"I hate feeling uncomfortable, but numbness drains my soul."

Boatyard, Kauai
December 1988

"It really sucks about the Ranch; life is just not the same now that it's over. That bitch Sheela really screwed things up for a lot of people."

Sundro was a strong man starting to thicken around the middle. Plopping himself down in the beach chair under the stern of *Elixir*'s hull, he removed his ball cap to mop the sweat off his high forehead. Putting the cap back on, his hand followed a habitual smoothing motion, down the long mustache that adorned either side of his wide mouth.

We were a year into the *Elixir* project. Sundro and Sargam, sannyasin friends from San Francisco, had come to the garden island to get married on the beach. They ended up staying with

us in the cliff house for a month and working on the boat.
Sundro, a carpenter by trade, was excited to be part of such a
challenging project. We were happy to have an experienced
woodworker on site. On his first day in the yard, he was talk-
ative, freely expressing strong opinions about our shared past as
participants in the Rajneesh commune in Oregon.

It was lunch time, the generator gloriously silent. The three
boys, Tosh, Kiran, and Wajdo had gone to the hardware store
for supplies, and Gavin now attended public school. This left a
rare opportunity for Sundro and I to have a private
conversation.

"Are you still part of the community in San Francisco?" I
asked, genuinely curious, but also stalling about how I was
going to react to his previous statement. He had basically
spoken the common party line about what had happened those
three long years ago. Unbeknownst to him, I had a different
experience and did not share his opinion.

"Yes, and we're living in a community house again. I like it
but it's not the same as the Ranch. That was such an amazing
time. What was your job there anyway?"

"At the end I was working in Sheela's house, actually."

"Really, you worked in Jesus Grove?" There was disbelief
in his voice. Like any large organization, there were only a few
hundred members who actually interacted with the leadership.

"Uh huh. How 'bout you?" Again stalling. The pressure to
speak up about the seamier side of the commune was growing
inside me.

"I didn't actually work there. I came in the summer to
attend Humaniversity.* I envied you guys that could live there
full time. What did you do in Jesus Grove? Were you part of
the underground tunnels? The wiretapping?"

After Sheela left the Ranch in September 1985, evidence
of wiretapping crime was discovered in secret bunkers

tunneled under Jesus Grove. In December of the same year, twenty-one members of the commune were indicted for wiretapping after intercepting oral and telephone conversations in Rajneesh Hotel rooms, restaurants, disciples' rooms, and pay phones. Twenty-five years later, in April 2011, Oregon Live reported it was the largest illegal wiretapping operation ever uncovered. I had known nothing about the underground rooms and illegal activities taking place below my feet, despite walking up and down the access hallway hundreds of times a day when I worked there.

"No, nothing that exciting. I was Sheela's receptionist. You know, answering phones, serving tea at meetings." I was weighing my words carefully and watching his expression as he bit into his sandwich. This conversation was a potential minefield. Sannyasins loved their Master and anyone who disagreed with His perpetual state of perfection risked being shut out. Instantly.

The party line was that Bhagwan knew nothing about the illegal activities that came to light. Wiretapping, assassination attempts, arson, and bioterrorism, just to name a few, were exposed after the Ranch disbanded.

Because of the intense controversy around our presence in Oregon, in the last two years of the Ranch in particular, we had ignored the rumors, assuming they were part of the state's propaganda against Rajneesh and His sannyasins. It would be many years and numerous court cases heard and prison sentences served before the extent of the real crimes was revealed.

"Oh, my God. How could you stand to work for her? She was crazy, power hungry, and hooked on drugs. She took the place over. And then look what happened to Bhagwan. She ruined Him. He ended up being arrested and the whole Ranch collapsed."

Most sannyasins had tremendous difficulty facing the accusations of criminal activities of their spiritual leader. Rajneesh, as their Master, had to be innocent to justify their trust and the choices they had made to follow Him. A favorite option was to blame Sheela, the spokeswoman and forewoman of the Ranch.

"Well, you have a right to your opinion, but what I saw gave me a different perspective on the whole scene," I ventured cautiously.

"He should never have trusted her. That was a huge mistake." Bhagwan had given Sheela the job of overseeing the Ranch and running the commune.

"You might believe that, but it's not what I remember, and she actually wasn't the bad guy." There, I said it, blasphemous words in the sannyasin world. I had to speak the truth and try to break the bubble that His disciples insisted on living in. They seemed oblivious to the reality of corruption, so often found in groups and organizations.

Sundro stopped chewing and looked at me, stunned. "What?" he asked with his mouth full.

"Sheela wasn't the bad guy ... at least not from what I experienced." I waited before continuing. "Do you know she met with Bhagwan every night, and He would tell her what He wanted her to do?"

"*He* told *her* what to do?" he repeated, struggling to hear through his idealized perspective. "Bhagwan said she went crazy with the power and took everything over. He said He didn't know what she was doing."

"Yes, He did say that. And I saw firsthand how difficult it was for Sheela, she would cry before going to see Him." My voice was getting stronger after being silent for so long, the truth at last forcing its way out of my mouth.

"Really? Why? You're lying." His lunch forgotten, his voice rose in righteous indignation.

"Because she was afraid of what He was going to ask her to do. Would He ask for another Rolls Royce? Then how would she pay for it? Would He ask her to speak with the media and what would He ask her to say? How outrageous and inflammatory would He ask her to be?"

"Oh, my God. That is totally not true. Bhagwan's enlightened. He can't lie. Of course, this is just more of Sheela's propaganda. Oh my God, you're one of them. Those Moms who ran the place with Sheela, one of those who betrayed Him." The words were coming faster now, gushing out and full of venom and hate for the women in leadership roles at the Ranch, the women known as the 'moms.' The need to blame won out over rational thinking to keep the illusion of a perfect Master intact.

"I know you don't want to hear this, but I have to say it. She was under so much stress, she started taking meds to get through the evening meetings. And yes, at the end she was a mess, completely distraught and possibly addicted. Maybe that was why she fled to Europe in the middle of the night with other Ranch leaders. She couldn't take it anymore. And Bhagwan lied to the press when He said He didn't know what Sheela was doing." I'd said enough, and I wondered if Sundro would even keep talking to me. The silence dragged on, filled only with the sound of the doves cooing in the ironwood trees.

A full sandwich later, he finally spoke, "Well, that's your perspective, as you said. A messed up one. One that I can't relate to. In my heart Bhagwan is still my Master, and I feel blessed to have known Him."

The truck pulled up at that moment, the three boys jumped out and unloaded the supplies from the back before pulling up their chairs and joining us in the cool shade under the boat.

"Whoa, what's going on here?" Waj, ever perceptive, picked up on the serious vibe between Sundro and I.

"Deb was just telling me about her betrayal of Bhagwan. And her version of what happened at the Ranch," Sundro replied after a brief hesitation, his voice saturated with derision.

"Oh, my God, you didn't." Waj looked accusingly at me. "Don't you know we need his help for the next month? Don't be telling him stuff that pisses him off." He was joking but not really.

I looked over at Tosh. He smiled that calm smile of his, grabbed his sandwich, and started to unwrap it. "Way to go, Deb. I can't leave you alone for a minute and all hell breaks loose. I thought we agreed we weren't going to talk about it." Seeing my furious look, he recanted, "No, you're right. It's been long enough, and I know how hard it is for you to stay silent."

"Don't look at me. I'm staying out of it." Kiran chuckled beside him, when my eyes challenged him to speak up.

"Don't get me wrong, Sundro. I loved Bhagwan and the Ranch, too. It's been a struggle to live a regular straight life, but I can't keep the idealism alive anymore. I saw too much. And even though I didn't understand what really went on, beneath the surface, I could tell that it wasn't as blissful as we disciples wanted to believe." I was done with my lunch and got up to get back to work. "And I'm not the only one either, ask the twins about their experience."

As I walked back to the workshop, the boys started to talk, getting more animated. *Good,* I thought, *get it out in the open. I love having sannyasins visit, but why does their high minded-ness and blind devotion to Bhagwan bother me so much?*

I picked up my canvas gloves, a clean rag out of the bin, grabbed a dust mask and went over to the dinghy davits resting on the sawhorses. They had three coats of Z-Spar Varnish already. The black six-hundred-grit sandpaper was folded in four and molded into my hand as I cupped it around the shiny golden wood, sanding it down before applying a fourth coat.

Before long, the noise of the generator faded into the background as I thought about my time in Sheela's house only three years before.

Rajneeshpuram
August 1985

"I don't want to go." Sheela was crying. "I just can't go." Tear laden smudges accented her dark eyes.

In addition to being Sheela's receptionist, I enjoyed helping her dresser with ironing and hemming for her many public appearances. I also served her meals. This assignment was a welcome taste of domesticity after construction and publications, but I had to get over my shyness about interacting with leadership of celebrity status. It was startling to see Sheela, who was so strong and vibrant in public, appear so powerless and overwhelmed.

I had taken dinner into the living room where she sat with her department heads, the Ranch 'moms.'

"I am so afraid of what He will ask me to do next. I just can't do any more, I just can't," she sobbed.

It was the fourth year of the Ranch and things had begun to fall apart. The land use lawsuits against the commune, initiated by the government of Oregon, stopped our expansion and we were unable to legally continue any further construction. The immigration cases against Rajneesh and his followers were also piling up, making it impossible for any new international residents to stay and participate. Sheela, the commune's spokesperson, was becoming more and more shocking and controversial as she was interviewed on local and national television talk shows.

When questioned about the 'free sex guru' she replied, "Free sex? We don't charge for it if you mean that." In response to the national guard threatening to take over the commune, she said, "Tell your attorney generals and all your bigoted pigs outside, if they touch any of our people, I will have fifteen of their heads, and I mean business."

The interviewer said, "We don't want the orange people in our town."

To which Sheela responded, "What can I say, tough titties.*"

My understanding at the time was that her PR circuit was to inform the rest of the country and the world about how Oregon's governmental and judiciary leaders were dealing unfairly with our community by twisting and changing laws to stop our city from not just growing but even existing. She railed against how they used the immigration system to harass and get rid of Bhagwan and his followers through deportation. She exposed the bigotry and religious intolerance we were experiencing even though we were in a country that had laws to ensure there were neither. As it turned out, the charges of criminal activity on both sides contained elements of truth. But at the time, any certainty was thoroughly obscured by volumes of extremely inflammatory rhetoric.

This evening, Puja, Sheela's nurse, was trying to calm her down. "It's okay, we will help you figure it out. Don't worry." The other moms all chimed in with their support as well.

"But you don't understand what it's like to be there with Him. He is constantly asking for things to be done and done in His way. I can't do it anymore, not another thing. I can't do another thing." Her voice rose, becoming shrill.

Puja again cut in with soothing responses and reassurances. "Here take this." She passed Sheela a tablet with a glass of water. "We'll be here when you get back tonight. We'll help you figure out what to do. Look, Gandharvo has brought your dinner. Let's eat something and get ready to go."

I placed the tray of beautifully arranged food on the small table beside Sheela and left the room as Puja handed her a delicate porcelain bowl of dahl and tore the Naan bread into smaller pieces.

Walking down the hallway to the kitchen, I wondered why Sheela was so upset about her nightly visit with Bhagwan and felt badly for her. They usually met each evening at seven p.m. Sometimes the sessions were short, only ten or fifteen minutes, sometimes they lasted several hours. We never knew when she would return, but her support team would have her evening snack ready for her. Her Ranch crew think tank would be there, just as promised, to review what Bhagwan requested and help to figure out how to make it happen. All I could think of was that I was glad I didn't have to meet with Him if it was this difficult.

Similar scenes played out over the next several months, making it harder and harder for Sheela to attend the nightly conferences. Repeatedly hearing her litany of Bhagwan's outrageous requests, and witnessing her distress, I was not as surprised as most when I learned she had fled to Europe. It was a top-secret nighttime operation at the end of September and most of the Ranch 'moms' followed shortly after.

It was true that I was not totally surprised, however, it was deeply alarming. While Bhagwan remained at the Ranch and was still our spiritual leader, the loss of our civic leadership threatened our way of life in a manner that all the lawsuits and media attacks had not been able to do. Sheela had been the 'head' disciple, tasked with being His face and voice in the commune and in the world. If she had fled in secret, her own relationship to her master in question, what did that mean for the rest of us? What would happen next?

None of us knew.

Boatyard
December 1988

Finishing the fourth coat of varnish on the dinghy davits that day, I thought about Sundro. I hoped we would be able to find some common ground about our contradicting stories before his month with us was over. Gratefully, my prayers were answered in just a few days. The crew helped us utilize our sense of humor and irrepressible sannyasin optimism to agree to disagree and the whole conversation became an endless source of bantering that continued good naturedly throughout his visit.

Chapter 16

Maha'ulepu & Krishnamurti Lake

"Soak up sunshine, swim in the sea and breathe in the open air."

Kauai
January 1989

"Yay, it's Sunday and since you guys are here, it might be a good day to check out Maha'ulepu Beach," Tosh suggested at the breakfast table. "What do you think?"

We were in our new Eleki Place house, a big three-bedroom rancher just up the hill from the boatyard. For a housewarming visit, my sister, her husband, and their three children had arrived from snowy British Columbia.

After unanimous agreement and preparations for a beach day completed, everyone piled into the vehicles and settled into a half hour drive over bumpy sugar cane roads. There was a short walk after parking the cars. We followed the twisted path, the ocean emerging into view and with it a profusion of colored sails.

The geographic location of Kauai's Maha'ulepu Beach provides strong currents and winds, making this a wind-surfing heaven during part of the year. The sails are like dozens of butterflies dancing in and above the wind-swept spray of the surf, a definite respite from the all-encompassing focus of our project in the harbor. My soul could fly in every direction when we came here: into the sea, the air, and the earth. Today, the rainbow sails, blue sky, and water reminded me of another beach and another time.

Rajneeshpuram, Oregon
Summer 1983

"Do you want to come to the lake with me?" I asked Geeta as we headed for the bus stop at lunchtime.

"You know what? I think I will," she said, surprising me.

Jostling along the gravel road in the yellow bus, we tried unsuccessfully to eat the morning's scrambled egg sandwich without wearing crumbs all over us. Coming around the last corner, a view of Krishnamurti Lake opened before us.

"Amazing!" Geeta exclaimed. "I had no idea it was so huge. I haven't been out here since it was completed."

The earthen Gurdijeff Dam had been constructed across the valley during the previous year. Surprisingly, the river had filled up the 330,000,000-gallon reservoir in less than six weeks; enough water to support our desert city. A towering eighty feet high, the front of the dam was landscaped with a huge replica of Rajneeshpuram's logo; a circle containing two flying birds, transcribed with flowering plants on a lush background of green grass. It was a stunning contrast to the rest of the brown and barren landscape with the blue expanse of the lake reflecting the brilliant color of a clear Oregon sky.

As we got closer, I could see the red clothes of hundreds of people laying on the shore and wharfs. The screams and splashes of water play careened into the open bus windows. A two-story diving board tower sported a long line of nervy souls awaiting their turn to hurl themselves into the air to fall thirty feet to the water. Windsurfers hung from the sides of their colorful sails, sharing the forty-five-acre lake with sailboats and canoes, residents, and visitors.

Piling out of the bus, we made our way down the beach, away from the crowds and laid out our towels.

"Race you," Geeta challenged as she kicked off her shoes and peeled off her red jeans and T-shirt.

Our red panties and bras doubled credibly as swimsuits. Contrary to popular belief, nude bathing was not allowed here.

"I'm glad you invited me," Geeta said after our swim in the sun-warmed water of the lake. "I miss the ocean where I grew up in Australia. How about you? Did you grow up on the ocean, too?"

"No, on a lake in Canada, and yes, I miss it. That's why I come over at lunch on summer days when the buses drive out here. It's almost like a holiday to get away from the warehouse and the cafeteria. Do you miss having days off?" I asked her.

She had been at the Ranch almost a year longer than I, as well as in the commune in India for many years before that.

"Well, not really, I mean, I have been living in the commune for so long, it is just natural for me to work all the time."

I tentatively ventured into more personal territory. "Do you have any space for a boyfriend, a steady one?"

She laughed. "No time for one, but I have a guy I see on

and off. Do you ever see the guy you came here with? You were so upset when you arrived, but now you seem pretty at home."

"I don't see Tosh very often. He's in construction and our hours are different, we don't even get to meet at dinner. And the Moms found a wife for him. That was pretty strange, going to his wedding over at the casino a few months ago. He's been away for a honeymoon, to meet her family and stuff. I'm trying not to think about it." I paused, my stomach starting to squirm as the memories flooded back.

I was in the Ranch casino. Shafts of afternoon sun streaked in the windows and fell on the blond parquet floor at my feet. Standing on the edge of a crowd of people, I was watching while the man I loved married another woman. I didn't want to go but couldn't stay away. It was one of those moments I wished I never went through and wished I could forget. But of course, it remains painfully embedded in my mind and heart.

There was a flowered archway at the front of the room and someone officiating as a marriage commissioner. I could hear mumbled words as they said their vows and then the crowd cheered and musicians started playing in celebration. Rose and Tosh danced together and made their way among the guests, kissing and hugging. A professional photographer was taking photos, his flash lighting up the room even more than the sunlight still pouring in.

The casino staff served champagne and snacks on small trays, circulating among the crowd. Still standing at the edge, I focused on breathing. Finding it difficult to stay present, feeling more alone than I could ever have imagined, I pulled on my reserves of why I was on the Ranch. The rationalization that he needed to marry for us to remain in Oregon felt abstract, insane.

Suddenly Tosh was at my elbow, whispering in my ear. "Are you okay?"

"Not really." I heard my voice, and it sounded far away.

"I'll come to your place tonight after work." And he was gone, dancing away with the next guest.

He did come to my room later that night. As he got into bed, I asked, "Are you going to have sex with her?"

"No," he said. "We aren't attracted to each other, not my type. And besides, she has a boyfriend. This is so weird. But I will have to travel to meet her family, a honeymoon of sorts."

I cried on his shoulder. "I wish this wasn't happening, you know?"

"Yeah, me, too, but remember, these are just the rules of this world. In our hearts we know that we love each other, and we don't need to be married on paper, right?"

"I guess," I mumbled into his neck.

"Gandi, you know that it doesn't mean anything to me, this marriage to Rose. If we intend to stay here, I have to do what the Manager Mom's say. We still want to be here, don't we? We gave up too much to just leave. Our whole life is here. There isn't anything to go back to. Anyways, it would be so boring after this," he continued, a weak attempt at levity.

"You're right. I know we can't really go back; we have experienced too much. But it doesn't stop how much it hurts, how confusing it is."

Yes, it's true that I love him, and it doesn't matter whatever else is going on. That piece of paper that they have doesn't mean anything, does it?

Somewhere in my heart I wished he would marry me, but I couldn't admit that, even to myself. Tosh didn't believe in marriage and, after so long, I didn't believe in it either.

But why did he marry her and not me?

It's a trap, it stops people from being authentic. My mind played over the arguments I had learned over the last years, arguments against traditional marriage. *Exclusive relationships keep partners bound to rules that they have to break to be real. It makes people lie. Why do I still feel so awful, confused, and emotional?*

Geeta's voice broke into my disturbing reverie, "Yeah, that happened to me, too. My boyfriend had to get an American wife. I don't call him my boyfriend anymore, but we still see each other occasionally. It seems easier to just go with the flow and be with whoever is available, don't you think?"

"Uh huh. You know, it's been interesting here with the guys ..." I hesitated, unsure how to proceed with this conversation.

"What do you mean?" she prompted.

"Well, before I came here, I was used to guys hitting on me. You know, whistling and making sexist remarks. All of that. It's quite different here. There isn't that constant innuendo from the men. I mean, some of them are actually quite timid." Uncomfortable, I rushed on, "I have to ask them out. And then when we do get together, not that I've gone out all that often, but sometimes they have trouble ... ah ... performing. Have you found that?" *Oh my gosh, did I just ask that?* I picked up a pebble and passed it from hand to hand before tossing it in the lake. It made a small splash, and I watched the ripples slowly spread out in ever widening circles.

Unfazed by my question, Geeta was thoughtful for a moment before responding, "Yeah, I think it's because this place is run by women, and it *is* quite intimidating for a lot of men."

"True, out in the world men are running the show. Here, the Moms head every department and carry all the authority." I observed.

She paused, a thoughtful expression on her face. "Or, maybe it's just because we are all working all the time, and everybody is too tired."

I laughed with her, thinking about the craziness of our lives in comparison to a nine to five job and having weekends and holidays off. As I watched the wind surfers speed over the water and flip their sails, I thought about Bhagwan's lectures.

"It's crucial to know yourself," He would say, and at the same time, He would expound on how difficult that actually is. "We are all conditioned and shaped by our pasts, our religions, our cultures, our families. Every reaction is unconscious, a mere reflex of patterned responses that we learned from the time we were born."

Bhagwan's teachings, as I understood them, continued to play repeatedly in my mind. *The real work of the meditator, the truly spiritual seeker, is to pay attention to how we are reacting, to start to separate what is a conditioned response, like Pavlov's dog, and what is authentically you.*

I believed that living on the Ranch, my responses would become authentic, that I would learn enough self-awareness to navigate through issues and situations with the real me, not the conditioned, automatic me that says yes when I mean no, for example, to ensure people will like me.

Geeta picked up a twig, drawing absently in the sand as she spoke. Turning toward me, she continued, "Bhagwan lectured to us for years: women are not property, and traditional relationships are out the window." When I didn't respond, she continued, "You can't just take a partner for granted and not pay attention to your own desires and attractions or get jealous and insecure when your partner goes out with someone else."

Thinking about Geeta's words, I could relate to them. Bhagwan had lectured for hours on why traditional relationships stop people from exploring their own selves, especially in sexuality. "Sex is the strongest drive in people, and our very life force," He often said.

"But it's so hard to do," I said aloud. "I still get jealous and hurt when my guy is with someone else. Don't you?" I felt exposed, admitting I wasn't free from entanglement. I picked up another rock to keep my hands occupied.

"Yeah, I guess that's why I'm not really with anyone here. I can't take it." She was frank.

Is this where I am headed? Is this what I want? There must be something else, there has to be a place where I can be authentic and hold my love for Tosh, and we can both have our freedom, and I won't feel hurt and suffer.

Is this what enlightenment is? Being beyond suffering? Is this the only reason I am here? Really?

"Yikes, the bus is loading, we have to get going," I said as I got up and pulled my clothes over my now dry undies. Shoving the towel in my backpack, Geeta and I ran to the bus and scrambled aboard.

Maha'ulepu, Kauai
January 1989

"Earth to Mars," I heard my sister's voice through my thoughts. "Where'd you go there, Sister?" She laughed as she pulled the towels out of the backpacks and started handing them out to the kids.

The water was deliciously blue, the waves two to three feet and the wind was up but not enough to blow sand all over us. And the windsurfers were in heaven, dancing across the wave tops and flipping the sails effortlessly as they turned and headed back out to sea. Back and forth, back and forth. My life was easier now. I was not confronted with the challenges of such radical lifestyle changes. I had a husband; my son lived with me. And my sister was here now, too ... my family together in paradise.

Chapter 17

Priming & Carving

*"It takes wisdom to know when to persevere
and when to alter course."*

Boatyard, Kauai
March 1989

"Looking good," Wajdo said as he stood in the road at a distance and took in the view.

"Can you believe we are actually getting some paint on this old hull?" I called across to him, excited. I rolled the roller in the paint tray filled with Benjamin Moore exterior house paint primer and whited out another four-foot square. The transformation was exhilarating; from dark brown mottled teak planks, to a white, smooth, homogeneous surface, like a real boat.

"Hey, Waj, can you get the camera from the car and take a shot for me from over there? This is definitely a milestone day."

I laughed, soaked the roller in the tray again, and went back to applying the thick white paint.

Last month the boys had finished refastening the planks, countersinking three thousand screws into the wood by a quarter inch. Traditionally these countersinks are filled with wooden plugs called bungs but placing Bondo and Marine Tex putty over the fasteners was quicker and more secure than bungs. With flesh-colored points of Bondo sticking out like zits everywhere, the hull had appeared like it had a bad case of acne until the Bosch mini angle grinder smoothed them off. Tosh had routed out the topside seams, revealing the shapes of the individual planks and accenting the graceful lines of the ship's design. Lastly, a mixture of linseed oil and turpentine, was applied with a lawn and garden sprayer to recondition the wood before priming.

Now, after all the deconstruction and reconstruction, we could do a task related to finishing and apply paint. Morale boosted immediately. Maybe, someday, this boat might be completed.

Once the paint went on there was an overnight change in the comments from curious onlookers and amateur boat builders. It was usually "a lot of work," and now we began to hear more "looking good." By this time, though, we were experienced enough to know both comments would be true for quite a while longer.

A few weeks later, standing on the ladder at the stern of the hull, I looked at the old name board fastened across the transom. *This is crazy.* The old lettering, *ELIXIR*, had been carved into the mahogany but was almost invisible now after thirty years in the weather, not to mention the countless times it had been sanded down and repainted. *Would I be able to redo this job and have it last as long? Could I make it look as professional? How could I make the sharp knife-like tools not slip into the raised areas of the letters? How could I not cut myself doing it?*

The wood carving tools I special ordered had arrived and were tucked into the tool bucket hanging off my belt. I had never done any wood carving, yet here I was up on a ladder, thinking I'd just go ahead and re-carve *ELIXIR* into the hardwood. Peering into the tool bucket, the carving tools intimidated me. I didn't even know which one to start with.

Tosh's voice interrupted my procrastination. "Are you okay?"

Momentarily avoiding the carving job, I looked over the edge of the transom and gazed into the hull. It was completely empty, like a giant rowboat, fresh white paint over everything.

"Yeah, I guess so," I answered, my voice hollow as it echoed inside the hull. "Just one more thing I've never done before. And ... it's so quiet and empty around the yard now," I added. Kiran and Miko had returned to Vancouver on the first day of spring a few days ago. After more than a year of living and working together with us on the boat, I was sad to see them go. Wajdo was still here but was at the beach today with friends. A much-needed day off for him.

My eyes followed the newly refastened beam shelves,* around the top of the planks, and the frame stringers,* a third and again two thirds of the way up, all keeping the empty hull in its correct shape; the last projects Kiran had completed before leaving.

"I guess I'm a bit melancholy today," I admitted. "How are you doing?"

"Trying not to think about them leaving by keeping busy,

my usual coping method for uncomfortable emotions." He chuckled. "Figure I can get the bulkheads* done today."

The empty hull was ready for them, the walls that would give even more structural support to the hull and separate out the staterooms and head from the main salon.

"You're happy with the new design now?" I asked, knowing how much he and Kiran had labored over redesigning the interior of the boat from the original drawings to accommodate one cabin with standing height throughout.

"Yeah, it'll be much more open than the original plan was. Two small salons separated by a crawl through cargo hold is crazy. Makes no sense to me. I'm going to put the generator on now, liven the place up again." He laughed for real this time, ready and excited to cut the 3/4-inch marine plywood into new bulkheads.

Taking a cue from Tosh, I put in my ear plugs to protect my hearing from the noise of his saw before blindly grabbing a wood carving tool out of my bucket. *I can do this. It's just calligraphy with a knife,* I told myself and started to redefine the E, the first letter of the name board.

Chapter 18

Caulking & Missing Tosh

"Don't go to sea with only one sail and no oars."

Boatyard, Kauai
April 1989

Is this how he meant? I asked myself as I tentatively pulled the thick fluffy cotton out of the bucket and tapped it into the second from the bottom seam of *Elixir*. With the hull repaired, refastened and the wood sealed with linseed oil and primer, it was time to caulk the seams.

In wooden boats, cotton is pressed into the gap between the planks. After launching, the cotton and wood expand as it soaks up water, making the boat watertight. The wooden mallet Tosh made for me felt awkward in my gloved hand. The caulking iron had to be lined up just so, in order to tuck the cotton accurately and evenly into the seam. I couldn't keep it straight. I was bashing into the wood and the edges of the planks were breaking. *This couldn't be good.* I was jittery all over as I began. *What if I do it wrong and it leaks?* This job could literally make or sink the whole boat. I pulled more cotton out of the bucket.

Originally, *Elixir* was caulked with oakum, a more coarse material than cotton. Another change from the original, but one dictated by necessity as oakum was unavailable. The cotton came in big packages wrapped in brown paper, think huge yarn. I had opened the package and gently unwound it into a five-gallon pail so it would feed smoothly out of the pail and into the seam. *Tuck, tap, tuck, tap, tuck, tap, tuck, tap,* making loose loops between the planks. Then back and *tap rock tap rock tap rock tap rock.* I rocked the curved caulking iron blade into the seam, tucking the cotton all the way inside. Light through the hull was no longer visible, cotton no longer visible, tight, hard packed. *Am I remembering how he showed me?*

I pictured myself back in the boatyard in Port Townsend, and I tried to remember the old master caulker and all his instructions from the previous summer. Shorter than me, he was nimble and strong at eighty-five, his fingers firmly guiding mine without hesitation.

"Just hold it lightly, just lightly, let the mallet do the work," he'd said, grinning crookedly to expose missing teeth. "Rock the iron, front to back, tapping all along. Here, watch me again."

And he did another section for me to watch. Again. *It looked so easy; how can I ever learn this? The mallet is top heavy, and my wrist is too weak.*

"Hey, pay attention, don't you get discouraged, girl. You'll have at least eighty seams to practice this on and get really good at it." He knew exactly where my mind was going after many years of teaching apprentices and watching them feel discouraged as they attempted a skill he had practiced into perfection for half a century.

"As you get higher up on the hull, it'll start to ring," he

continued, "like a big wooden bell. Tighter and tighter, the hull gets really tight and rings, just like a bell," he repeated.

I wasn't sure if I knew what he meant. I did hear tapping, but it didn't sound like a wooden bell to me. *What's a wooden bell sound like, anyways?* I thought, frustrated, coming back to *Elixir* and my first seam. *What were we thinking to have me do the caulking?*

This job was mine because it was a job I could do, theoretically. Many tasks I could figure out and do on my own. Some, like the caulking, Tosh and I figured out together, but I did the task. While dentistry, and the teamwork required for a successful and fulfilling practice, had trained me about synchronicity, and two heads being better than one, this project took that sense to a whole new level.

On this boat, two heads together made more than two, an exponential advantage. He would talk with me about a challenging task and sometimes I would ask a few questions and then suddenly he would see another angle and have it all figured out. And as I think about it, this element of working together as a team to produce "something" is what is most precious to me. The "something" that is produced is a byproduct, not nearly as valuable to me as the experience and feeling of being immersed in and sharing the creative process itself.

An aha moment floods through me. I have been curious why the boat itself did not bring me, or Tosh, the satisfaction I anticipated. People were always admiring her and saying, "You must love having such a beautiful boat." Tosh and I would look at each other, vexed, as it didn't feel like anything. The process itself was the whole point of the exercise, and I felt the truth of the well-known quote, "It is not the destination, but the journey that is the point of our lives."

The many facets of the boat reconstruction took us on a fantastically diverse, varied, challenging and all-encompassing journey; one that was easy to confuse with the end product, because the boat was such a beautiful object.

Another understanding from the project that has remained with me is the unwavering awareness of the temporariness of "things." For example, *Elixir* would have fresh varnish on the rails and look amazing but within three months, the sun would have destroyed the brilliance of the finish, and I would have to redo it all. Just like house cleaning, things look beautiful for a few hours and slowly the dust, debris and disarray settle in for the rest of the week.

I was nervous about this caulking job as it felt crucial to everything. I mean, if the seams leaked, then the whole boat would go down, right?

An hour later and only halfway down the seam, this could take more than a month, but the movements started to feel more natural. *Well, I got this, I guess, and only launch day will tell if I am doing it right. Stop stressing about it and trust. You really are doing your best.* Slowly I let my hands get into their rhythm, *tuck-tap-tuck-tap* and *rock-tap-rock-tap.*

Tired of worrying about leaking, sinking boats, my mind shifted to Tosh, my lover still after more than ten years. *It has been so sweet these days.* While we missed Kiran and Miko, Wajdo was still here living his own bachelor life. We were enjoying the quieter days with just the three of us, Tosh and I and Gavin. The end of the day found us tired from the physical work but also exhilarated from learning new skills and watching *Elixir*'s recreation. She was beautiful. Elegantly, classically so.

I loved to curl up in bed together with my husband at night. Without the other people in the house, there was more privacy. It was more intimate. I was reveling in our new closeness and felt a rush go up my spine, thinking of our sweet time last night. Knowing I would see him every day and share his bed every night was precious and something I treasured after our time at the Ranch.

Tuck,-tap,-tuck-tap and *rock-tap-rock-tap.* I started a new seam, the second one of the day.

At the Ranch, while Tosh and I did sleep together sometimes, we also slept with other partners. Hard to imagine now, here on Kauai, how different the lifestyle at the Ranch had been. Spiritually, I didn't completely understand why there were open relationships, why it was set up like a kibbutz, with the men, women, and children all housed separately. Part of me thought that it was to cultivate freedom from attachments and exclusivity, both bad words in the seventies and eighties. Both words believed to limit our ability to love without restriction. At least this is how we, as cohorts, viewed it at the time. Personally, I struggled with these ideologies, not knowing if it was just because they were going against my conditioning or if they really were false ideals. I was determined to experience it all and learn for myself what was true.

Rajneeshpuram, Oregon
1983

While I had known my relationship with Tosh would change, I could never have imagined how much. It was difficult to arrange to sleep together as our houses were far apart, a bus ride at late hours, and our varied work schedules. Both of us had entirely different groups of friends, mostly those with whom we worked each day. Sometimes we would meet by chance in the cafeteria, have an opportunity to talk, and share a quick hug in the food line. There were no private phones, and cell phones were still science fiction.

Surrendering to the experiment I was part of, I tried not to focus on him and how our relationship seemed to be slipping away. I had no control of him or us in this environment. I focused instead on the dream we were all creating of a city of peace and love where all could live together in plenty and realize our common dream of spiritual enlightenment. But tonight, I was missing Tosh and couldn't distract myself with other connections.

I piled onto the yellow bus when it stopped, one of forty colleagues leaving the publishing house and heading for Magdalena Cafeteria. Beer and a hot vegetarian meal awaited us. I slid into the first vacant seat, my thoughts preoccupied for the fifteen-minute ride.

The bus stopped. I gathered up my backpack and scooted down the bench seat to the aisle, waiting for a chance to stand and nudge my way into the line of unloading puffy red jackets, bags, and scarfs. There were shouts of "see you in there," "save me a seat" and, "see you tomorrow."

I wondered who I would run into in the cafeteria line, or who would be at the table where I sat. It was always a surprise. As foreign and uncomfortable as it was in the beginning, I became more flexible and learned not to make plans. It was too difficult to keep them and there was always disappointment when Tosh or any other man you planned on meeting never turned up. They always had a good excuse, "I had to work an all-nighter, sorry" or "I ran into an old lover of mine from Poona and the energy was really good." If you expressed your dissatisfaction it was met with, "Hey, no expectations. That's a setup for heartache. You gotta go where the energy takes you, right?"

Right. Tosh was probably working late as usual. *Maybe I'll go over to his house after supper and meet him there. I miss him so much. Stop it. Just go get dinner,* I told myself, using self-discipline to stop my mind from freaking out.

I sat with friends from the publishing house and joked around on the outside, but inside I felt lonely and powerless. Finishing up, the young woman on my right asked if I was going dancing later.

"I don't think so, I'm kinda tired tonight," I answered as we piled our dish trays in the racks, our small contribution to clean up after dinner.

Walking mechanically to the bus stop outside, I passed my own stop and instead found myself waiting by the one that went in the opposite direction, to the trailers where Tosh shared a room with another swami. Eventually climbing aboard the bus, I tried to think up a plan. *If he isn't there, I'll just leave him a love note on his pillow. Or maybe just crawl in his bed and wait for him. But what if he doesn't come home? And what if his roommate's there?* My head hurt as much as my heart did, it was just too complex after a long workday. *Focus on the positive, Gandharvo, only the positive. He will be there, and it will all be okay.*

When the big yellow bus stopped to let me off, it was suddenly very dark, the Oregon heaven filled with millions of brilliant points of light in the blue-black of the night sky. I paused for a moment, marveling at the immensity of our universe, and then I noticed the small lanterns marking the pathways to the double wide trailers in Saraha Grove. The gravel was suddenly noisy under my boots, the still air frosty and my breath visible as I made my way up the slight incline to Number 9.

Letting myself in, the doors were never locked, I removed my boots, placing them neatly in the rack with the other dozen pairs. The house was quiet except for hearing the rustling sounds of sleepers behind their closed doors as I walked down the hall. My palms were sweaty. I paused outside his door, the last one on the right side.

There was soft light showing under the bottom of the door, illuminating a wedge of beige hall carpet and my own wool sock covered feet. *Yay, he's home. Or maybe it's his roommate?* I took a few deep breaths as I put my hand on the door, turned the knob, and pushed. There was candlelight and soft music playing on the stereo. *Ahh, sweet. How did he know I was coming? It's all good. See? You were supposed to come over here.*

My eyes scanned the dimly lit room finding the stereo and yes, his clothes on the floor by the bed. He was in bed already. *Oh my God.* My breath stopped in my throat, my stomach clenched, and my heart screamed. His naked back and legs were fully visible to me and so were the naked legs and arms of a woman, wrapping around him from underneath. Gasping with shock, I quietly closed the door and leaned against the wall outside in the hall for ages until I could get it together to leave.

My mind raced. *Should I go back in and confront them? No, this is the way things are here. You knew that when you decided to come. I can't just leave, he's my man. Is he? Does anyone own another human being? Am I his? No, you're your own person. You also can do what you want. But I only want him. Do you? Is that true?* It had been true but now? *Don't melt down here, get yourself outside, get some air.*

Numbly, I watched my feet walk themselves down the hallway to the foyer. I noticed them step back into their boots, and march out the door into the night, a night still and shredded with distant starlight. Sitting on the bench by the bus stop, my eyes filled with tears, and my chest heaved with my sobs. It was late, and the buses didn't run as frequently. I didn't mind, because I needed the space and the darkness.

Boatyard, Kauai
April 1989

Tap rock, tap rock. *Damn, I missed the seam.* My eyes blurred with tears. I tried to pull the splintered wood out of the seam and tidy it up. *Almost at the end of this one,* I thought. *Thank goodness. I'm tired.* Waves of gratitude washed over me. I had survived the experiment.

Tosh and I were still together, actually even married now. And living in paradise, on a tropical island, working on our dream project. As I worked my way down the last few inches of the seam, I pulled my mind back from the past, remembering just last night and the sweetness of feeling connected to my true love, enjoying the feeling of his body wrapped around me. Free from the worry of him being with someone else.

"Are you ready, Mom?" Gavin interrupted.

"Perfect timing, kiddo," I responded as I tapped in the last bits of cotton up around the stem, where the planking met with the structural timbers of the bow.

He already had his yogurt container filled with paint. He'd rescued a tiny brush from the can of turpentine, drying it off on the rag he had learned to hang from his waistband.

"Hey, were you sorry to leave the Ranch back when you were six years old?"

"Where did that come from, Mom? Wow, that was so long ago."

"It's only six years ago." I laughed as I worked the cotton smoother, in front of his paintbrush. "Were you?"

"Really, Mom? I was glad to go live with Daryn Dad. I remember having fun at the Ranch, but I missed you a lot. Remember when I came to your A-frame?"

"I do. Ajhad brought you over there, right?"

"Yeah, and I waited around on your porch until you came

home. You gotta admit, Mom, it was pretty weird not seeing your mom whenever you wanted to." His brow was thoughtful as he painted over the cotton, remembering his younger self trying to find ways to visit his mom.

"Are you sorry you had that experience?"

"No, not exactly, but I'm happy to be living with you again in kind of a normal life." He laughed. "Mom, you guys are just not the usual parents, you know what I mean? Here I am hanging out in a boatyard, pretty much permanently skipping school. Not really normal."

"Yeah, about that ..."

"Don't start, Mom, I will get it done, I promise ... eventually." He knew how important it was to me that he completed his school assignments.

And we finished our seams for the day. "Time for a swim?" I asked as we put away our tools.

"Yeah. Can I go see my friend at the bar?" he asked.

"Sure. Tosh, we're on our way home," I called up onto the deck of *Elixir* where he was gluing in the beams.

"I'll be there in a couple of hours," he responded, his head appearing over the side for a moment as he waved goodbye.

And the next day it started all over again. Tap tuck tap tuck and tap rock tap rock tap rock. My mind once again mulled over how I had managed such a different lifestyle.

Rajneeshpuram, Oregon
1983

Eventually the ride arrived and picked me up from the bus stop bench. My eyes were still running, and my body felt wooden, still stunned from what I had seen. I climbed up the three steps, nodding to the driver as he pulled the handle to shut the door. There was only one other man on the bus at this late hour. I sat in the row in front of him.

"Hey, what's up? You look pretty upset. You okay?" he asked, leaning forward, his chin resting on the metal bar across the back of my seat.

"'Pretty upset' is pretty accurate," I responded, unable to contain the tears rolling down my face. I hoped the dark would hide them.

"Don't tell me, your guy is with somebody else?" The stranger behind me spoke gently.

"Yup ... that's it. Man, it sucks. I hate it."

"Yeah, it's the worst, ever. I agree." He put his hand on my shoulder, protective.

"Did it happen to you?" I asked after a while.

"Uh huh ... more than once." He sat quietly in the dark, the noise of the bus as it bounced and rattled along the uneven dirt road toward my subdivision of town houses the only sound for several minutes.

"Do you want to talk about what happened?" he eventually asked, his deep voice conveying familiarity with heartache.

"What's to talk about? I just walked in on him making love with somebody else."

"Shit, that's the absolute worst."

"Yup, pretty much."

The bus was slowing down. "This is me," I said, reluctant to leave his sympathetic company.

"Me, too."

"Oh, good."

He followed me off the bus, and we stood by the side of the road for a bit. It was a clear, cold night, and a half-moon was rising, climbing higher in the dark sky, subduing the stars.

"Hey, you feel like company for a bit?" he asked. "You

know, to get your mind off stuff? Let me hold you for a bit? ... no pressure at all." I noticed he was tall, and handsome in a rugged way, his hair hidden like mine, covered with a warm knitted cap.

"That feels like a good idea. Which town house are you in?"

"I'm in this one." He gestured to the first house at the bottom of the hill, his gloved hand steady as he pointed. "My roommate's in Portland for a few days, by the way."

"Wow, lucky you." It was a coveted luxury to have a room to yourself, even for one night. "Okay with me, if it's okay with you," I said.

I suddenly realized how tired I was, my day catching up with me. It had begun before six a.m. and it was now more than seventeen hours later.

"To be honest, the thought of hiking up the hill to my town house and dealing with my roommate right now ..." My words trailed off as we slowly made our way to the nearest house and climbed the steps to the porch.

Chapter 19

Lover, Coving & Press Conference

"A person who tells you they don't make mistakes is in denial."

Rajneeshpuram, Oregon
1983

The townhouses all had the same layout, so despite the dim light I knew where to take my boots off and where the shoe-rack was in the foyer. *What am I doing? It's okay, this is a gift to you. Be here, stay present. Do this a different way. You don't have to be by yourself right now. Allow yourself to have some comfort tonight.*

I followed the tall narrow shape of the swami I had just met on the bus. Unspoken Ranch etiquette decreed silence as we carefully made our way up the stairs to the second floor, the sleeping house softly lit with baseboard night lights.

In his room, we took off our coats and dropped our day packs. His hat came off, revealing long hair in a low ponytail. It was thick and blunt to his shoulder blades. He took notice of my hair, shoulder length with soft curls, flattened from being in a hat. My fingers ran self-consciously through it.

There was a soft light in the room, purposely left on by the house cleaners to welcome home the weary workers every night. A futon rested on the floor. A small pile of laundry rested on one corner, all of it immaculately folded and precisely placed. The house cleaners did laundry daily, our red clothing all labeled with a name to help sort the many loads of wash. The only evidence of a roommate was the empty futon bed, identical, on the other side of the room. Soft beige carpet had fresh vacuum tracks evenly spaced over its entirety, pristine, peaceful.

He walked over to the low table by his bed and put music on, soft folksy music, the green light from the dials playing on the bare creamy walls. Kneeling, he turned on a small lamp beside the stereo in front of a framed photo of Bhagwan. His hand paused on the fresh flower in a slender vase, another aesthetic touch from the house cleaner.

Rising, he gracefully made his way across the room to a narrow closet and passed me a fresh towel. Still without words, we both made our way into the hall, he went left, and I went right into the matching bathrooms adjoining the four bedrooms on the second floor.

I tried not to think, attempting to erase from my mind the image of Tosh with someone else. I took off my clothes, tied up my hair, and climbed into a steaming shower. The water calmed me. Drying off, I made my way back into his room.

He was already in bed, setting the alarm on a small folding clock, his fingers long, precise and careful. He had broad shoulders, with muscles that were well defined in the lamplight, his skin wintery pale. My heart was suddenly pounding harder. *What is this? How can I be feeling attracted to someone else in the middle of all this grief?* In my heart was suffering, pain, anger and a flicker of interest in the possibility of some delight, some attraction.

I put my clothes down in the corner and unwrapped the towel from around me, draping it over the closet door handle to dry.

Feeling his eyes on me I was conscious of my body, the pale skin covering a slender, long frame with small breasts and tiny waist. His eyes seemed to approve of what he saw. I tried to breathe slowly to stay calm and focused on the excitement. Suddenly heartache and panic came over me as I knelt onto the futon and sank into his arms. I was grateful not to be alone. He didn't say anything. He just held me, knowing I was crying. My tears ran down his chest, and he didn't seem to care. He had been where I was. I sensed it, and that gave me permission to feel it all. The night light got dimmer and, in time, died. The music played softly and still he held me, caressing my hair.

Time passed and my tears stopped, the anguish spent, allowing the energy to shift into the present moment and awareness of the compassionate man I was with. He was thirtyish and strong from hard physical labor. His long brown hair was soft, unbound and smelled fresh, like outside. The outline of his clean-shaven face was angular in the blue light of the moon as it fell in through the window.

My lips slowly found his neck, his chin, and lastly his mouth. Our breathing was even and slow, our bodies drawn together in a nourishing, sweet communion before sleep swept us away.

The healing tryst ended with the sounds of feet in the hallway and running water in toilets and showers. We were too late to make it to the cafeteria for breakfast, so we piled on the bus for our work sites, me to the publishing department, and him to the construction site.

I was quiet at work, my mind in turmoil again. The gut punching emotion and searing visual of my partner with another person opposite the spontaneous, nurturing experience of being with Sami. Which scene would my mind fixate on? Which feelings would I allow myself to indulge in? I was not aware then of having a choice, so my mind jerked me here and there, dragging my heart and soul with it.

Eleki Place House, Kauai
Summer 1989

Sitting at the dining room table and sipping my breakfast tea, I still found it hard to believe that I was living in paradise, working on this old boat, and amazed at where my life had led me. To this place. To this time. To this project. I was calmer four and a half years after leaving the commune. My heart was no longer whipped here and there. Time, space, and simple repetitive tasks worked wonders for my mind and soul. I was coming to terms with living a simpler life, immersing my desire for connection to the Divine into physical sensations of tropical air and sunshine on my skin, and seawater soothing my entire body during long swims across the bay.

Later, as I sat up on the newly completed decks, my eyes traveled out over the yard visible from under my protective blue canopy of reinforced plastic. The trade winds blew under the improvised roof, cooling me despite the intense tropical sun. I was filled with peace, the raging rivers of questions and angst turning to a placid lake, devoid of ripples. Even the yard was still and hushed. Empty of tourists exploring the harbor, there were no clouds of dust from their noisy rental cars on the dirt road that circled the yard. Gavin was visiting his buddy north of Lihue and Tosh was in Honolulu seeing a specialist for a sore elbow.

The Coast Guard was out in the cutter, doing boarding exercises, firing blanks across the bow of a play-acting non-compliant vessel. Except for those occasional sounds of gunshots, it was quiet. Even the generator was off.

I had assembled my tools on the deck. It was exciting to sit up here, imagining this boat in the sea again. *What would it be like to be on the water? Would the caulking leak? Stop it.* I told myself, chuckling at the constant question in my mind, a question that would not be answered until launch day. *When would that be?*

I had mixed the runny, clear epoxy with filler and sawdust to make a thick brown paste to fill the sharp angle between the bulwarks and the deck, the whole eighty feet of the perimeter. Instead of a flexible quarter inch bead of silicone around a door or window, I was laying down a two-inch bead of epoxy that would be rigid when it set.

It took me about four feet until I mastered the exact amount of epoxy to load into the seam and the accurate angle to hold my wooden paddle to smooth the coving uniformly. Scooting along the deck on my bum was slow but the work was pleasant. No noise and dust today, although I wore a mask and gloves to keep the toxic epoxy fumes out of my lungs and off my skin.

With the tranquility of the day, and the familiarity of the task, my mind wandered and wondered at the twists and turns of fate. If the Ranch hadn't failed, I'd not be sitting here working on this boat.

Why had the Ranch failed? When exactly did it end? When Sheela left? Was it that press conference, the one that Bhagwan held after her departure?

Thinking about it made my heart race.

Rajneeshpuram, Oregon
October 1985

"Sheela has done terrible things," Bhagwan ranted from His air-conditioned podium, "things I knew nothing about."

Local and state government bodies had been closely monitoring all the activities at the Ranch as local people were furious about all the 'red people taking over the county.' Sheela's clandestine departure was the perfect excuse for immediate government action and all commune financial assets were abruptly seized and frozen.

With His spokeswoman gone, Bhagwan himself quickly held a large press conference in the massive meditation hall.

"She bused in all the homeless people in America and registered them to vote," Bhagwan continued from his chair, speaking strongly, enunciating the words more quickly than His usual slow rhetoric. "I knew nothing of this. She took over the town of Antelope. I knew nothing of this. She was power hungry, and I didn't know. She was out of control. I have been in seclusion and in silence for two years, trusting Sheela to take care of my people for me. And she has betrayed my trust ..."

"He is lying," I whispered vehemently to Tosh, who sat cross-legged beside me amid thousands of other people, sannyasins and outsiders alike. I started to uncross my legs to stand up.

"Shh," Tosh hissed at me, quickly grabbing my arm and forcefully pulling me back to a seated position.

"But He's lying," I repeated, incredulous as I remembered the many nights at Sheela's house and the conversations before and after her nightly visits with Him.

"Shh, be still. Don't draw attention to yourself," Tosh whispered anxiously through clenched teeth.

I struggled briefly until I became more aware of my surroundings. Security was on high alert for these meetings as the local people were outraged and volatile, the Peace Force* stood vigilant around the perimeter of the auditorium, ready for any outburst with automatic weapons.

Boatyard, Kauai
Summer 1989

The first press conference was problematic, an experience that would not let me rest. A memory that continued to prick and prod and question, vexing my soul. Rajneesh was my teacher, and I had personal experience to the contrary of what I heard Him say about Sheela and things that had happened on the Ranch. Spiritual people are not supposed to lie. My Master was not supposed to lie.

My inner framework and moral navigation system were massively, irretrievably not just shaken, but irreparably broken. I was left not knowing which way was up, without confidence in my ability to discern right from wrong, or light from dark. It seemed I had terribly miscalculated the intended plan and trajectory for my life. Not only my life, but my children's lives, as well. How could I make it right?

The altruism of thinking and living the big communal picture had failed. Was working for ourselves, on a personal dream, the right course? How could this possibly be of benefit to others?

Chapter 20

Move Along, Ma'am

"Develop resilience and learn to sail in rough seas."

Rajneeshpuram, Oregon
October 1985

Something wasn't right. I had just tried to call Gavin and there was no answer. I had tried over the last few weeks with no response. Had they moved? Were they away? I called Mom. She'd seen Gavin the previous week. As far as she knew, they hadn't moved or changed their phone number. Trying to find answers and my heart in a panic, I couldn't sleep, which left me distracted and worried throughout the next day. I had a new job managing fifteen attorneys in the legal department. The legal briefs were one big tangle of words that I couldn't seem to connect together. Somehow, I got through the hours in the law office until dinner time.

The climate of the Ranch was in disarray. At the end of

September, Sheela and her leader 'Moms' left in the middle of the night. Shortly after, Bhagwan held a massive press conference to denounce her. *Maybe that was why I was so unsettled?*

I was as shocked and confused about what was happening as everyone else. Imagine a huge community of ten thousand people just suddenly losing their leadership. While Bhagwan was still here and continued with his daily drive-bys, He was not part of the everyday running of the commune.

I met Tosh at the cafeteria at dinner. He was sitting with some friends from Nelson, our hometown. They were taking a six-month course in bodywork at the Humaniversity.

"Hi, Tosh. Great to see you, Melanie and David," I greeted them with hugs before sitting down at the table.

"How are things going, sweetie?" Tosh asked as he energetically dug into his dinner.

"Actually, I'm worried about Gavin, I've called over the last few weeks, but there's no answer. I called Mom, she's pretty sure they haven't moved."

"That's odd ..." He stopped chewing as the information registered.

"Tosh, I have to go up there, I can't stand this anymore. I need to see him." My lip quivered, and I struggled to stay rational. *Damn these emotions, it makes it so hard to think straight let alone talk. I've held it in all day, just a little bit longer.* But my tears finally spilled free.

"When did you see him last?" Melanie asked, her hand empathetically on my knee. Her daughter was also up in Nelson, staying with friends while she and her husband were studying.

"It's been two years. I can't believe it's been so long. I usually talk with him every week but something isn't right." Tosh put his arm around me, which made me cry even more. "I need to go up there and see him, but I don't know how," I'd been thinking for a few weeks about this. How could I get off the Ranch? Our van had broken down by the side of the road when we arrived, leaving us without private wheels. There were buses and Ranch and vehicles going into Portland almost daily, but then what? Nelson was in the other direction without direct bus or airline connections and across an international border.

"Hey, Gandi, you can use our car. It's just sitting out there in the field. It should run okay, get you the five or six hundred miles or whatever it is," David, Melanie's husband, said.

I was momentarily stunned. I'd been so lost in a hamster wheel of trying to figure out how to get off the Ranch, I'd never even considered borrowing somebody's car. I didn't even think I knew anyone with one any longer. "Really? You guys have your car here? And you're okay with me taking it on a long road trip?"

After a simple discussion it was arranged, pending a meeting with Vidsy, the Ranch 'Mom' in charge of personnel. She, for some unknown reason, had not run away with the other 'Moms'.

Meeting Vidsy the next day, I simply stated it was time for me to leave for two weeks to visit my son. Expecting a lecture about it not being the time to leave, and if I left, I couldn't come back, I was shocked by her gentle response.

"Yes, it's been a long time. Have a good trip, and we will see you when you get back."

What? Did I just hear that correctly? What's going on here? Not wanting to discuss it further in case she changed her mind, I responded simply. "Thanks, Vidsy. See you in a few weeks." I was going on a road trip. I needed to remember how to drive, and I hoped my driver's license was current.

Now, two days later and several hundred miles away from the Ranch, I focused on my driving, keeping within the speed limits, stopping only for bathroom breaks and gas. I'd remembered how to drive and my license was still current.

The brown Pinto wagon ran smoothly and hadn't seemed to be the worse for wear after sitting for months in a field with hundreds of other cars, literally out to pasture, as private vehicles were not part of the commune. Now that I was on my way, I was consumed with visions of a reunion with my son. How much had he changed? It was as if all the longing of the last years were concentrated into one big desire to get there yesterday already.

Looking at the forests as I whizzed by, the scenery barely registered in my mind. I had attempted calling again but there was still no answer. I tried to not think about what that meant. I would get there and find out what was going on. There would be a simple explanation for the lack of communication.

After our divorce seven years ago, and while I had sole custody, Daryn and I had agreed to talk about Gavin and his living arrangements openly, without binding legal contracts. I would honor the fact that Daryn was his birth father and important in his son's life and I expected Daryn to do the same for me. Until the last few years, Gavin had always lived with me, Daryn not even visiting or calling. But I'd kept my end of the promise when Gavin requested to go and live with his dad three summers earlier. *How could it be two-and-a-half years already? How could time just fly by so fast? But it had ...*

Ten hours later I drove into my hometown in the late afternoon. Barely able to contain my excitement, I drove straight to Daryn's house and parked on the street. There was a vehicle there and the lights were on in the house. *Good, they're home. Whew.* I smoothed my hair back as I got out of the car, stretching my cramped muscles. Walking stiffly to the door, I rang the bell. *Oh my gosh, I can't wait to see him. What a rush, after such a long time away. Hey, why isn't anyone answering the door?*

I walked around to the other side of the house. Yes, there were lights on, and that was definitely a car parked just outside. I rang the bell and tried to open the screen door to knock on the inside door. *Maybe the bell isn't working? But yes, I can hear it. Why isn't anyone answering?* I went back to the car and climbed inside where it was warmer. October is cold in Nelson, the beginning of winter. I took a few deep breaths. *Okay, calm down, there must be a perfectly good explanation.* But my belly felt sick. And I'd just driven six-hundred miles.

Knock, knock, knock. I jumped. Someone was knocking on my side window, just a foot from my face. Turning, all I saw was a dark colored uniform.

I rolled the window down and saw it was a police officer. He had parked his patrol car right behind me. The sick feeling in my stomach intensified, my breath suddenly jerky.

"Are you Deborah Cavanaugh?"

I nodded. *Oh, thank goodness, he knows what's going on.*

"You need to move along, ma'am," the officer spoke firmly, clearly.

"I don't understand. I'm just here to visit my son. No one is answering the door ..." My heart was beating too fast, my mind racing. *A cop? Why is there a cop here? And he knows my name?*

"You need to move along, ma'am," he repeated, but his tone was softer.

I just stared up at him, he was bending over to speak through my window. Suddenly he squatted down beside my car. "You don't know what's going on?"

"What do you mean? I've been trying to phone for weeks and now I'm here and why aren't they answering the door? The lights are on, the car is here ..." I took another deep breath, to keep from crying. *This wasn't what was supposed to be happening right now. I was supposed to be with Gavin right now.*

"Listen, lady, there's a restraining order against you, you need to move along," his voice was softer, but still clear. His eyes were searching my face for something, but he wasn't finding it, whatever it was.

I just stared at him blankly. I had no idea what he was talking about. My heart was pounding. My palms were sweating where they rested at the bottom of the steering wheel. *Was I being arrested? What did I do?*

He shifted his position a little, still squatting outside my car door, adjusting his height so he could talk to me eye to eye. "There's a restraining order against you. You can't be here right now."

"I don't understand what that is," I said softly, the words barely getting past my dry lips, my heart jumping all over the place, smashed and speared, hurting. "Where is my son? Where are they? Why don't they answer the door?"

"Ma'am, there are papers filed down at the station saying you cannot see your son. You really don't know anything about this, do you?" His eyes and his voice were soft now, compassionate. He could tell I was completely caught off guard, without any clue as to what was happening to me.

"No."

"Well, you can't stay here, follow me down to the station, and we'll see if we can get this straightened out."

I rolled up my window, my body shaking and not just from the cold. *What's going on? Just take a deep breath, follow the policeman, you can do this...* And I could, even with my eyes running, I kept breathing in and out, *just one foot in front of the other, you'll figure this out.*

The officer left me in the foyer of the precinct and told me he would research the situation. The seats were plastic, hard and cold. As I sat, the sound of metal chair legs on the concrete floor scratched my ears, echoing in the bare utilitarian waiting room. An oversized wall clock ticked as the second hand jerked its way around the face. The roar in my head had stopped, it was like I was dead, just a shell, watching myself sit in a limbo of the bizarre, following the inner instructions to *breathe, just keep breathing.* Upon his return, the officer's face was concerned.

"It seems like a Daryn Cavanaugh filed this restraining order over a year ago. You knew nothing about it? You were never informed?" His voice was incredulous.

I shook my head, unable to speak as I struggled to comprehend what he was telling me. The roar in my head returned. *There must be a mistake. This can't be happening. Stop it, listen to what the man is telling you. It's important.* I forced my ears to listen, his voice gradually growing clearer as the noise in my ears faded, allowing me to hear.

"Usually, the person to be restrained receives a citation delivered by a sheriff or at least a formal notification in the mail. This is highly unusual." He shook his head. I could tell he felt badly for me. "I suggest you get yourself a lawyer right away."

Finding my tongue, ungluing it from the sides of my mouth, I heard myself ask, "How do I do that?"

"Do you know where the courthouse is?" he asked, kindly.

"Yes."

"Do you know where the government offices are next door?"

"The new white building?"

"Yes, go to the family court clerk in the morning, first thing. I think they open at eight. Ask for a copy of the court orders against you and a list of attorneys who specialize in family law. You got that?" He sounded genuinely concerned now.

"Yes." *Lawyer? I need a lawyer? I have court orders against me? What did I do? Stop, breathe, pay attention. You need to get out of here.*

Aware of his concern and that he had been as shocked as I as the last hour unfolded, I somehow found myself thanking him for helping me. I walked out into the street, clutching a small piece of paper with a court order number handwritten on it. It was dark out now, the air cold, people walking past on their way home after work.

I had been in touch with my parents before driving north. They expected me. I cannot even imagine what went through their minds that night after I arrived. They were surprised I hadn't picked up Gavin, and as stupefied as I was that there was a legal proceeding against me. My father, the principal of the largest elementary school in the town, was well known and highly respected. My mother, also well-known and respected, was a registered nurse in the local hospital. Our family hadn't had any dealings with the law or legal issues, ever. It was completely foreign ground.

They had been to visit me at the Ranch the year before, stayed at the hotel, ate in the cafeteria, met Sheela and her parents. It had been a positive experience for them as they were impressed with the city and all we were doing there to be self-sufficient and self-sustaining. They had enjoyed the interesting, well-educated people they met, but most of all, could see that I was happy being part of a huge social experiment.

That night my feelings swirled around my belly and chest like a whirlpool, drawing tighter and tighter, making it painful to breathe. I was very afraid of not being able to see my son. I had made a terrible mistake somehow, obviously, or my son would be with me. I didn't understand anything about what was happening, but a huge gaping maw of terrible recrimination and guilt chewed in my belly.

I should never have stayed on the Ranch. I should have returned before now. Oh God, what have I done?

Before collapsing into bed that night in my childhood bedroom, my father said, "Don't worry, dear, surely there is a mistake. You'll see, it will all be sorted out in the morning."

———

The next morning the doorbell rang at eight a.m. I answered it. A stranger stood on the porch. He asked, "Are you Deborah Cavanaugh?"

"Yes," I answered.

He handed me an envelope and said, "You have been served." He abruptly turned and walked away without waiting for a reply. *So rude. What's going on with this place?*

Standing in the doorway, I noticed the plain white envelope had my name on it, and the return address of a law office. My heart threatened to stop beating. *Oh, no, what now?* With shaking fingers, I ripped it open. It was indeed a legal document: a subpoena to appear in court in ten days.

Chapter 21

Unfit

"Don't wait for easy times, learn to dance in the storms."

Nelson, British Columbia
October 1985

Arriving at the government buildings later, the family law clerk handed me a handwritten list of ten family law attorneys with numbers discreetly written in the margin. Numbers on a scale of one to ten on their skill and efficacy. I noticed that the attorney Daryn had used for the restraining order, Bryce, was number one. I pointed that out to the clerk.

"Oh dear, I'm sorry," she said, "of course I can't say anything but if that is his attorney you better for sure get number two on the list. Mr Bryce is known for getting dirty, not that you heard that from me, of course. Number two is very ethical, a straight shooter."

"But he lives in Trail." I panicked. Trail was an industrial town about fifty miles away.

"Oh, he comes over here all the time, honey. Don't worry about that."

Two days later my newly hired attorney, number two on the list, pronounced with conviction, "This is just a straightforward case of religious freedom." He was maybe ten years older than I with neatly trimmed brown hair and a regular build. Definitely on the preppy side appearance-wise.

In his office in Trail, I'd handed him the copy of the restraining order, the subpoena and answered a few questions about my past and my current lifestyle. He informed me I was charged with being an unfit mother for being part of the commune in Oregon, and my ex-husband was demanding sole custody. Mr. Smith hadn't seemed perturbed in the least. It was obviously a case of religious discrimination. Having worked for the attorneys in Rajneeshpuram, I was not so confident. Not at all. Things that were totally legal, as everything we had done there was by the book, were somehow turned about by our adversaries, convoluted. I was smartening up that this may be true here as well.

"Well, straight forward or not, I just need to tell you that this is a 'hot' subject currently. Rajneesh has been on the news a lot lately, and there is an immense amount of anti-red-people sentiment across the states."

"This is Canada, it's different here. Obviously, you are well educated, are a professional, and come from an excellent family with a stellar reputation. This won't be a problem. You'll see."

I wanted to believe it was true. Canada has a more tolerant, fair-minded culture. He would write up the response. I told him I would get evidence of the benefits to children who are raised in a community, kibbutz-like culture. My calls to the Ranch the day before revealed the Rajneeshpuram attorneys had mountains of precedents they had amassed over the years from similar family law cases. There was a huge body of evidence from psychologists, doctors and scientists, proving the children of sannyasins excel in every aspect of their lives, because of their alternative lifestyle.

In the meantime, my heart was breaking to be so close and not to be able to see Gavin. It seemed to be the cruelest punishment imaginable. I spent my time at my parents' house, on the phone to Rajneeshpuram, being coached on how to handle the upcoming court date. Tosh was on his way up to bring court documents the attorney would use.

My heart hammered in my chest as I walked into the courthouse, my feet wobbly on small heels I'd borrowed from Mom's closet. Brown leather. To match the brown and white plaid dress I'd also found there. I knew by this time it was crucial to wear other colors besides red. The news, even in Canada, was full of footage of Bhagwan's arrest just this week.

There were continual breaking news updates with images of Him in chains, wearing a prison jumpsuit, without his knitted hat, his beard still hanging past his waist. It seemed that He had followed Sheela's lead, boarded a plane and left suddenly and unannounced in the middle of the night. But His plane had been intercepted in the eastern states when they landed to refuel. Federal agents arrested Him and took Him to prison. The media frenzy was at its height, indoctrinating the public about this Indian guru and his followers dressed in red that practiced free love, took over towns and carried machine guns. This guru and his followers were a threat to the very fabric of North American life.

The courthouse was old, with a round turret on one corner, like a fairy tale castle. The three stories of granite blocks were covered in red ivy with wide shallow steps leading to paneled glass doors. Inside, the smell of old papers and stagnant air assaulted me. I followed the signs to Family Court up the stairway. My heels caught and clicked on the shiny metal strips fronting each battleship linoleum covered tread. Steadying myself on the thick oak banister, my hand slipped along the wood, clammy as I climbed to the second floor. My attorney waited for me. Taking my elbow, he guided me into a small conference room.

"How are you doing today?" he asked, considerate as he pulled out a straight-backed chair for me to sit.

"I guess I'm okay," I managed, although my hands trembled. I clasped them together in my lap. I felt completely other than myself. Strange environment. Strange clothes, a dress and heels. I had never worn clothes like these. Straight, ordinary clothes. I pulled my knitted magenta jacket closer around me. It was soft, warm, and smelled like me. He was pulling a thick legal brief from his case, placing it in front of me.

"As you are aware, I submitted this to the judge last week, to give him time to read it and familiarize himself with the case. This is far more detailed and professional than any brief I've ever submitted for this type of family law case. Excellent work. I'm sure everything will be very straightforward. The judge will go through the affidavits and ask questions and both sides will be given a chance to respond. It may take a few hours. Do you have any questions before we go in?"

"Is this judge a fair one?" I asked point blank, aware that

there could be very different outcomes for a case depending on which judge was hearing it.

"Well, actually, the judge that was originally scheduled would have been better. I see on the docket today, that we have a different judge, a last-minute change for some reason. Highly unusual in this court." He looked puzzled for a moment before his confidence in the rightness and fairness of the Canadian legal system took over once again.

I looked again more closely at the docket and the name of the presiding judge. My mouth went even drier as I recognized the name.

Noticing my face as it paled, he quickly got me a glass of water, assuming it was the usual pre-court appearance jitters. Pushing his hand away, I spoke.

"I think that Daryn's mother is this judge's secretary."

"That doesn't make sense," he stated matter of factly, not quite getting the implications through his absolute faith in the fairness of the law, "that would be a conflict of interest, of course." Looking at his watch, he stood up. "It's time to go."

I couldn't feel my feet as I walked down the hall to the courtroom, the fair and just minded attorney at my side. He held open the heavy paneled oak door for me. As I passed through into the room, I was shocked to see Daryn's whole family present.

On the left side of the room, I was alone with my attorney. My parents and Tosh had offered to come but I had said no, assuming that the court hearing would be a private affair with just Daryn and his attorney. I couldn't have been more wrong. One side of the room was almost filled with plaintiff support-ers. My side empty. *Holy crap. Looking worse than I imagined.*

"All rise." The judge was announced as he filed in. "With the Honorable Justice Blake presiding, the Supreme Court of

Canada, Nelson, British Columbia, is now in session." The gavel banged down and we all sat.

After addressing the two attorneys, who both stood, the judge lifted up his copy of the thick document defining the defendant's response to the plaintiffs' charges of unfit mother-hood and request for sole custody of Gavin and slammed it on his desk.

"There is absolutely no question about this case. Total and sole custody is awarded to the plaintiff, Daryn Cavanaugh with absolutely no visiting rights for the defendant whatsoever except with two weeks written notice and complete supervi-sion. Case dismissed." The gavel banged again.

My attorney started to stand up.

"I said, Mr. Smith, case dismissed." The judge got up and walked out of the court.

There was intense buzzing all around me. People stood and walked around, smiling, congratulating each other.

What had just happened? Not even five minutes had gone by. Did the judge even read my submission to the court? My attorney quickly gathered his papers and shoved them into his briefcase. He took my elbow and steered me smoothly out into the hall and back into the small conference room, carefully closing the door behind him.

Tears poured down my face. The tension from the last days erupted into sobs. A Kleenex box appeared in front of me. And then a glass of water. I took a few moments, allowing the river to flow, then forced myself to pull it together.

"What does this mean?" I asked, blowing my nose with unsteady hands.

"We lost the case, Daryn has sole custody of Gavin, and you do not even have visiting rights. If you wish to see him, you must write to Daryn and request a meeting two weeks before.

And when you do meet with Gavin, you must have Daryn present with you. You cannot see your son alone."

When I didn't respond, he added, "I have never experienced anything like this. This is entirely unprecedented." I noticed his face was drained of color as he sat across the table from me, his head in his hands. *Shit, is he breaking down right now?*

"What can we do about this? Options?" I asked pulling myself together even more.

"Yes," long pause, "yes, um, yes, we can appeal, but this ruling is in the Supreme Court, not just family court, so ..." He wouldn't look at me. He cleared his throat, obviously overwhelmed. He blew his nose into a handkerchief he'd removed from his jacket pocket.

"And?" I persevered, my brain taking over, realizing my knight had just crashed.

"Well, the chances of changing it are very slim to none, actually." He still had his hand over his face, his elbow on the table, not looking at me.

"Do you remember when I told you this was a 'hot' case when we first met?"

"Ah, yes ... but I didn't think that would apply here. I honestly have never experienced anything like this before," he repeated, shaking his head.

"Okay, but what do I do now?" I asked, trying to push him out of his shock, and back into his role as my solicitor, my counsel.

"Um, you need to make the required request in writing if you want to see your son," he sat straighter, his hand now resting on the table instead of hiding his face. "I can do that right now and will pass it to Daryn's attorney before we leave. In the meantime, you are free to do as you wish, your son will remain here. Oh my gosh, I am so sorry." His eyes teared up; his face flushed.

Somehow, I made it home. Shared the devastating news. And went into my room and closed the door. I removed the offensive shoes, the foreign dress. Pulling on my red pajamas, I fell onto the bed.

The sounds that escaped from my mouth sounded animal-like. Deep screams of pain, agony, the sounds ripping up from my guts, forcing their way out. No longer controlled, no longer afraid, no longer wondering. My whole being realized this experience was the worst, the most catastrophic of nightmares. No longer holding back. I pressed my face into the pillow, stuffing it into my mouth, trying to muffle the awful sounds. The sounds would not stop. Like emotional vomit, a reflex born of grief.

My mother came into the room and laid against my back, holding me for hours while I mourned. Not a word did she utter, knowing there were none. The pain only a mother can recognize, and silently tolerate, unconditional love.

By the middle of the night, Mom quietly left me. My sobs were softer, gentler. The grief slowly retreated to a deep inner place. My breathing was still convulsive from sobbing but easing. And there was razor sharp clarity left in my mind. A laser beam of knowing Gavin was the most precious thing in my life. There was nothing that mattered more to me. Not my pride, not the desire for revenge in the face of betrayal, not the powerful drug of victim-hood. It was all a trap, and one that I would not be caught in.

I had visions of my wrists eternally in handcuffs, if I allowed myself to be a victim, if I allowed myself to make Daryn wrong, if I focused on how unfairly I had been treated, if I focused on how much I hated him and what he had done to me and to our son. I resolved I would burn through it all in one night, one night only of rage and hate and revenge. One night was all I would allow myself.

And while I screamed and cried that night, the clarity remained with me. Only the love, only Gavin, only the truth, please help me to see, to be the best I can for him, to be an example of living for freedom, an example of taking full responsibility for everything in my life, finding my own part in the events that led to this day.

Focusing on Daryn and what he had done would never help me, or Gavin. I could only be culpable for my own part in this drama. Gavin would grow up, and when he was older, we would have a relationship. We would catch up on our lives. He would know I had fought for him in a court of law and lost. I had done what I could. Gavin had his own destiny. I had to trust in the bigger picture of his soul's evolution.

This was part of it, as excruciating as it was to own this, it was the truth. Or it wouldn't have happened. There was something bigger than me and my petty desires, yes even my desire to have him close to me and be part of my life. All my resistance to this manifested as a scream of *No. It can't be.* Then it wouldn't be happening. You have to trust in what is happening to you. You gave it your best shot, the best attorney you could find, the best legal experts advice in the world from the Rajneeshpuram attorneys. *Oh, why did Bhagwan have to get arrested this week? Why was it all over the news?*

I had only been with Daryn for sixteen months. He had never helped me to support Gavin. And he had been mostly absent until these last three years. How could this happen? This is totally unfair. And my family is a good one. Daryn ran away from home at fifteen, his siblings all drank and smoked pot. How could the judge award them custody over my teetotaler, well-educated family?

There were no answers, nothing made any sense. I was

trapped in the hamster wheel of hate and blame and being a victim. Would this help Gavin? Would this be a good example for him to observe as he grows up? Am I going to be a crying, hard-done-by, resentful woman? *No. No. No! Get it together,* I told myself. There is only another eight years before he will be sixteen years old, before he starts to ask his own questions.

You better have a life he can be proud of, be a person he can learn from, be an example of higher consciousness. An alchemist who transforms the lead of hate and revenge into the next level, the gold of love and light. I had visions of a fire, and I was burning in it. I was burning but I wasn't dying. I was burning, and like the iron in the blacksmith's fire, the heat and the pounding of the hammer make the blade stronger and sharper. All the things that were not really me, were burned in fire that night.

The dross burned away, leaving me spent, and incredibly calm. The compass of inner guidance, the voice speaking to me, was constantly pointing out the trap of falling into blame. The trap of forgetting to stand tall and own that I made the choice to be at the Ranch, wanting a different life. Own that I ignored the little voice inside, the conflict of having to choose to be at the Ranch versus leaving and being with Gavin. Own that I had given little regard to the rules of this world, thinking I was above it all, that if I focused on love and trying to make this world a better place, I would be protected somehow. Own that, by ignoring societal norms, I would now pay the price for those choices.

And this was it. I needed to keep my values; however, I was part of this material world, and there were consequences to running off and living in my own idealism. The world does not treat nonconformists well. I would have to learn a balance. I would have to learn to pay better attention. My lack of regard had cost me my son. The highest price imaginable.

And so it was. I had times of great duress, but I heard that inner voice telling me that love was the most important thing, more important than being right, more important than my pride, more important than getting even or making someone else hurt as much as I was hurting. Daryn would have his own lessons, someone else was in charge of his soul, and it wasn't me. It wasn't my job to teach him or even make him know how much he had hurt me. It was all out of my hands. It was in God's hands. Leaving me free. Free to continue with my life, free to grow, free to love.

It was finally arranged to meet with Gavin. I spoke with him on the phone. I told him I was deeply sorry but my case in court had not been successful, and he would be living with his dad from now on.

"Can I see you, Mom?" he'd asked me.

"Yes, but only with your dad or Gina present," I answered him. "But Gavinooski, you know the big maple tree in front of your house? How about if I meet you there?"

Later that day, after a phone call with Daryn ensuring I could visit with Gavin, finally, I walked up Cedar Street and low and behold, Gavin was up in the big maple tree beside the sidewalk. I quickly climbed up, too, and we had our reunion. Maybe Daryn was watching from his window, maybe they never knew, but I had time with my son again held in the arms of a tree. The tree holding us together in its massive brown branches, shaded in privacy by the orange and yellow leaves of fall.

We met several times in that tree over the next weeks. I slowly got myself reassembled into the new reality of being an 'unfit mother' as I was now officially labeled in the world. I decided to return to Rajneeshpuram with Tosh and met with Gavin again just before I left.

"I am going back to Oregon for a little while, Gavin, and I'm so sorry I wasn't successful, but I want you to know I did my best. There isn't anything else I can do as the papers are filed in the highest court. I know you are young to have this conversation, but if you want to live with me again, it will be up to you to make it happen."

While I don't recall his words, I do remember feeling that he understood me perfectly well.

Chapter 22

End of the Ranch

"We followed our hearts and left the old world."

Boatyard, Kauai
December 1989

"What the heck?" I exclaimed as I climbed the ladder up onto the deck.

Tosh stood where the cockpit would be, surrounded by huge pieces of cutout cardboard and plywood. With his hand on his hip and a pencil over his ear, he was deep in thought, a clipboard with drafting paper carelessly cast to one side.

"I'm trying to redo the cockpit design," he announced after a moment.

"Uh huh." By now I was used to the drill. No sense discussing it. He had a plan, just go with it.

Tosh excelled at using wood and cardboard to mock up his designs, a skill he had developed while renovating many of the dental offices we had worked in. Accommodating the new deck layout, new engine and steering gear, he was also working to incorporate stowage, better drainage, and comfortable seating.

"Come over here," he beckoned. "Can you reach the wheel from here? When we are on a starboard tack, this is most likely where you would sit." He paused, moving to the companionway hatch, "And can you grab the lines here? As we adjust the sails, I want to be able to reach them easily from a sitting position so we can brace our feet securely."

I followed what he was saying. He watched me as I sat and reached and measured where my feet were stable.

"Sit here." He placed a piece of plywood against the temporary stanchions, then adjusted the angle. "Is that comfortable? Better than just a ninety-degree angle?"

I sat where he instructed, grabbed the front of his shirt, and playfully pulled him toward me. "You sit," I said as I laughed, "and kiss me, you monomaniacal man." And he did. But the moment was short lived.

Releasing me, he had the pencil out from behind his ear and his clipboard in hand, quickly sketching the new seat back angles and cockpit floor, any playful flirtation completely out of his mind.

Eventually a design emerged that included a large lazarette (storage locker), comfortable seat backs that lifted for stowage and provided protection from the sea. The new cockpit was shallower than the original with large drains that emptied directly to the outside of the hull. All right angles were sealed with the same radiused epoxy coving as the bulwarks to prevent any standing water in corners and mitigate the potential for dry rot.

Leaving him to his drawing, I made my way down the ladder, saddened. I missed my husband. After almost two years, the project was slowly absorbing more and more of him. Like an obsession, it was all he thought about. *Isn't this what it takes to complete such a huge undertaking?* I rationalized. The feeling of being invisible and undesired threatened to take over, but I resisted. I, too, wanted to be successful in completing this boat. *It wasn't that bad, was it? Every marriage goes through cool times, right?* I focused instead on my plan for the day and a sannyasin friend due to arrive at the airport in several hours.

Later, waiting in the cool breezeway of the airport for Sargam, I remembered her beach wedding with Sundro here on Kauai almost a year earlier. We'd met in the early eighties at the Ranch. I thought about the last time I had seen her there, near the end. She was just one of dozens of daily goodbyes as the dream of utopia in the desert crumbled and the Ranch family dispersed, sannyasins departing for all continents of the world.

Beyond the goodbyes to my friends, memories of what Tosh and I did during those last days rushed forward in my mind, intruding into my current reality.

Rajneeshpuram, Oregon
December 1985

My hands shook as I typed the document. *Could I really do this? Would this work?* I knew it would. I knew it was legal. *But it was so...* My mind couldn't grasp just what it was. *Way outside my comfort zone?* I laughed cynically to myself as I typed.

I was in the law office of the Rajneeshpuram attorneys. There used to be fifteen of them. Today, only a few paralegals and secretaries remained. Most had gone to Portland where the courts and government offices were, still fighting legal battles despite the loss of leadership. Some had left altogether during the preceding four months, while Sheela and her group had departed in September and Bhagwan at the end of October. The media had been all over it. Huge news. Huge anti-sannyasin sentiment.

While there were still a thousand sannyasins left on the Ranch, the population was sparse in comparison to the ten thousand that had filled the streets during the summer. People left daily, unable to continue without leadership, and consumed with fear from the unannounced, intermittent raids by the National Guard. In less than two months, the smooth routines of the highly functioning commune were in disarray, the purpose of everything we were doing in question. No, not in question. Pointless. Over.

I was only halfway through the document. *What if someone sees what I am doing? That's nuts, there is no one here who cares. Besides, there is no one here who would recognize what you are doing.* Despite the cold of the office, my armpits were wet with nervous sweat under my red wool sweater.

For the previous nine months, I had worked in the legal department, managing all the lawyers and their court appearances, filing dates, and the production of their documents. Under their supervision, I also wrote and managed all of the corporate law, bylaws, mission statements, and board meeting minutes. That is what I was doing now. Composing a sale agreement between the Rajneesh Medical Corporation and Doctor Robert Rudell, aka Tosh, my partner. We had a meeting scheduled at the medical center with the head of the Medical Corporation in an hour. This document needed to be completed and printed on official letterhead, reviewed and ready for signing beforehand.

As I readied the papers for printing, I waited for the machine to warm up. It had been off for days. If this plan worked, it would be a godsend. Tosh and I would have a leg up in our reintegration into the real world. *Who had come up with such a plan?*

It was just a few days ago. Tosh and I had gone to bed together, happy to have space alone, at last. My roommate returned to Chile as soon as Sheela left. The townhouses were almost deserted. It was like having an eight-bedroom house to myself. Almost. We still had a cleaner, my laundry was still on my bed, folded immaculately when I got home at night, the vacuum marks fresh in the carpet.

"What do you think, Gandi? Time to leave?" Tosh asked me.

"Yeah, it is. But we don't have any money." I'd never thought it would end so I'd never given any attention to plan B. Of course, that was part of the spell of the place. We could all be free to be in the moment, leaving the regular cares of the world at the commune gates. Now those cares of the world crashed through the gates every day with National Guard raids, people searching for suitcases and backpacks, and their long unused car keys. A steady stream of vehicles wound their way along the twenty miles of muddy road, out of the gates and back to another reality.

"Such a waste." Tosh sighed, smoothing his longish hair back from his forehead. "All the equipment, supplies ..." His voice trailed off in the darkness, his motions shadowy in the light, gray from the uncovered window. A winter moon was barely discernible through the snow threatening overcast. "Millions and millions of dollars. Nelson doesn't have resources like this." He referred to our hometown of ten thousand people in the mountains of British Columbia.

"Few small towns do," I responded. "Speaking of the

resources, what's going to happen to all the medical and dental equipment?"

"Don't know. The government has frozen all the assets. Maybe it will all rot here."

"Well, I know you could sure use it." I laughed a little cynically as I snuggled into his chest, teasing him. I laughed, proud because he had designed the cabinetry and ordered the supplies making the three operatories match and set up with the best and most efficient equipment of the time. My words were playfully teasing, knowing that he ran hot and cold when it came to dentistry.

"How about in a few days? Can you be ready to leave in a few days?" The sound of his voice rumbled in his chest under my ear, the rumble radiating out into my body, like ripples from a stone thrown in water.

"Yeah, not much to pack. Where will we go?"

"I'm thinking we can go to Laguna Beach in California. The guys from my construction crew are heading there. We've been talking about getting a house together and doing home renovations for a bit, you know, get some money together."

"Not go up to Canada? Where you can practice dentistry? I can see Gavin?" I asked, suddenly worried even more, reminded of my loss of Gavin and how was I ever going to live so close to my son and not be able to see him without duress.

"I want to make some money first, and besides, it's the middle of winter up there right now. The kids are settled into their school year. Wouldn't you rather go south to the sunshine for just a bit?" His voice gentle, he understood my concern. I missed the children, and I would never forget the nightmare of losing custody of, and visiting rights to, my child.

"Good point, now that you mention it. We won't be much good for anything without money. If we go north in the summer we can stay at the lake while we look for work. That feels better, actually." And it did. My body relaxed again, the sunshine and warm weather really did sound like a good idea right now. And I could put off confronting the awful situation with Gavin just a little while longer.

The next morning in the cafeteria, Tosh and I ran into Arup, the head of the Rajneesh Medical Corporation, and sat down at her table.

"I'm so happy to see you two together. How are you doing?" Arup asked, remembering our arrival four years ago. She'd met us in Sheela's trailer amid all the excitement and enthusiasm about this amazing communal adventure on the Big Muddy Ranch. Most couples that arrived together, didn't leave together.

"We're good, thanks, Arup. How about you? You are one of the few 'Moms' still here," I replied, aware that she'd become the target of anti-authoritarian sentiment as people became disillusioned and resentful before leaving.

"Yes, it's certainly a different scene here these days. Will you be leaving soon?" she asked softly, vulnerability evident in her posture and speech.

"I think so, we are just trying to arrange the logistics, rather challenging without a car and no money," Tosh joked. It was the situation for most of us.

"You made a donation when you came, didn't you?" Arup asked.

"Yeah, we have ten-thousand-dollars' worth of shares in Rajneeshpuram Financial Services Trust, those assets are all locked now," Tosh stated, then continued, "I would like to know what will happen to the dental equipment. Do you know anything?"

"No idea. All the assets of the Ranch will be turned over to the government as far as I understand." She shrugged, seemingly in the dark, too.

"If we can think of a way to get the dental equipment out of here, it would help me get back on my feet after all this." Tosh took the final bite of his pancakes and eggs.

Arup suddenly put down her coffee cup, her shoulders squaring. "You know, Tosh, there might be a way, after all."

And here I was printing up the sale agreement between the Rajneesh Medical Corporation and Doctor Robert Rudell. The printer had finally warmed up, I had loaded the correct letterhead into the machine and the last page was emerging, warm from the paper tray. I quickly checked the documents for accuracy, sliding them into the appropriate ten by twelve-inch envelopes. Carefully locking the letterhead cabinet, and replacing the keys in my desk drawer, I wondered whatever would become of this desk and all the other furniture and supplies in this immense, abandoned office.

Noticing the wall clock, I quickly slipped my arms into my jacket and pulled my hat over my wavy hair. Running down the stairs, I let myself out of the empty building. The bus approached. *I really was doing this.*

The bus stopped and I climbed on board for the short ride to Pythagoras, the medical center.

"I can't thank you enough, Arup," Tosh gave her a hug, sincerely grateful for the strange turn of events.

I had presented the sale agreement and the signatures were enthusiastically executed. In return, we had presented Arup with the ten-thousand dollar Certificate of Shares in Rajneesh

Financial Services Trust, signing it over to the Medical Corporation.

"I am so glad that I was able to help with this, and that the equipment won't be lost in some warehouse of government confiscations somewhere." Arup laughed, happy to oversee something positive during the collapse of our carefully built commune.

"And you thinking of the handicap van to transport the equipment was brilliant, just brilliant." Tosh grinned and shook his head, amazed at our good fortune. Not only did we have dental equipment, we now had a vehicle, too.

Lihue, Kauai
December 6, 1989

After picking up my friend at the airport, we both relaxed in our beach chaises in the late afternoon sunshine. Sargam fell asleep, exhausted from her travels. Behind my sunglasses and under my visor, I watched the waves rolling onto the shore, their frothy tops left behind on the sand, sinking into the wet gold in tiny bursts of bubbles. Like my dreams of the Ranch, my dreams of a Utopian community, my dreams of living a spiritually connected life, all bubbles submerged beneath the surface of my current life. Bubbles that burst and sunk deeper with every mile Tosh and I drove in that old ambulance as we left the commune and entered a new reality.

Rajneeshpuram, Oregon
December 1985

I was looking out the window of the ambulance, the dull gray of winter permeating the landscape, trees a greenish gray, sky a Paynes gray out of the Winsor Newton watercolor box, even the mud of the road stretching in front of us was brownish gray. The windshield wipers did their best to clear the freezing rain from the glass, but the edges created a frosty frame to view the dirty patches of snow that dotted the surrounding hills.

Tosh concentrated on avoiding the many potholes of the road, while I fiddled with the silver knobs and levers on the wide dash. "There must be more heat somewhere," I moaned.

"You got it, that's the one," Tosh acknowledged without taking his gaze from the road.

The anticipated warmth emerging from the vents hit my face. I removed my gloves putting my hands up to the small square. My fingernails were blue from the cold. Gradually warming up, I settled back into the seat, taking some deep breaths. *Just yesterday we signed an agreement with Arup and packed up the dental equipment. And just last night I had hastily thrown all of my belongings into the same trunk I had arrived with three years earlier.* My mind couldn't think about that. I focused on the last few hours; it was easier.

Tosh and I had gotten up early, unable to sleep, thinking about the journey we were about to embark upon. Showering quickly, it was the last time I would be in that bathroom, with all the soaps and creams and shampoos provided for me, all without chemicals and fragrances. *What would it be like to have face cream that smelled like strawberries again?* I thought, remembering my Rachel Perry cosmetics from before the Ranch.

I had walked through the whole big house, checking closets,

everything was empty, save for a portable sewing machine in the cupboard under the stairs. My roommates. *She'd forgotten it. Would it be alright to take it?* There was no one to ask and no one to give it to. It would be left here. Saying a small prayer for forgiveness, I dragged it out of the cupboard and into the hall.

"What do you think, Tosh? Is it stealing to take this?" I asked, already feeling guilty.

He quickly knelt and opened the case. A metal Singer, not plastic like the new ones. After refastening the case, he looked up at me and smiled. "You just got a present, sweetheart. I know you'll be able to use it. Your roommate couldn't take it with her back to Chile. I think she would be happy for you to have it rather than a stranger."

The guilty feeling in my stomach dissipated with his sensible words, replaced with excitement that I would have a sewing machine to start my new life.

As the van bounced along, I thought about it wedged into the back with all the professional equipment. I smiled, just faintly. I'd be able to sew again. It was a good machine, hardly used, and I'd been sewing since I was six years old.

With the van all loaded we drove over to the service station to check the tires, fluid levels and get gas. The attendant smiled and joked, "You, too? You're leaving? Who will be my dentist now?"

"Not sure, Hari. When are you leaving?"

"Venu and I don't want to go just yet. I have a feeling we will be here for a while. You know, last man standing, or something."

Without private vehicles on the Ranch, there was no money exchanged for the gas, it was all managed through the corporations. *Another priceless gift from the Rajneesh Medical Corporation,* I thought to myself.

And here I was. Once again in a van, albeit a much larger

one, driving away on a winter day into yet another unknown. But this ride didn't carry the tears and broken heart from leaving a family life behind, the fear and anticipation of losing my love and my partner. For this ride, Tosh was still with me. A miracle despite the experiences of separation over the last four years. His presence and the fact we were making changes together, made it tolerable, as well as possible to face whatever was coming, including a life outside without my son. My initial fear and dread began to dissolve into more calm.

With less emotional turmoil, I felt pensive, letting the knowledge that the Ranch was finished slowly sink in. It was over, the lifelong experiment now cut short. And although I could barely admit it to myself, I felt excited about the future. I had arrived in a commune in a van that died by the side of the road, and I was leaving that same commune in an ambulance, less healed and more broken than I ever knew.

All the activity and anticipation obscured any awareness of the depth of disillusionment and despair in my soul as it transitioned to a purely material existence. And this awareness didn't fully emerge for several years, not until I began work on the boat.

Chapter 23

Laguna Beach & Redemption

"Surrender to what is, let go of what was, and trust in what will be."

Portland, Oregon
December 1985

"Do we have enough gas to make it to Portland?" I asked. The Big Muddy was an hour behind us and the paved roads were a novelty. I felt easier in my heart, too, my breathing less restricted. As if we'd driven out and away from a heavy fog, dark with distress and disillusionment.

"I think so, but this old ambulance likes to eat gas, that's for sure. It has a big engine. When we get to the city, we'll stop at a payphone to call the dental equipment warehouse and head straight there," Tosh said, laying out the plan we'd discussed.

"We should get there before they close." I checked my watch.

We were quiet, each of us in our own thoughts, immersed in wondering how to navigate the next few days, especially how to get some money, crucial for our reintegration into a cash-driven society.

Later, in Portland we emerged from the dental equipment warehouse with a check for five-hundred dollars, an advance for the dental chair, two operator chairs, a light, and x-ray unit we had unloaded from the van and left for them to sell on consignment.

"How are we going to cash it?" I asked. "We don't have a bank account anywhere anymore."

"The guy told me they bank right there on the corner."

We made it to the bank before it closed, and they cashed the check. We had money for more gas and food.

The next morning brought more freezing rain and dark skies. A storage place nearby was happy to rent us a cubicle, and we unloaded the rest of the dental equipment. Fastening the brand-new padlock on the locker, Tosh put his hand on the closed door, speaking to the contents, "We'll be back to get you soon, and when we do, we'll be ready to put you back to work." He carefully attached the small brass key to his key ring, one that contained only one key for the van. I had the other one.

"Here we go again," he said as he laughed. "This is how it starts. One key at a time until you have a whole ring of them, keys for a life back in the world, and they weigh your pockets down." Handing me the second key on its thin wire, he added, "And here's yours."

Continuing to California the van was almost empty now, hollow and echoing, like part of my heart. *Don't think about it. The next days of our lives will unfold how they do.* Taking a deep breath, I looked back into the cargo space behind me. Tosh had placed the futon from his room at the Ranch across the back and made up a bed, just like pre-Ranch times, but I could stand up in this van. It would make a perfect camper. To ease the inner feeling of free falling, I allowed my mind to consider easier, more familiar things, things and actions I could actually envision myself participating in again. I began designing curtains to cover the windows all around. I could sew them with the new machine.

The tension in my chest eased up a bit. I took more deep breaths as I stared out the window. The drive down the freeway was a social update. Newer models of cars, billboards advertising things I'd never heard of, as well as newer versions of products and services that had changed during our four years of isolation from the culture in general. We listened to the radio, amazed the news heralded new names and specific world issues yet still sounded so much the same.

"How is it to be driving again, Tosh?" I asked, genuinely curious.

"In one way it's as if I never stopped driving for four years, but in another way, it's kinda stressful, everyone is going so fast. Damn. That truck was close." The van shuddered from the side winds as a huge semi passed us at eighty miles an hour. A wave of anxiety hit my stomach at the same time. Internally, I was sideswiped by the knowledge I was once again on the precipice of a new life, one I had no way of anticipating. I was changed. Tosh was changed. The world outside was changed.

Lihue, Kauai
December 6, 1989

Later that night after Sargam's arrival, seven of us gathered around the round dining room table, enjoying our dessert, tea and cookies. We stuck candles in guava ice cream, an early celebration for Tosh's forty-second birthday. Gavin was reading in the living room. As usual when sannyasins gathered, discussions included the Ranch, Sheela, Bhagwan and especially what had happened at the end of it all.

I got up to make more tea and refill the cookie plates. Turning on the tap to fill the kettle with fresh water, I hurriedly took a deep breath. It was ragged going in. *Damn, my pulse is up, too. Why do I still get so triggered in these conversations? It's all still so real even four years later.* I turned off the tap and carried the full kettle to the stove, igniting the gas under it. In the dining room, I could hear the soft cadences of voices, their rise and fall animated as the inquiry and exploration of the events around the end of the Ranch were considered.

I returned to the table with fresh tea and cookies as Tosh said, "We moved in with Ranch friends in Laguna Beach. Oh, and we had to get rid of our orange clothes. Remember that?"

"Oh, yeah, what a trip. We went to thrift stores to buy clothes that were not the notorious red or orange indicative of a sannyasin," Kali reminisced. "I loved picking out other colors to wear. I liked green. How 'bout you, Deb?"

"Yellow and turquoise." I smiled. "It was so freeing to just get any color in the store after six years of orange and red. But I must admit, it made it harder to shop as there was so much to choose from." But inside there was so much more. It truly was a freedom, an outward sign of the release from the dogma and rules of the group, freedom from a code of thinking and behavior that was no longer required or even valid.

"Yeah, with all the negative publicity about sannyasins, we didn't wear red again and purposely kept well under the radar. Even now I don't talk about that part of my life with just anyone. People have too many judgments, it feels bad," I admitted.

"Me neither," Shakti admitted, "it gets too complicated

answering all the questions and knowing they don't really want to know. They just like feeling superior, because obviously being a sannyasin was really fucked up. Oh, and the sensationalism."

"Well, it was sensational, that's for sure. The hundred Rolls-Royces come up every time, even before the 'sex guru' stuff." Vardo chuckled softly.

"We made enough money to return to Canada and ended up in Silverton." Tosh picked up his ice cream bowl, licking it clean. "And you guys know the rest of the story," he concluded.

Washing up the dishes later that night, I thought about our conversation. Well, there was just a bit more to the story.

Nelson, British Columbia
October 1986

"Can we meet for coffee?" It was Daryn, my ex-husband and Gavin's father, on the phone. Tosh and I had returned to British Columbia after eight months in Southern California, and I had sent the required letter requesting permission to visit Gavin. Now I had a phone call.

My hand was sweaty on the receiver, my pulse quickened. *What could possibly have gone wrong now? It can't get any worse, Deb, calm down. Could he deny my request?*

"Is Gavin okay?" I asked, forcing my voice to stay matter of fact.

"Yes, Gavin's fine. Can we meet tomorrow at four?" He came straight to the point.

"Sure." A million questions flooded my mind

"Okay, see you then."

I hung up the phone, my heart thumping loudly in my chest.

"Everything okay, Deb?" Tosh asked from across the room, concern in his voice and on his face. Since leaving the Ranch, he called me by a shortened version of my given name.

"Don't know," I confessed. "Daryn wants to meet me tomorrow after work. He says Gavin's fine."

Later, sleep eluded me, my mind running wild with scenarios, trying to guess, to prepare for the worst. *But honestly, you've faced the worst already, just relax.*

The next afternoon, I parked the car at the mall after an excruciatingly slow drive in from the lake. Slow because there was so much traffic and excruciating because of the apprehension about what was coming. I prayed I'd be able to see my son. *Maybe Gavin would be with him.*

Walking into the mall, I spotted Daryn immediately. He was alone. Conspicuously tall, he stood at the coffee kiosk, already holding a lidded cup in his hand. He scanned the entrance. Seeing me, our eyes met. I was seeing him for the first time since that shattering day in court almost a year earlier. Returning his gaze, I walked confidently toward him, determined to at least fake calm, self-assurance.

We hugged. It was natural and how we had always greeted each other. However, I felt wary and guarded, almost stiff, as if encased in a suit of metal armor. *Remember, someone else is in charge of Daryn's evolution. His actions have nothing to do with you. Any blame or feeling like a victim will keep you bound, trapped. Your job is to remain centered and certain that only the love will prevail. Even if you don't get to see it before you die. You have everything you need to get through this meeting. You are not alone.* I took a deep breath. Determined to prove to myself that civility and communication are possible despite all obstacles.

"Can I get you a coffee?" he asked, his voice low.

"No, thank you. I'm good for now." I smiled a small smile before turning to walk to a table.

As he took off his dark fleece jacket and hung it on the back of the chair, I noticed he seemed agitated, out of his comfort zone.

"Gavin is good? Gina and the kids are okay?" I asked, making conversation, wondering why he was nervous. He settled into his chair at the table across from me.

"Yes, everyone's good," he answered distractedly as he carefully placed his coffee cup on the table. "So you are back? You guys have a job up here now?" he asked.

"Actually, yes, and yes. We'll be doing a locum up in Silverton." I answered, reiterating what I had said in my letter requesting visitation.

"I'll just get right to the point," he said. An audible exhale followed his words.

I still couldn't tell what was coming. *Good news? Bad news? Why did he seem so uptight and jittery?* I pulled the zipper down a bit on my jacket to offset the warmth of the mall. I adjusted myself on the edge of the hard chair.

"Um ... well ... This is harder than I thought ..." he admitted, his gaze off to the side and down at the floor, anywhere but at me.

I waited, breathing, not moving. *What was it?*

"Um ... well ... Gavin has been driving me nuts. I can't take it anymore. Can you take him off my hands?" The words spilled out fast, as if under pressure. Daryn fell abruptly silent, still looking down at the table.

I stared at him, momentarily unable to speak. "Ah ... can you repeat that ... just to make sure I understand what you said?"

"Yes, it's been crazy at the house with Gavin. I need you to take him off my hands. I need a break." He spoke more slowly, clearly. And obviously with great relief. He leaned back in his chair. His eyes slowly met mine.

What the hell? Is this possible? My heart did a cartwheel. I wanted to jump up on the table and dance. I wanted to throw my arms up in the air, tip my head back and scream *Yes* at the top of my lungs, disrupting the world with my joy, my relief. I'd thought I'd have to wait until he was sixteen or grown up. I'd thought I'd go through the next years with only occasional moments with my son. Even so, Tosh and I had returned and found a job in the area to be close to him, so I could see him whenever permitted. I'd only been in town a day. What a miracle. I was in awe.

Quietly, all I said was, "Sure. Of course."

"Thank you." He reached for his coffee and took a small sip before replacing it back on the table.

We both stayed quiet, the silence stretching out, loaded with emotion. The newness of the situation settled into my brain, the altered paradigm sinking in. Slowly the ramifications made their appearances, clearly and with precision.

"Does this mean we're changing the court order?" I asked.

"Yes."

"Can I go to my attorney and have him begin the reversal?" I repeated, just to be sure.

"Yes."

"When can this happen?" I hardly dared ask, in case I was mistaken, in case there was a catch.

"You can pick Gavin up tonight if you like."

"Seriously?" I took a deep breath. "That's wonderful, Daryn. I can't wait to see him," I paused. "Can you write me a letter to carry in my wallet saying I have your permission to have Gavin with me? You know, just in case I get stopped by the police for any reason ..."

"No problem, good idea." He seemed more at ease as he reached for another sip of his coffee.

There were long silences and a few more words. As logistical questions emerged, I asked them. He answered. The whole meeting wasn't more than twenty minutes.

A short time later, parked outside Daryn's house, I waited, pinching myself. This was a miracle. My eyes were glued to the door. *Would Gavin emerge? Would I really get to see him again right now?*

"Hi, Mom," he called to me as he ran down the walkway to the car a few moments later.

"Hey, kiddo. Great to see you again." I knelt in the street outside the car and hugged him. He was taller than last year, more grown up at eight years old. My throat constricted with emotion; my eyes overflowed. I squeezed him tight.

"Hey, I can't breathe, Mom." He laughed as I released him.

"Bye, Dad," he said, giving Daryn a hug before he climbed into the car.

Daryn put a duffel bag in the trunk and handed me a folded sheet of paper. "This should work until the legal papers are complete," he said.

I quickly unfolded the paper and read it, not taking anything for granted.

To Whom it May Concern,
I, Daryn Cavanaugh, with sole custody of my son Gavin Cavanaugh, grant permission for him to stay with his mother, Deborah Cavanaugh.

Signed: Daryn Cavanaugh Dated: August 20, 1986

"Thank you," I reached up and hugged him.

Gavin lived solely with Tosh and I after that. I could never figure out what had really happened. *Had Daryn realized the error of the litigious path he had chosen? Had Gavin taken my parting words in the tree that day to heart and consciously made life hell in Daryn's household? Was it a gift and a blessing from the Divine, an answer to my prayers, a reward for owning my own responsibility for the situation and ferociously resisting the urge to blame others?*

And maybe it was not so much a reward as the natural order of things, of how this place works. Divine Law. We are completely responsible for everything in our lives. And truthfully, consciously owning this is excruciating when dark things happen, and overwhelmingly worth it as I was being shown. Looking back on it, having my son back was the one thing that could heal me faster than anything else. The one thing that could help me integrate back into a new life after living through the traumatic events of the previous years.

Even with Daryn's consent, it took two years before the court reversed its order. Only then did I remove that letter from my wallet.

Chapter 24

Bhagwan Leaves His Body, Dinghy & Knees

"The dancing of the waves and the rocking of the sea will set your soul free."

Kauai
December 1989

Gavin plopped himself down on my towel and drank his juice. He was covered in sand, the color of his swim trunks indiscernible. It had been three years since that miraculous day when he'd arrived unexpectedly back into my life. *Yes, I feel very blessed.* I could never have guessed during that awful night after the court hearing, that I would be here in paradise with him today. An active part in the boat adventure, he was enjoying his beach boy life.

"Can we have some chips, Mom?" he asked. As I looked into his blue eyes, peeking out of that sand covered face, they were the same eyes from the tree all those years ago, but the concerned sadness, so out of place in a seven-year-old gaze, was gone from them.

Suddenly, 1989 became 1990, January bringing winter storms of wind and deluges of rain. The boatyard would be squishy and wet with deep puddles in the potholed access road. The tarps over the roof framework around *Elixir* would take a beating. Tosh would patiently redo them, keeping the sun and rain off us and our unfinished boat.

Another quieter storm passed through after a phone call from Kiran in Vancouver informed us that Bhagwan had left his body. He had been ill since his deportation back to India in 1985. While I had let go of a great deal in the last years working on the boat, it was still a thoughtful time as I pondered His spirit, His soul, and where He was, and how that affected me. Would He be all around in the air I breathed now?

He had told us that when He passed, we were to move on with our lives. No fuss, the transition out of physical existence a natural one, one to celebrate. He had also said He would forever live on in the essence of his disciples, and wherever we went and whoever we met would be touched by His presence.

Sitting up on the deck, I thought about this as I sanded down another coat of varnish on the cap rail,* the wood that sat atop the strip planked bulwarks. They were a finishing piece, following the curve continuously around the perimeter of the decks and fashioned out of merbau, a hardwood from Southeast Asia. It was extraordinarily beautiful wood, a deep red brown with golden highlights coming alive under the magic of the oil and varnish.

Now that He was no longer confined to His body, did I feel His presence differently? Was this the finishing work for our souls? Would His presence jump shift us to the next level of consciousness, enlightenment? In spite of my disillusionment, I still sought a way to value His guidance, a vestigial hope and remnant of my previous spirituality.

So far, I felt the same. Or did I? I didn't feel as driven. Maybe I was mellower than I had been about the Ranch, slowly accepting the changes life had delivered to me. And I was no longer processing the past. Perhaps this need had been resolved by time and death? Now, the present moment was all consuming.

"Hey, Deb, come out here a minute," Tosh called in the front door of the Eleki Place house a week later. In the middle of preparing dinner, I dried my hands on a towel, and encouraged Tiki, my winged sous chef, to fly off my shoulder and up onto the stationary blades of the ceiling fan.

Gavin, after helping with the bird show at the Westin Kauai when we lived in the cliff house, had been determined to have his own birds and Tiki and Kiwi, white cockatiels, had arrived in our lives. They flew free in the spacious open floor plan of the house and reveled in sitting on my shoulder, pecking the shiny stones out of my earrings, or perching on the model of *Elixir* and chewing the rigging, or landing on the dinner table at mealtimes. While Gavin held one end of a length of spaghetti in his mouth, Tiki would eat the strand all the way up to his young master's face.

Making my way to the front door I could hear the rain deluging down, on the roof and against the windows. It stormed during the last days in January, and I had been unable to work in the yard, varnishing the cap rails and stanchions didn't go well in the wet weather. If the rain blew in under the tarps it made permanent little ripples in the surface, and even if it didn't, the varnish dried with a milky finish from the high humidity, like old rheumy eyes.

"What is that?" I asked, incredulous as I looked out the front door, through the sheets of rain.

"Will this work for our dinghy?" Tosh grinned widely, standing there in the pouring rain, unconcerned that he was soaked through.

"Well, it's as derelict as *Elixir* was when we started. A perfect match." I laughed. It was a seven-foot shell, with two opposing diagonal layers of eighth inch cedar strips, unfinished, the epoxy yellowed and chipped. The uneven ends of cedar strips were sticking up and ragged, like broken teeth in a pirate's wicked grin.

"With all this rain, I can work on it here in the garage and at least get something done this winter."

For the next month the small, orphaned boat was restored in the comfort of the garage, out of the wind and rain. In the end, it was fully assembled in the living room, including raising the custom sail I'd sewn, a perfect match for the mother ship.

Boatyard, Kauai
Spring 1990

"Hold it," Tosh called down over the side of the boat, giving the crane operator the closed fist signal. It was deja vu this April of 1990, the second time on this project we hired a crane. The new 42 HP Perkins Diesel Engine with attached Borg Warner Reverse Gear was hanging in the air, suspended over the aft end of the boat.

"Got it, Ron?" Tosh asked my dad, who stood in the engine

room, guiding the machinery into its new home. Visiting for a month, my parents were thrilled to be put to work. The floor of the cockpit was hinged on one side, opening the whole engine room for easy access, another of the modifications Tosh had incorporated when redesigning the cockpit. We had poured a new concrete bed in the engine room with hardwood supports cut from brown-heart wood, extremely dense and rot resistant.

"Yep, she's right on target," Dad responded as the crane lowered the huge engine the last few inches into place. "We got it."

Tosh undid the hook from the strapping, and let it go, up into the sky, over the side, and down to the truck. After checking that the engine bolts were accurately lined up on the supports, he scrambled over the side to pay the crane guy.

"See you in a few months, to step the masts," Tosh promised.

"Sure thing," Crane Guy called as he climbed up into his cab.

"Wow, sure you got a heavy enough engine?" Dad laughed as he assembled the sockets and wrenches to bolt the new gear in place.

"Actually, the Perkins Company tried to sell us a new aluminum model that was half the weight of this one, but we decided to go with the old heavier one," Tosh explained.

"More ballast?" Dad asked.

"Not really, although it's a definite advantage, especially since we jackhammered all that cement out of here. It was the last available older style diesel engine and has been used in tractors around the world for years."

"Of course," Dad followed, "parts readily available no matter where you are."

"Yeah, and that wouldn't be the case with the newer lighter

engine," Tosh continued as they tightened down the big engine bolts.

"You know, we sure have a lot more room than with the old engine, I couldn't even squeeze in here. It was a 50 HP Detroit Diesel. They don't make 'em anymore."

"Are these the original fuel tanks?" Dad asked, his back up against one of the two stainless steel tanks that fit snugly aft up to the transom on both sides.

"Yeah, we sure lucked out with those. The previous owner had taken them out and we found them lying under mountains of crap below the hull during our original cleanup. I sent them to the local metal shop to be pressure tested and repaired. Lucky for us, they were salvageable. I wouldn't want to know how much seventy-five-gallon custom stainless tanks would cost to fabricate right now. Got that, Ron?" Tosh checked that the last bolt was done.

"Yeah, all done. What did you finish them with?" Dad asked. A builder himself, he was interested in every detail.

"Epoxy metal paint to protect them from external corrosion. We finished and placed them in the cockpit prior to building the deck around them. We weren't so lucky with the original stainless-steel water tanks. Unsalvageable, we had to fabricate two fifty-gallon containers out of plywood and epoxy to adjoin these fuel tanks."

Besides the milestone of installing the engine during their visit, my parents also helped with sail restoration. Mom scrubbed them down in the driveway and Dad seized (sewed) the hanks (clips to hold the sail onto the forestay) on the jibs while I replaced the leather chafe guards on the corners of the sails. Structurally almost done, we had begun work on her propulsion systems; diesel and wind.

"What are you working on today?" I asked Tosh one morning after their departure, genuinely curious as he had two-foot strips of mahogany and rosewood piled around him.

"Hey, there," he greeted me with a saw-dusty hug. "How is Nicole doing?" Tosh's daughter had an audition today for a fashion show in the big shopping mall in Lihue.

"She's all set, totally excited about it." While I had no interest in modeling or that lifestyle, it was something she loved. I was proud of her and glad she, too, was part of our lives again. She'd just turned twenty-one, was living in her own place on the island and thoroughly enjoying her job at the Westin. As a stable hand, she cared for the carriage horses, harnessing and unharnessing dozens of them each day.

"Good for her. And how does it feel to be thirty-five?" he teased me as he returned to his wooden strips. Birthdays continued to pile up along with projects, and he'd taken us all to dinner to celebrate mine the previous night.

"The same as thirty-four." Although it sounded old to me, I wouldn't admit it to him. Instead, I teased, "How does it feel to be forty-two?"

"No, really. What are you working on?" I persisted. The cabins, decks and rails were complete. He was working on something for the interior.

"This is a jig for the knees," he announced, as if it was as everyday as mashed potatoes.

"Okay, what are they?" I laughed as I pictured a boat with knobbly knees, cracking up at the mental image in my mind. "Sometimes this boating vocabulary is just too funny."

"Now that you mention it, I guess it is pretty funny," Tosh agreed before continuing with an explanation. "In order to reinforce the strength of the decks, cabins and the whole rig, we need to fabricate knees, or braces, to install port and starboard of both the main and foremasts."

"I still don't get how these strips of wood could possibly be strong enough or big enough for that kind of stress," I said, still puzzled as I pictured two masts, towering sixty-five feet above the decks and supporting sails full of strong winds. It would take a lot of strength to hold that magnitude of force.

"Well, traditionally, knees are grown structural pieces of a wooden boat," he explained. "They are the part of a tree where a big branch grows out from the trunk, very strong and curved because it grows that way. There isn't a forest here to supply a tree for the knees, and unfortunately, I've used all the big pieces of hardwood so I can't cut them out of a solid piece. But there's lots of mahogany and rosewood to use if I utilize the strip plank method of fabricating them."

"That wood is so dense and hard. How will you bend them?" I seriously doubted the viability of his idea.

"I figure I can steam them the same way we did the deck beams and carlings, you know, make the steamer again. These pieces are much smaller, so it won't take up the whole counter in the kitchen the way the deck beams did. And with the alternating mahogany and rosewood, the red and black, they'll look amazing in the cabin," he added, excited.

"So, what's this jig?" I asked.

"Once the wood is steamed and softened, I'll assemble the strips together into the correct order, bend them around this custom form and clamp them all in place. After some days, when the wood has dried into its new shape, we'll take the clamps off, and reassemble the wood with epoxy between all the layers, re-clamp it onto the jig again and leave it to set."

A few weeks later, Tosh cleaned up the completed knees, then epoxied and fastened them into position inside the cabins. As I completed varnishing them in situ, I allowed myself to imagine all the forces they would have to tolerate, to hold the masts up with the sails full of wind, maybe even in a gale.

There were the light layers and in between were the dark layers, almost black. The black layers were even more dense a wood than the lighter ones.

My mind returned to ponder how the darkness could have penetrated our Shangri-la of the Ranch. Is our world like this? Everything and everyone layered with light and dark? Does this make us stronger? Like these knees? Is this what helps us keep our masts out of the water and our sails filled as we navigate complex lives?

Besides being incredibly robust, the laminated knees ended up as stunning additions to the interior decor. These knees were just like us. The thought wafted into my mind like a powerful perfume on evening air, the layers of our darkness and our light are what make us interesting, beautiful and unimaginably resilient.

Chapter 25

Painting, Upholstery & Trailer

"A ship is not just its components or a vessel to get from A to B: a ship embodies true freedom."

Boatyard, Kauai
May 1990

"How's it going up there, Deb?" Tosh's question floated up under the tarps from below the cradle, interrupting my thoughts. "Just got back from the hardware store with the primer, are you ready for it yet?"

"Great, thanks. I'm taping the last section and will be down in a minute." I had finished sanding all the decks and was carefully masking off the varnished cabin tops and rail caps. It had gone faster than I expected. Picking up my guides, tape, scissors, and utility knife, I gathered them in a bucket before heading down the ladder to collect the paint.

At the bottom of the cradle, I reached up to give Tosh a hug, but he was busy focusing on his next project.

"Tosh, can't we hug for just a second?" I asked, instantly feeling rejected.

"Yeah, sure," he answered, giving me a distracted one armed one.

"No, I mean, I want a real hug. I want to really feel you," I persisted, holding onto his arm.

"I'm right here," he answered, frustration starting to show through.

"No, you aren't. You're thinking about the boat. Do you even see me?" My voice was rising and sounding desperate. This wasn't good but I couldn't stop myself. "Come on, Tosh. Are you okay?"

"Look, I'm fine. Let it go," he responded, pulling his arm away.

"Please, Tosh, just a little break here together. It's too much boat all the time, I miss feeling close to you." *Crap, the tears are starting. Damn it.* I looked like the needy, neurotic wife. I hated feeling emotional and wished I could be as cool and detached as he was.

He went back to work; I took a walk across the yard. *Shit, this was hard.* I sat on the big, jagged rocks of the breakwater and let the wind blow the tears off my face. I didn't have to stay here; I could leave but then what? I sat there for a while, breathing, and letting the sound of the crashing Pacific waves calm me down. I still loved him, and I had so much invested in this boat I had to keep going. It would get better. This boat would get done some time. It had to.

I was glad to have the hard reality of the decks to focus on, the tape was stuck securely where it was intended to go, and I was in control of exactly where that was. Walking back to the shed and mixing the paint, I noticed that a precise paint job was much easier than understanding my emotions, cultivating my inner ideologies and my soul's values.

"Welcome back," Tosh said, giving me another one-armed hug as he walked by.

Why did I love this guy so much? Don't think about it. Stir the paint.

This was it. I was finally applying white oil-based under-coating on the decks and cabin tops. Dipping the new brush into the primer, it soaked slowly into the gray foam. Laying down those first strokes, the cloudy brown of the epoxy covered plywood transformed into a uniform, bright white. And slowly the rest of the resentment was whited-out of me, too, allowing small bits of excitement to take its place.

The following day the layer of exterior enamel house paint unified the topsides, cabin tops, decks and cockpit into a whole ship, the individual, separate pieces of her construction and foundation forever erased from view. The high gloss paint made her bristol, the nautical descriptor for immaculate, new, and polished.

Eleki Place House, Kauai
A few weeks later

The new heavy-duty sewing machine whizzed as the thick velvet fabric fed through it, stitching the piping for the cushions that would furnish *Elixir*'s salon. I was working at the dining room table, surrounded by open windows, the tropical breezes of Kauai wafting in, and once again showering me in stephan-otis fragrance from the vines outside.

Gavin was at school, Tosh, Wajdo, and I working at the house and in the boatyard. Everyday. As I carefully guided the sewing machine through the six-foot seams of the cushion covers, I thought about the last months and all the pieces of the boat that were coming together at last. The inside layout was coming alive. Marine plywood and epoxy had transformed into bunks, lockers, counters, and cabinets, everything sealed with anti-mold enamel paint.

While paint was drying in the boatyard, I was at the house wrestling with six-foot slabs of eight-inch mattress foam. I had made newspaper patterns of the settees and used a serrated bread knife to cut the cushions to size. After a successful on board try-in, I returned home and wrapped them in one-inch polyester batting, painstakingly basting it in place by hand. The slabs resembled giant fuzzy butterfly cocoons, all piled up in the corner of the living room, a colony of chrysalises awaiting metamorphosis.

My body was relaxed, relieved to be without masks, safety glasses, ear plugs and gloves; at ease to be sewing and engaged in a familiar task. Reaching the end of the piping cord, I started in on the twenty yards of heavy-duty nylon zipper. Using a special attachment, I sewed it into the back seam of each cushion cover.

My mind was calm. I had almost transitioned out of pondering the unanswerable questions of what had gone wrong at the Ranch. Instead, my quiet hours of sewing began to be filled with contemplation of what it would be like to be at sea. Would we sail around the world like the families in the books I was reading? Would I get seasick? Would Tosh find a remedy for his now well-known affliction with that malady?

Could I provision and cook to maintain proper nutrition without access to fresh food? I made lists of staple foods and how much would be needed for two years, the minimum amount of food to have aboard in case of shipwreck. I had started collecting food storage containers large enough for the amounts I had calculated. Storage lockers on board were constructed to fit specific containers, all planned for ease of use, just like a highly functioning, procedure driven, dental office.

Boatyard, Kauai
A month later

"Hey, what's going on?" I had just arrived in the boatyard and the generator was still in the shed, not yet drowning out the cooing of the doves in the woods next to *Elixir*. It was early, the sun still low as it laced its way through the acacia trees, sending long shadows across the harbor. Tosh sat slumped on the tailgate of his truck, an open letter resting on his lap, his knee exposed through the rips in his work pants. His face lacked its usual enthusiasm for the day.

"Just got notice from the Port Authority. We have to move the boat."

"And? We have to launch her sometime, don't we?" I was confused. Of course we would have to move the boat at some point.

"No, you don't understand. They are redesigning the boatyard, and the road is being re-routed straight through here," he motioned toward *Elixir*. "We have three months."

"Can we launch in three months?" I tried to keep the doubt out of my voice. We had been working solidly for two and a half years and had accomplished a lot, but were we ready for launch? The hull was refastened, caulked, and sealed. New decks and cabins were completed and finished along with the bulwarks and rail-caps. Even the bulletproof Lexan hatch covers were built and in place.

She had a brand new 42 horsepower Perkins diesel engine in her engine room. After salvaging the rudder from the original piles of debris under the hull, it had been refurbished and the custom stainless-steel strapping and rudder post had been welded in place last week. The interior was done except for the locker doors, wood trim, and sole.

"We could, but it would be a lot easier to completely finish her before launching. I mean, we need our workshop and tools, and tramping down the dock with all this equipment would be a huge drag." His voice was flat, unconvincing. Long pauses.

"We need more than three months?" I asked for clarification.

He laughed, cynically. "Since when has anything on this project been done in a few months?"

I was relieved to see him smile, as wan as it was. He had been subdued since Wajdo had decided to go back to the mainland. For the first time on the project, it would be just he and I in the yard. His brother and his wife had returned to Canada after the first year. Our morale was low, not surprising with the amount of love, time and energy that had already gone into this labor of insanity. "But there is a bigger issue," he slowly continued, leaving me hanging in another of his verbal canyons.

Tired of coaxing him, anticipating I would be stressed about what was coming next, I went back to the car to get the water jugs and ice chest. I placed them deliberately in the makeshift 'break room,' the space below the aft end of the hull, where it was cooler.

He got up off the tailgate and slowly walked over to sit in the shade. "Sit for a minute." He could tell I was on autopilot to get the workshop productive and moving, not wanting to hear about any further setbacks. I didn't know if I could take it. This project was taking so long our savings were almost gone, not to mention that I was tired of being alone, without girlfriends, and ignored by my husband.

"The bigger problem is that the original crane that put her up in dry-dock has been moved to Oahu. Right now, there isn't anything on the island strong enough to lift *Elixir*, let alone drive across this soft, bumpy field of grass between her and the launch ramp."

"So how are we going to get her back in the water?" I was taken aback at this news and barely stopped myself from screaming ... *What were you thinking? Stupid, stupid, stupid.*

"Well, I was hoping I had more time to figure that out."

"Well, while you are figuring that out, I have a lot of locker doors to strip down and refinish." I walked resolutely over to the shed and yanked open the doors, slamming the padlock inside on the workbench. As I jerked the heavy generator out of the shop, I tried to take deep breaths and calm down. The only thing my brain could do was stay focused on my present job, otherwise my mind would spiral into pits of anxiety about what we were doing. *Could we do it? Why were we doing it?* It seemed crazy and completely impractical.

The project was so much bigger than I could ever envision accomplishing. I did not know how to do any of it, let alone move seventeen tons. Oh, but yes, I do know how to put gas in the generator, I can lay the original locker doors out on the workbench, I can soak them with paint stripper, I can scrape off the old varnish, using metal brushes and steel wool to get the mahogany stain out of the grain. Oh yes, and plenty of rags.

Slowly, as I immersed myself in stripping the old red stain, my mind stopped racing, my heart stopped panicking, and I found a calmer place. Yes, the project was bigger than me. Before this project I did not know how to do anything I was currently doing. I learned. I figured it out. And I was part of a team. Somehow, with Tosh, we always figured stuff out in the end. Yet why did I still get so angry and anxious? Why was it always the last minute when we figured it out?

Later, when the generator sputtered and stopped, I automatically went over to refill it. *Where was Tosh?* I thought, looking around. He was still sitting in the funky chair, but he had company. I took off my gloves and pulled down my face mask as I made my way over to them.

"Hi, Shakya. Wow, great to see you. And perfect timing for a visit." He'd been at the Ranch with us. A big, stocky man, mild mannered and understated, he was an engineer and welder who, like Tosh, could fix just about anything and solve the most complex problems. And, like Tosh, he thrived on it.

"So I hear." He chuckled as he got up to give me one of his massive bear hugs. "Don't worry, we'll figure it out. We always do, somehow." There was no bravado, just a quiet, resolved assurance in his lisped speech.

"Great," I responded, feeling relieved as I returned to my locker doors.

In my peripheral vision, I could see the boys walking around *Elixir*'s cradle with the tape measure and graph papered clipboard, the constant motion of Tosh's hand to the stubby pencil behind his ear, so familiar.

And figure it out they did. They designed a new cradle on wheels fashioned from steel I-beam and train wheels, the parts clandestinely acquired from a night visit to the piles of rusting equipment on one of the old cane plantations. A fork-lift assisted by a one-ton truck pulled her across the boatyard a month later.

It felt surreal, watching her slow, stately progress, the trailer and supports barely visible. A huge apparition. A little bit like the Peter Pan movies where Captain Hook's tall ship is flying through the air. It messes with your mind and the proper order of things. The whole project was larger than life. This moment in time allowed a rare glimpse of that, an eagle's eye view instead of our usual field mouse perspective.

At the end of the day, safely parked in a row of ironwood trees next to the boat ramp, *Elixir* rested solidly in her new launching cradle.

Chapter 26

Rigging & Rejected

"If you don't know your purpose, it doesn't matter where you go, nothing will feel quite right."

Lihue, Kauai
September 1990

"Bedtime already?" Tosh stood in the lanai at the workbench, his gloved hands full of unraveled one-by-nineteen stainless steel wire, the standing rigging for *Elixir*. With the boat in her new site in the boatyard and the success of the ingenious trailer-cradle, it felt like we might be, at last, approaching the end of the project. There was a faint glimmer in sight at the end of what had been a circuitous tunnel. The shelf-paper-on-the-walls project management system had worked well, most of the major tasks crossed off with big black felt marker with comments like, *DONE*, *WHEW*, and *NEVER AGAIN*, written over them.

RIGGING. This page had arrows moving out to additional pages, taped haphazardly around it. Another milestone would be getting the masts raised and reassembling the rig. Now that we didn't have to launch her right away, it would be much easier to complete this job in dry dock. But I was tired.

I stood in the screen slider between the lanai and the living room, my hand on the door frame watching Tosh splice the back stay. I remembered the challenge of unraveling the old standing rigging three years earlier. Using the four-by-six prints the previous owner had taken, Tosh had figured out every piece in that nasty pile of corroded wire, deciphering where it went in the rig and its exact dimensions.

The warm trade winds carried the fragrance of stephanotis through the screens, filling the house, erasing the memory of mold and cockroaches, reminding me of something other than this boat, and why I was standing here. "I don't know how you do it, Tosh. You've been in the yard all day until dark, and then you work on this wire all night. Aren't you tired?"

"I don't think about it, actually." He continued twisting and working the strands back into the lay of the wire, creating a loop that would go over the end of the mast.

Tosh learned how to splice stainless steel wire out of a book he bought on rigging. Setting up a vise and waist high bench in the screened lanai of the Eleki place house, he was able to do one stay or shroud per night, splicing both ends. It was a perfect task for the winter months when the nights were longer, and he couldn't work in the dark in the boatyard. Using wooden blocks to protect the wire from scoring from the vise, an awl, and needle nosed pliers, he teased the stiff wires into their new positions.

The muscles of his upper arms strained, working hard, exposed by his sleeveless T-shirt. I loved his muscular arms, whether here tonight as he spliced wire, wearing heavy leather work gloves or in a dental operatory, wearing thin latex ones and gripping delicate dental instruments. His forearms were also strong and masculine, well-tanned, his skin damp from exertion. I wished they were around me, holding me, caressing me. He briefly glanced in my direction, his gaze missing me as it returned to the intensity and detail of his task. "How many have I done?"

"Fourteen." My voice was flat, resigned. He didn't notice that I had swapped out my boat yard work clothes for something more feminine.

Once we had the inventory of wire, we were able to calculate how much to order and what dimensions it should be. While the original rig had been galvanized steel, we decided to use the stronger and more permanent stainless for the restoration even though it would be much harder to work with.

Eventually a giant spool of rigging wire arrived on the island and was awkwardly maneuvered from the back of the Mazda and into the Eleki Place garage. Gathering up our courage one evening, we began rolling out the wire into the long driveway. Labeling as we went, a hundred-foot measuring tape precisely measured all the pieces we had recorded from the old rigging. To make the cuts in the thick wire, I closed the bolt cutter using all my weight to press it closed against the concrete driveway, like a giant pair of scissors as tall as my waist.

"And how many are there again?" His face once again focused on his task, oblivious to my attempt to be feminine, provocative, alluring in a lacy teddy, longing for a break from working on the boat; longing for some intimate time with my husband. Longing to connect with him in other than the mechanical details of splicing the wire into dead eyes at one end or mast or spreader loops at the other.

"Twenty." How to get his attention? I missed feeling his

eyes on me, feeling his desire for me, feeling his love and appreciation for me. I missed seeing that sparkle in his eyes when he was excited about sharing time with me. "It's been two weeks straight on this rigging," I continued aloud, *and almost three years straight on this project,* I screamed to myself. *And we had been through this before. Why don't you learn? He isn't interested in you. If I try to talk with him, we will end up in a big fight, like we had last week. What can I do?*

"Yeah, well, one a night, only four left." As each piece was completed, it was coiled, labeled and hung on a rod in the garage, waiting for the day we would raise the masts.

"How much longer tonight?" I tried to keep my voice light, feigning carefree, like nothing was going on. I didn't want to fight.

"Half an hour or so. You will finish the leathering on the rest of those tomorrow?" He was serious, thinking only of the project. The leathering* was the last in a four-step process to prepare the wire before the actual splicing could begin. I tried to go through the process in my mind to distract me from wanting his attention so much. *I am going crazy. I can't do this anymore.*

Feeling close to bursting into tears of anguish and screams of rage, I bit my lip and quietly turned away, switching off the lights on my way through the living room. Locking the front door, my bare feet were silent on the floor tiles of the hallway. Entering the bedroom, I closed the door part way, kneeling on the thick rose-colored carpet to blow out the candles burning on the low end tables next to the futon. I left the music on. Maybe it would help me sleep. I loved this bedroom. Spacious with a high ceiling, there were floor length windows on two sides. With the lights all out, I could see into the garden and out over the moonlit canyon beyond. It was beautiful.

Discarding the useless outfit on the floor, pulling the covers back, I got into bed. Laying there, feeling the ache in my heart I tried to put my attention on my breathing, to keep it connected, but it was ragged and jerky, my throat constricted and painful. My eyes burned, the tears escaping down my cheeks and running into my ears. I turned my face into the pillow, sobbing.

While I could have long talks to my sister about the boat or the kids or cooking, this was private, this lack of intimacy in our relationship. And soul mate or not, it would be the end of it. The breathing helped a little, and the Gibson Girl in the silvery moon kept me company until I fell asleep.

I awoke to the sound of the roosters in the canyon below the house. Without curtains on the huge glass door windows, the light was pale gray, truly colorless. It was very early. Tosh had eventually come to bed and was sound asleep on his side. I snuggled closer to him, pressing my naked body against his back, reveling in his warmth and the softness of the hair on his form, breathing in his familiar scent. I loved him so much I wanted to be in the same skin. No separation. Ever.

Lihue, Kauai
October 1990

"What was that about?" Tosh asked as I got off the phone with my sister. Even though I was unable to share with her about the times of deep loneliness in my relationship during the project, our weekly talks buoyed my spirits. She kept me up to date with the happenings in my family, and I regaled her with stories from the boatyard, the latter helping me to find humor and fulfillment in the telling. Both she and Willem wanted to build a boat someday and were living their dream vicariously through our unplanned and extended adventure with *Elixir*.

"Willem just got laid off for a month."

"Oh no, that's not good. What's he going to do?" Tosh asked, concerned.

"He's on unemployment for a few months and wants to come down here and help on the boat," I responded.

Tosh was instantly brighter. Since Wajdo had returned to the mainland in August, he missed having another guy in the yard and Willem, a master woodworker, would be a significant help.

"Looks like he'll arrive on the weekend. You have some stuff for him to do?" I laughed.

Yes, there was plenty of work for Willem. When the old cabins were dismantled, the salvaged woodwork and hardware were incorporated into the new cabin design. His fine craftsmanship made art of the repairs and revisions on the original cabinet doors and drawer fronts. Gallons of paint remover and steel wool stripped the old finish that had been hiding rich yellow oak, spruce, and Philippine mahogany. Following multiple coats of varnish, Willem attached the refinished bronze hardware, gleaming gold everywhere and adorning the old boat like the royal queen she was.

The old companionway ladder, corner pole and doors emerged from under numerous layers of old paint, revealing vibrant golden spruce that contrasted dramatically with the deep red of the mahogany cabin sides. The doors were further showcased by the original twelve-inch bronze strap hinges, polished to thick tapered strips of lustrous gold.

As the finishing work progressed and more and more boat parts were reassembled, I, too, began to feel rejuvenated and re-inspired by how graciously this boat was coming back into herself.

Chapter 27

Stepping the Masts

"A sailboat is animated by the breath of the wind."

Boatyard, Kauai
May 25, 1991

"Do you have any comments for the record?" Gavin asked me from behind the huge video camera balanced on his slim thirteen-year-old shoulders.

"Yes, I do," I responded, playing along despite the anxiety in the pit of my stomach. "This is the biggest day yet in this project, because we are installing two sixty-five-foot masts in this boat. It's momentous, because we don't really know if all these restored pieces of rigging will actually fit together," I admitted. It was true. It had been so much work, but what if it didn't fit? I couldn't bear to think of it.

"How did you figure out how all these pieces went together?" Gavin asked as he panned the immediate area around the dry-docked ship. Two fully rigged masts lay on their padded sawhorses, beside the fifty-foot schooner, *Elixir*, under the palm trees of the Nawiliwili boatyard. Surrounded by several dozen friends and fellow sailors, many of whom were giving last minute advice about how this should unfold.

"We used old pictures and rigging books to figure it all out. While we have been meticulous in our planning, research and calculations, we are still operating on a lot of faith." I watched nervously as the crane finished extending and locking four stabilizers. The wide outrigger pads sank several inches into the soft earth beside *Elixir*'s cradle.

"In your opinion, what will be the trickiest part of this process today?" Gavin continued professionally, focusing the camera back onto my face.

"Well, you know those toy games? The ones in glass cases where you put in your money to gain control of small tongs so you can pick up the toy that you want? It is kind of like that except much bigger. This crane guy is going to pick up these long poles and hover over a twelve-inch hole in the cabin roof. The hole is just a quarter inch bigger than the diameter of the mast. His job is to thread it through the opening and down through the cabin and have the square butt land perfectly in the mast step* that is bolted to the inside of the keel," I elaborated.

"Wow, that does sound critical. Like simultaneously threading two needles a few inches apart with welding gloves on. Thank you for speaking with me. I am now moving on to talk to the skipper of this operation." Gavin walked steadily away from me while he narrated, off to intercept Tosh amidst the last-minute adjustments prior to lifting the main mast.

After a celebratory picnic in the boatyard last night, the boys had continued working until four-thirty in the morning. They wired the spreaders with navigation lights, finishing three hours before the extension crane arrived for the third and last time on this project.

The yard was suddenly quiet. This was it. I wiped my sweaty hands on my shorts before re-gripping the camera from around my neck. The bustling and banter from a moment before subsided, leaving only the drone of the crane's engine, and the chatter of the palm fronds in the trade winds. All eyes remained on Tosh as he stood back and gave the anxiously anticipated thumbs up signal.

Crane straps, wrapped just below the spreaders, slowly went taut. The wood creaked as it felt its weight against the fabric bands, slowly lifting off the sawhorses. The mast was almost vertical now, the base hanging loose for a moment until two men on guy lines steadied it. And then it rose twenty feet in the air, dangling precariously above *Elixir*'s deck.

My stomach knotted. *How could that thing just hang there?* Tosh and Shakya had scrambled up the side of the cradle and reached up, trying to catch the massive spar as it swung overhead. My breath stopped. *What if the strap breaks?*

"Okay, we're good, go ahead and lower it," Tosh yelled after he and Shakya had the base of the mast gripped firmly in their hands, ready to guide it through the hole in the deck. My breathing resumed, shallowly.

Climbing onto the deck to join them, I steadied my grip on the camera and started shooting again. As tense as it was to watch, I was amazed at the degree of accuracy the crane operator exhibited as he lined up the mast for precise insertion. But my brain tormented me with images of a missed target and shattered mast and cabin. And even more terrifying, a single wrong move could smash Tosh and Shakya as they guided this massive object hanging awkwardly above them.

In those moments of suspense, mind cameos of disaster alternated with the thousands of steps (plus three and a half years) it had taken to get the schooner rig completed and assembled.

The lines for the running rigging* had filled the cargo bed of the Mazda like a massive serving of spaghetti, all coiled after being cleaned, measured, spliced, and labeled. The deadeyes,* with their alien facial features, had been reconditioned with turpentine and linseed oil after sanding the gray sun bleached wood off their ancient cheeks. They were lined up in orderly rows in newly fabricated, stainless-steel, chain plates* amidships on both sides of the boat.

The spreaders had been restored and attached to the masts, the mast collars with their blocks hanging like giant beads on thick white chokers. Standing rigging was draped over the masthead like long flapper necklaces around the mirror on a dressing table.

The shroud line bars, name boards, port and starboard lights were restored and varnished, waiting for their belaying pins.* During restoration, while I polished these bronze bars with a rag wheel and rouge, my imagination conjured images of pirates brandishing swords and bashing their foes over the head with the heavy pins. The counterpart of a traditional pirate ship, this old schooner was worthy of Captain Hook and his ruthless crew.

"Whoa," Tosh yelled, using the slicing motion across his throat as he did. The mast had successfully navigated through the narrow aperture in the cabin top. Tosh, Shakya, and I quickly climbed down the companionway into the cabin, leaving a man on deck to relay directions from below.

The butt of the mast was suspended above the galley counter, just hanging there. I blinked a few times before snapping the surreal image. How it missed the delicate joinery and fiddles of the immaculately finished counter was beyond my comprehension. Imagine putting together jigsaw puzzle pieces that weren't on the original plans and having them fit.

"Ready, Tosh?" Shakya asked, bracing his strong body around the suspended mast and balancing his bare toes on the edges of the floor beams.

"Okay, let her go," Tosh called up to Kenny. The whole thing started to move down through the hole in the counter, missing the fiddles by millimeters, not a scratch on the glossy varnish, they didn't even touch.

"Stop," Tosh yelled and immediately it stopped just six inches from the mast step. I could see the issue, the square butt was twisted about two inches to starboard, think puzzle piece off by a quarter turn.

"Turn the load two inches counterclockwise," Tosh directed.

Could a crane do that? I wondered. The mast slowly rotated to the left. Amazing. I took another photo; it was so close. I focused my lens on the shiny new penny resting in the square receptacle, the year of the coin a message for the future, recording when this mast was stepped.

"Good, let her down," Tosh yelled again. The mast slid into its socket, just like that. It had taken about twenty minutes for the mast to descend those last six inches into position.

To secure the mast in its new home, we fastened the shroud lines to the chain plates on the hull before releasing it from the crane. The foremast was stepped in the same way. Both masts were then secured into their mast partners* with the original, restored, hardwood wedges, filling in the half inch gap between the partner and the mast.

Lastly, before the crane left the boatyard, Tosh, securely tied into the bosun's chair, was attached to the crane's hook, and hoisted to the top of the masts. Judging by his yells from the stratosphere, it was immeasurably higher than he'd imagined.

I laid on my back on the deck and watched him, the trapeze artist, high in the sky, as he hooked up the stays that go between the masts. After taking some camera shots, I let my hands fall back and took some breaths, letting in the powerful significance of this day.

These masts were like plugging *Elixir* into her animator, the wind, the breath of the earth. She was no longer just an inanimate, wooden shell but a giant step closer to realizing her purpose, her life. Once she was launched, these masts would be drive shafts to the sky, supporting her air-filled sails, and transferring their elemental power to the keel, propelling her forward across the seas into unknown adventures and destinations.

Chapter 28

Launch

*"Don't be driven by all the work. Instead, be guided and inspired
by your heart's desire for the sea."*

Boatyard, Kauai
June 12, 1991

"I christen this vessel, *ELIXIR*. May she travel long and far on
the seven seas of this world!" I shouted as I swung the champagne bottle hard against the dolphin chain plate on her bow.
With my hand inside a thick oven mitt and the bottle safely
enveloped in a nylon stocking, there were no flying shards of
glass, but masses of white bubbling foam ran down *Elixir's* bow
and my arms, soaking my feet and the wood of the pallet I stood
upon. The smell of the wine filled the air immediately around
me until the ever-present trade winds gently wafted it away.

Gavin came up close with the video camera.

"Do you have any comments for this occasion?" he asked,

once again playing the news anchor. He took his role as documentary filmmaker seriously.

"Where to start?" I joked before adding, "No comment," with a smile, my mind full of all the work that had gone into the last few days. The boot stripe above the water line was masked off and painted, and lastly, the heavy metal bottom paint was applied. Hundreds of capsules of tetracycline were emptied into the five gallon can of paint and then mixed up with the electric drill. We'd been told the antibiotic kept the bottom free from barnacles and seaweed for much longer than just the copper alone. The bottom needed to be painted within three days of launch to help prevent sea life from attaching to it. Finally, the big day had arrived. After four years of planning and hard work, *Elixir* was going to be launched back into the sea and her true environment.

I stood back and looked up. All the way up, just like the narration to the children's TV show about the friendly giant. Two masts towered high above the deck, their tops and the cross of the spreaders silhouetted delicately against the blue of a tropical sky. Strands of colors, long strings of colorful triangular shaped flags, fluttered from the mast tips forward down to the tip of the bowsprit and aft to the end of the main boom, where it rested on its cradle, protruding several feet out over the stern.

The varnish on her rails and cabin sides shone a deep red, ten coats of varnish bringing the grain of the mahogany iridescently alive in the sun. The bright white of the hull was accented by long straps of bronze trim, shining like gold. Each plank was carved on both sides, defining its whole length and further accenting the long slim hull clearly outlined at the water line with the black and gray of the boot stripe. The maroon color of the bottom paint almost matched the mahogany of the cabin sides, the deep full-length keel, a strong foundation for the rig aloft.

For a moment, taking in the magnificent sight of her, the feelings of the last three and a half years of working in the yard, of figuring out how to reconstruct her, of all the small failures and victories, slammed into my soul. My throat involuntarily gulped for air, eyes briefly blinded as my emotions washed over me. The struggles for my husband's attention melting backward in time, minimizing as my being drank in the bigger picture of such an accomplishment. I was proud of him. Proud of his vision and his ability to transform his vision into reality. A man of few words. A man of action.

Thinking about it now, I don't remember feeling my part in it all. As if I wasn't a solid participant, but a liquid, energetic component, somehow tying together Tosh's vision to this material world. A home. Food to eat. A family to be part of. A component that I had not valued as important as his, always searching for ways to be equal and always feeling I was falling short. This wasn't his perception; this was my own.

The people gathered around us clapped and cheered and talked amongst themselves, reminiscing about how long *Elixir* had sat on land, how it was a miracle she was actually going to taste the sea again, stories about their own launchings, and the inevitable worst-case scenarios about launchings gone terribly awry.

There were neighbors and fellow boat builders, a team of three, who had been watching our progress through the long three years. They had shown up early, before we arrived, and surprised us with eighty feet of purple orchid leis. The rails, the entire length and breadth of *Elixir* were garlanded with these exquisite flowers.

Our new age friends from all over the island, friends who lived in their own realities apart from the status quo, believed in extraterrestrials. They watched patiently, awaiting launch day when they could witness a small miracle. There had been a rumor amongst the new age group on the island about strange star people from Pleiades, who one day just showed up out of the blue and worked unceasingly on the old boat in the harbor, the old boat that had been abandoned for six years before we showed up. That rumor, I had been shocked to find out, was about us.

The small sailing community was glad to welcome *Elixir* back to the water after more than ten years ashore, since well before we acquired her. And the Coasties, the crew of the Harris Cutter stationed in the harbor who had watched us over the years, as well as trained me in water safety, heavy weather sailing, coastal and celestial navigation, and issued my ham radio license. They had their inflatables out in the water fully crewed, watching for *Elixir* to roll down the ramp toward them, like a debutante coming down the wide staircase before a ball, escorts waiting, and in awe.

Gavin moved among them all, a large, rented video camera resting professionally on his narrow shoulder, interviewing and making jokes as he panned wide shots of the scene and zoomed in on the patiently waiting hull. *What's a few more minutes after all these years?* she seemed to say, looking huge and oddly out of her place in the middle of the tarmac, so exposed after being tucked away for years in her grassy boatyard spot beneath the ironwood trees.

It was 1400 hours, and the tide was the highest of the month. With *Elixir*'s full keel and five-foot draft, we wanted the water as high up the ramp as possible for launching. If anything went awry, it would be another month, and the next full moon, before the tide would be this high again.

Frank, the forklift driver, was in position, chains attached to the trailer, and *Elixir* positioned stern first at the top of the heavily corrugated concrete ramp. The plan was to let her roll backward down the incline, the forklift acting as a brake, controlling her descent into the sea.

Moving the pallet I had stood on for the christening off to the side, Tosh, Shakya, and I climbed quickly aboard using a hastily positioned step ladder. Running to the fore deck, Tosh threw the prepared guy lines (ropes) down to the four men he had commandeered to assist him, two lines on each side. They would hold the boat steady until we got the engine started to motor to our berth, empty and awaiting us.

Prior to launch day, two one-hundred-pound batteries were hoisted aboard using the halyards, the block, and tackle put to good use well before they had to raise a heavy sail. We'd started up the brand-new engine and made sure it functioned. Shakya's job was to make absolutely sure. Today it would be started for real, with sea water circulating for coolant instead of a hose, and securely attached to a propeller, drive shaft, and wheel.

"All set. Let her go!" Tosh yelled up the ramp to Frank, giving him the thumbs up signal that everything was in place.

Slowly, she started to roll, and the attendees inched forward, voices hushed, intent on the next momentous seconds. As she rolled over the edge down the steep ramp, Tosh yelled, "Whoa!" He made a slicing movement with his fingers across his throat. My stomach lurched. *Now what?*

"She's going crooked, off to the side, pull her back up," he directed Frank.

And so it went, inching down the ramp, trying to steer her straight but with great difficulty as the tongue (trailer hitch) was now dragging on the ground, attached by the chain to the forklift. They needed to stop every few feet and pull her back up to straighten her out. The crowd moved with the men with the guy lines, everyone paying close attention to each nuance.

Gavin continued to film, walking and providing running commentary in a soft voice, like the announcer for a high stakes golf game.

I sat in the cockpit with my shoulders and body hanging over the rail, watching the concrete twelve feet below slowly move under us, my mind all over the place, my fears constructing a mental hamster wheel. I was afraid the boat would slide off the trailer before she could settle in the water. That she would tip over because of the steep ramp, causing her to keep going sideways, that the engine wouldn't start, that the steering gear wouldn't work, that the waterline would be off, that when she finally got in the water, she would leak, and sink at the end of the ramp.

Breathe, Deb. Breathe.

"The first kiss of the sea," someone yelled, "her keel is in the water." There was more clapping, and the voices were less hushed now. We'd almost made it down the ramp.

"Let her go, Frank," Tosh yelled.

She started to roll faster, picking up speed. The swoosh of the hull slicing into the water for the first time filled my ears. *This is it.*

I ran forward and swung the big white plastic fenders over the side, checking the lines were secure where the men held her steady. Shakya was in the cockpit, turning the key for the engine. It started immediately, the exhaust belching blue smoke, the big diesel growling and coughing up seawater.

Back in the cockpit I went ahead and cast off the two aft lines into the sea, the men calmly winding them hand over hand into a big loop on the concrete pier that we would collect later. Amid ship lines were cast off on the starboard, the port lines pulling us up to the pier so Gavin and Nicole could jump aboard for our first motor around the harbor. Slowly, the bow was past the end of the pier, and I tossed the last lines overboard. Standing on the bow, I stretched my hands up to the sky, and gave a huge "Whoopee," waving at all our well-wishers as they cheered back.

Not able to wait another minute I dashed aft to the cockpit and down the companionway ladder into the salon where I quickly pulled up the sole (floor). The bilge was bone dry. Not a drop of seawater anywhere. The months of caulking were a success. Now I could breathe for real.

"How'd the water line look, Gavin?" Tosh asked as I returned topside.

"Just a tad high at the bow, I think," Gavin answered.

"Pretty darn good, if you ask me," Shakya commented, pulling himself back into the cockpit after hanging over the side to check it himself.

"And the bilge, Deb?" Tosh asked, not waiting for me to volunteer my good news.

"Dry as a bone. We'll see how she is in a few hours." I laughed, sitting on the cabin top as we headed out into the main harbor for the first time, proudly accompanied by two Coast Guard inflatables, one on each side.

Feeling the wind across my face and in my hair, it blew straight through my skull and into my brain. The last vestiges of doubt and uncertainty about this project ever being done were zephyred away. We were afloat, freed up from the confines of land and a dry dock cradle.

We were launched, not in the originally planned six months, but almost four considerable years later. We were free and buoyant, slipping seamlessly into the next stage of a monumental dream. It was an open, wild and ecstatic moment, our first taste of the wind on the water and the feel of my feet on her decks, alive with the motion of the waves carrying her, and all of us, forward.

Part Three

THE REALITY

Chapter 29

Aftermath & Malcolm X

"On this sailing ship I return to the sea and sky, the sun, the stars and the wind's song in the rigging."

Nawiliwili Harbor, Kauai
End of June 1991

"Knock, knock, knock, Harbor Police."

I started, suddenly awakened from a deep sleep. There were men outside, thumping on the hull.

"Shh, stay still. They'll go away," Tosh whispered in my ear.

My heart pounded and my palms were sweaty with fear. I was trying to orient myself from the world of sleep and dreams. *Is this a dream? Where am I?*

Feeling Tosh holding me tight, I gradually remembered. We were aboard *Elixir*. She had launched a few weeks earlier, and we'd moved aboard two days ago. In the dark, my eyes made out the shadowy outlines of boxes piled everywhere. *It was illegal to live aboard here.* My belly clenched tight. My ears heard footsteps outside on the concrete dock.

"They're leaving," Tosh whispered.

"What time is it?"

"Four-thirty a.m. They are doing their pre-dawn patrol, I guess." He rolled over onto his back, his hands clasped behind his head, staring through the dark at the ceiling.

"Well, we kinda knew they don't allow living aboard here in the harbor." I was fully awake now and the situation we were in was getting way too clear. *We could be fined, imprisoned, and the boat could be impounded.*

"Yeah, but I didn't actually believe they would be doing rounds checking on the boats," Tosh sighed. "At least now we know what time we have to bail out of here from now on." He chuckled in a frustrated way. Reality crowded in on his world, affecting us.

I sighed, too. It grew more challenging by the day. I was not as cavalier as my husband about rules. I momentarily remembered our launch day and that first motor cruise out into the harbor, accompanied by the Coast Guard. It was a glorious feeling to be out on the sea, the wind on my face and in my hair. I had hoped it would be 'smooth sailing' once we were in the water, but since then there had been more storms to endure and we weren't even at sea yet.

Despite the harbor rules forbidding living aboard, without money left for rent, we had no choice but to move out of the Banyan Court condos. While we had been downsizing over the last year in preparation, there were still things that needed to be trimmed from our ballast. Hence the boxes piled everywhere. Condensing four years of life and a four-bedroom house onto a forty-foot boat was one thing, but doing it covertly was an even bigger challenge.

We'd cleaned up the workshop, getting rid of old wood and supplies we no longer needed. The shed was still under the palm trees with the trailer parked next to it. At that moment, little did we know how much we would use it over the next year, making money hauling out and repairing other people's boats.

Working in the boatyard over the last four years, Tosh had made a name for himself as a master craftsman, the evidence showcased in *Elixir*. As a trusted member of the boating community, people wanted their boats to benefit from his expertise and they were willing to pay for it.

Other boats aside, we still weren't done with *Elixir*. Her water line was a nautical engineering issue. With the new lead keel, she was sitting stern heavy and bow light, the imbalance drastically impacting her handling. We 'borrowed' huge plastic garbage cans from around the boat yard and loaded them on the bow before filling them with water until our painted water-line matched the actual water line. Using weight per gallon of water, Tosh and Shakya figured out that we needed about fifteen-hundred more pounds in the bow, almost a ton.

We also discovered during our motor cruises in the harbor that the propeller was not balanced and the drive shaft was bent. Marine engine experts recommended buying a new propeller and realigning the drive shaft, which meant removing it and shipping it to Honolulu. Both of these issues required a haul-out. We decided to wait until October for this, giving us some time in the summer to return to Canada to see family. In the meantime, we lived aboard.

I eventually heard the slam of car doors as the Harbor Police slowly left the boat launch area, their tires crunching on gravel strewn tarmac. Rolling on my side, I gingerly extended my bare feet onto the cold glassy surface of the hardwood cabin sole (floor).

"Time to go?" I asked Tosh, who continued to stare at the ceiling. "Hey, what are you thinking about, sweetie?"

"I was wondering how to get us out of here sooner rather than later." He paused, smoothing his thick hair back with his hands again. "But there is no way we can be prepared for an ocean crossing in a month." We spoke just above a whisper, aware that sound carries everywhere on the water and not knowing who might notice we were aboard.

The window of good weather for sailing north was June and July and would take three to six weeks. While all the standing rigging was in place, there was a lot of running rigging left to do. Not to mention that we still needed to learn to sail the rig. Like Tosh, I wished we could be ready to go immediately, but there was still much preparation ahead before undertaking such a crossing.

"We're going to go north, right?" I reiterated our decision to take the boat north rather than south.

"Yep, much as I love sailing, I sure get sick out there. At least if we go north, we'll have the boat up in the shelter of Vancouver Island and, hopefully, we can enjoy sailing in calmer seas." He sighed, feeling conflicted and frustrated by his body's frailty. Crewing here in Nawiliwili Harbor, Tosh had not done well, vomiting over the rail and taking several days to recover after just a few hours aboard small sailboats.

Sailing the South Pacific had been our original dream, of course. Warm water sailing with the prevailing winds, and beautiful azure anchorages. The reality of Tosh's seasickness was now apparent. The thought of being stranded in the south Pacific without work or an economical way to bring the boat north had required us to revise our plans.

Heading north was not as appealing. Cold water and air temperatures, as well as sailing into the wind, proved much more challenging. But if we went north, at least we (and the boat) would be in Canada where we could work and make a living again.

"Gavin," I directed my whispered voice forward to the V-berth where he had made a serious teenage hideout. "Time to get up."

"Ahh, Mom, it's still dark out," he moaned from under his covers.

"Yeah, well, the Harbor Police have come and gone already. We need to get going before they come back for the day."

I had left my clothes ready at the foot of our berth, folded on the navigation table, and started pulling them on in the dark. Tosh slipped out of bed, quickly jumping into his. He'd claimed the companionway ladder as his clothes rack.

"You know, I read about this special medicine they use for the astronauts," Tosh commented, "to help with motion sickness, I'll ask Jerry if he can get me some." Jerry was a fellow boater from Florida who had worked for NASA before retiring to the sailing life.

"That's a great idea. It must work as those guys get thrown around in zero gravity more than sailors do, and they don't survive if they get sick."

"All set?" Tosh asked, noticing me picking up the bag I'd packed the night before containing all our toiletries, towels, breakfast food, and drinks.

"Yeah. Hey, Gavin?"

"I'm here," I heard his sleepy voice in the dark and the three of us made our way quietly out the hatch and up onto the deck. Jumping over the two-foot space between the boat and the concrete pier, we landed quietly in our bare feet before pausing to slip naked toes into flip flops.

Without speaking, we walked down the quay to the shore and found the little Subaru waiting in the parking lot. Not wanting to alert the Coast Guard of our presence in the harbor, we drove out of the harbor with our lights off, only turning them on when we were out of view of their station.

Driving through Lihue in the predawn stillness, we all stayed silent, too sleepy to talk, on our way to Hanamaulu Beach Park and the old wharf. After parking, we laid our seats back in the car to sleep another few hours before the sun came up. *Well, this will be something to talk about sometime*, I thought.

It's strange thinking about this now. I didn't feel homeless, but we learned where the bathrooms were open all night and where there was good drinking water. We washed up in public wash houses, brushing our teeth and combing our hair in the metal mirrors of state park facilities.

It was a strange mix, this boating life, living outside the box, accepting the inconvenience as well as deeper unsettled feelings of not having a stable place to call home; both feelings we tolerated for the opportunity to live a different, less conventional life. *Besides, it was temporary, and we would be sailing away in less than a year*, I reminded myself.

Sitting at a picnic table later, I unpacked the breakfast bag, laying out a cloth before I put the food out. Today was a treat, I had bowls for granola and small vacuum boxes of milk.

"Where are the bananas, Mom?" Gavin asked. He'd helped me pick out the short stubby apple bananas at the market the day before.

"Bottom of the bag. Here you go," I said, passing him one.

After breakfast we'd drink tea from a thermos and read our books for a bit before showing up in the boatyard around eight a.m.: just normal islanders getting to work for another day in the harbor. I didn't know then, but we would continue to hide out in plain view for nine more months.

Lihue, Kauai
Spring 1992

"What'd you think, Deb?" Tosh had his arm around me as we walked back to our car after the movies. Gavin was up ahead.

"Yeah, I will be thinking about that one for a while, that's for sure." My head was spinning. We had just watched Spike Lee's production of *Malcolm X*. "Did I get that right? Did his spiritual master try to assassinate him?"

"That's what it looked like, and we thought we had it bad with a few lies and abandonment." Tosh laughed as he opened the car doors, and we piled inside for a ride back to the harbor and our boat. While boat break-ins and crime were rampant on the island, she was safely secured in a slip next to the Coast Guard station, a trade off we were grateful for despite the inconvenience of hiding the fact we illegally lived aboard.

Making our way through the pale lamp light in the harbor parking lot, my mind was in overdrive. So many things to think about. After months and months of not thinking about Bhagwan and the Ranch, thoughts of our time there were alive and swirling around in my head. All over again. *Who would have guessed that going to see a regular movie would trigger me into the past so much?*

Walking through the gate to make our way out over the water to the slips, the air was almost still, the clanging of the halyards on the metal masts of the boats a mere whisper tonight. It smelled fresh, and felt moist, like the warm air of the Hawaiian Islands always does. I was soaking it all up. In just a few more months, we would sail away, our time at an end here. I wouldn't be able to just walk ashore to a car parked nearby; the car would be sold.

How many days would it take to cross the Pacific? How would it feel? Would I be able to handle my fear? Would I flip out? Would my lessons from the Coast Guard have prepared me well enough for such a crossing? Would the weather be kind, or would it be extreme? Would we have enough water? Enough food? Enough fuel? The mental inquisition was always with me these days, relentless.

Finally reaching *Elixir*, we slipped our flip flops off on the dock before stepping aboard her pristine white decks with bare feet. They were slippery with condensation. Tomorrow I would apply the non-skid coating, the weather forecast was good, a prerequisite for painting.

"What did you think about the movie, Gavin?" I asked as we brushed our teeth. We'd turned on the twelve-volt lamps and the cabin was cozy, glowing gold from the linen shades.

"That guy was crazy," he answered with his mouth full of toothpaste.

"Which one?" I asked.

"The teacher guy. He was insecure. What a trip, and he was a grown up," Gavin continued, disdain evident in his teenage voice.

"You think so?" Tosh asked.

"Yeah, he didn't like that his student was getting more famous than he was. What kind of a teacher is that, anyway?" He shook his head as he made his way forward to the V-berth.

"No pulling the wool over on that one," Tosh muttered under his breath.

"I heard that, Tosh," Gavin called from his bunk. "I have really good hearing, too," he teased.

We all laughed. It was true. He did have good hearing, and it was also true that he had surprising insights on human behavior. My fourteen-year-old going on thirty-five.

"Good night, kiddo. Thanks for coming to the movies with us," Tosh said, genuinely happy to spend time with him these days. They were getting along better since last summer, the constant adventures and challenges of life aboard bonding them.

Tosh and I climbed into our berth, tired but relaxed after an evening out.

"Good night, sweetheart," I whispered in his ear, kissing his neck.

His arms enfolded me, holding me close. "'Night, Deb, love you," he whispered back.

The next day was clear and dry, the sky a deep tropical blue, the trade winds balmy. We'd awakened at four a.m. and made our way over to the park for washing up and breakfast, dropping Gavin off at the high school on our way back to the harbor. It was a routine now, a quasi-homeless morning habit, but one that I would be glad to be rid of when we sailed away.

Tosh was hauling another boat out today. He would do repairs and then repaint the bottom before relaunching it in a week or so. Having reached the end of our savings a year ago, we both made ends meet by working on other people's boats. I did bright work, refinishing internal and external wood, including masts. Tosh used the trailer he and Shakya had built to haul boats out of the water, repairing and repainting hulls.

Today I got to work on *Elixir*, our boat. Getting my supplies out of the lazarette, the storage locker behind the wheel, I started taping off the perfect shapes with rounded corners, where I would apply paint and then sprinkle the non-skid, glass beads evenly onto the wet surface. They were round, less than a millimeter, and smooth, but their addition to the deck provided an excellent grip. No more slipping, at least that was the hope.

As I worked in the early morning sun, measuring and taping the decks, I kept thinking about Malcolm X. Maybe the role of a Master is to set their disciples free, to push them out of the nest, to abandon them so they can find their own independent destiny in the world as well as their own unique connection to the Divine.

Suddenly my body was filled with tremendous gratitude, for Bhagwan, for my Master, for His actions, which had forced me to find my way. His lies compelled me to question and ponder why He had done such a thing. He had driven me to question my life. He had forced me to question the rightness, and accuracy of my decisions. I had doubted and felt misguided and led astray, a victim, a failure.

And now, brilliantly, I could feel the perfection in all of it. All of the thousands of hours I had spent sanding, painting, sewing, and polishing, my mind had been thinking about the Ranch and my spiritual journey. Trying to make some sense of it. Trying to integrate and digest the experiences into something positive and useful, not just a misguided quest, not just a waste of a life and resources. The last years of inner torment and anguish were suddenly transformed into a bright light, a light of knowing it was all as it should be. I was doing what felt right. I also knew beyond any doubt that I could never have found this rightness without my journey with Bhagwan and the commune.

Chapter 30

Shakedown & Lost

"I won't allow fear to stop me from learning to sail."

"Mom, look, the dolphins are here," Gavin called to me from the bow of *Elixir*.

It was very dark as I made my way forward, keeping my balance by gripping the hand holds on the cabin top with one hand and the foremast shrouds with the other. My feet were bare, I wore shorts and a harness over a T-shirt, the tether's metal carbuncle sliding along the cabin top, loud over the muffled purr of the diesel engine.

A windless night, the sails were uncovered but still furled on their booms. Kneeling on the tidily coiled bow lines to protect my bare knees from the hard deck, I peered over the bulwark, my eyes following the snake of Gavin's tether as it disappeared over the bowsprit. I could make out his shadow in the dolphin net below and watched him reaching through the netting into the frothing curve of the bow wave.

Gradually the shapes of spinner dolphins became apparent, the pod frolicking right below us, leaving a phosphorescent vortex of shimmering rainbow brilliance in their wake, a stunning light show in the darkness. Breathing in the sight, my shoulders relaxed a little. This two-week shakedown* cruise, just a month prior to our planned ocean crossing, would bode well. The dolphins were here, playing.

An hour earlier, at 2130 hours, we had thrown off the dock lines from our berth in Nawiliwili and slipped gently out of the harbor into the full face of the Pacific Ocean. We decided to leave at night when sea and wind conditions were calmer in the notoriously difficult-to-sail channels between the islands. Looking up from the phosphorescent-bathed dolphins, my eyes were unable to make out anything at all, it was so black. *How would we be able to see other boats or even the islands as we approached them?*

Feeling the butterflies in my stomach start to fly around, I quickly pushed the thoughts aside, replacing them with new ones. *We're finally on our way. You're at sea, at night, and you will sleep aboard while underway. This is the dream, the whole reason for the last four years.* It was starting to sink in.

Momentarily closing my eyes, I let the soft wind caress my face, and felt my hair blowing back gently, and with it, the endless lists of planning and preparation were swept away into the night. I felt the sparkles of chi slowly make their way up my legs, through my torso, almost dispelling the knots of anxiety that had permanently lodged in my belly over these last months. A dolphin let a breath out of his blowhole, a fine spray gently catching Gavin and I in our faces as we continued to watch the glistening light show at the bow.

Shakya and his wife Anuprada, a nurse, were aboard as crew along with Tosh, Gavin, and me. Were we prepared enough? Had we remembered everything? As I looked into the darkness ahead, I prayed we had. As Tosh liked to remind me: we'd done our best preparation, and we'd have to trust we'd be able to ad lib the rest. He had a natural self-confidence about going into the unknown, a gift I envied.

The rigging was complete, the sail and hatch covers sewn and in place. Provisioning for two years was labeled and safely stowed aboard. I had completed heavy weather sailing certification from the Coast Guard, along with coastal and celestial navigation courses. The satellite navigation equipment and antennas were installed and functioning. My ham radio license, with Morse code, was proudly posted beside the new VHS radio. Now it was time to put all this information and newly acquired skill into practice. What could this boat do? How would her neophyte crew respond to her needs underway?

Several hours later it was nearly midnight. "Hey, we've got some wind. Let's raise some sails," Shakya, who sat in the cockpit with Tosh, suggested. They were finishing up giant insulated sippy cups of hot chocolate that I'd passed out the hatch earlier.

"Good idea, let's see what an old boat can do tonight on this first leg, and maybe get to Oahu before next week." At a slow four knots, Tosh joked about our sluggish progress over the last hours.

Standing at the starboard foremast shrouds, I found the peak halyard in the shadows, the line that was attached to the tip of the gaff, the wooden spar across the top of the mainsail. Shakya was on the throat of that same twenty-foot gaff. It was so heavy, it lifted me off the deck before I could raise it. Another reason to be grateful to have Shakya and his superior weight and strength aboard.

"Go ahead," Tosh yelled from the cockpit when he saw we were in position with the lines free flowing at our feet, released from the belaying pins that kept them unsnarled and orderly. He had turned *Elixir* into the wind and kept us underway with the engine as we began raising the sails.

And the sailors' dance began, a dance that had been going on since man started sailing the seas thousands of years ago. Shakya and I on deck, on the halyards raising the sails, and Gavin and Anuprada in the cockpit controlling the sheets, the lines attached to the sail bottoms. All of us were harnessed with tethers to the boat for safety. The synchronized raising of the sails, the team all working together in unison, to harness the wind and propel this beautiful boat forward through the water into the unknown and into the next chapter of our lives.

"Looking good," Tosh yelled when the fore and mainsails were up. They were luffing and flapping gently in the light air, not yet filled as Tosh kept the boat into the wind. "Let's get the two jibs up."

Shakya and I quickly made our way further forward, grabbing the correct lines out of the inky mess and getting them raised to the top while Gavin and Anuprada controlled them from aft. Tying our halyards off on the belaying pins to secure the sails, we made our way back to the safety of the cockpit in a hurry, knowing as soon as the sails filled, the boat would heel over on her side, slicing through the seas. The Pacific swells would splash and wash over the bulwarks; the booms, all three of them, would swing powerfully to one side, knocking anything in their path overboard.

Turning the big wooden wheel so *Elixir*'s bow headed off the wind, Tosh adjusted his body, his feet against the downwind seat, as thirty-four thousand pounds tipped thirty-five degrees to one side. The booms swung over, sails instantly bulging out and filling with wind. Anuprada and Gavin trimmed the sheets, tightening the foot of each sail just enough to hold the air without luffing. The hull shuddered, shouldering the impact of air on the thousand-square-feet of sail as it hit the rig. Tosh turned off the engine. Suddenly, it was silent except for the swoosh of the water slicing along the hull and the hum of the air moving along the Dacron of the sails. A magnificent feeling, a heavy full keeled wooden boat under a powerful schooner rig.

My heart soared with pride in this beautiful vessel, her huge rig now filled and pulling us forward through the dark sea. I couldn't quite comprehend the occasion with my mind and even with my eyes, in the dark, the rig was shadowy and high, towering above me. She was something so new and foreign from even my wildest imaginings during my long hours of intro-spection while I sanded and varnished all her bits and pieces. As the whole picture was now fully assembled, working and underway, I was breathless.

"Are you and Anuprada okay for the first watch?" Tosh asked after settling into our new course heading.

"Sure thing." Shakya sounded enthusiastic as he crawled over to take the wheel, bracing his heavy frame around the lazarette and seat backs.

"Can I make you two some more cocoa?" I asked from the stability of the companionway hatch, enjoying the view of Shakya's face slightly illuminated by the red glow of the compass, encased in its pedestal in front of the wheel.

"Sounds good," Anuprada answered from the uphill settee, her hair silhouetted, blowing softly around her face, her feet solid against the compass stand.

They passed me their mugs and I disappeared below, strap-ping myself into the galley to do simple tasks made challenging with one hand and everything on an angle. Filling the kettle with water by pumping with one foot and trying not to fall over, putting the mugs in the bottom of the sink to keep them from jumping over the counter fiddle* onto the floor, opening the cocoa can after two tries as I needed two hands and kept needing to grab the overhead hand hold to stay upright. *Yes, this was different from our day cruises, where I had things prepared beforehand in a thermos, with daylight and the boat was not heeled over as far. The shakedown has definitely begun.* I grinned to myself. *Playing house with a twist, or on a slant.*

With Shakya and Anuprada on the first three-hour watch, the rest of us prepared for our first sleep in our berths while underway.

"Wow, it sounds cool up here," Gavin was already in the v-berth, just two inches of wood between him and the swoosh of the sea. Tosh went forward to make sure his lee cloth was secure, holding him in his bed.

We undid ours and fastened them overhead, crawling awkwardly into bed from one end.

"We did it, Tosh. We are underway; we cast off from Kauai. Congratulations, Skipper." I reached around the lee cloth to give him a kiss on the cheek, another challenge with all the motion, and was nearly thrown out of the bunk.

"We sure did. Congrats to you, First Mate, for hanging in there." Tosh chuckled from his side of the cloth. "See you topsides in three hours."

I lay awake, the newness of all the motion keeping my senses engaged. A steady stream of faces marched behind my closed eyelids, recent memories of friends who had come to wish us well and buy our precious boat-building equipment. The workshop and tools were gone now except the few pieces needed to maintain *Elixir*. At the very end, we'd sold the vehicles, our last ties to the land traded for a life at sea.

The weather window for the northern crossing, June and July, was here and it was basically 'shit or get off the pot,' as the saying goes. After taking almost five years instead of the original six months, I was truly glad to be done with this project, amazed and relieved that we had pulled it off despite the challenges. But I also knew there was more in store for us on this nautical adventure.

I needed to stay present and focused on the myriad of details for this next leg with *Elixir*, the seaborne part, the sailing part, the life aboard part, all new, all demanding the full attention of my mind and emotions. There had been no time for nostalgia, for regrets about leaving Kauai, and there was no time now, either. I swallowed the lump in my throat. *You really do need to sleep, Deb. It's going to be time for your dawn watch before you can blink.*

Saturday, May 30, 1992 (Day 2)

"How are you feeling, Gavin?" I asked.

After uneventful night watches, Gavin and I watched the sun come up with an almost imperceptible north wind. But, as the morning grew brighter, I felt odd, lethargic yet hungry.

"Okay, why? Are you feeling sick, too?" It had been a constant question for all of us. Would we get seasick? Or would we be lucky, with a stomach of steel?

"Well, I think I'm okay, maybe I'm just tired from no sleep." *Was this what getting your "sea-legs" felt like? Was this my style of sea sickness?*

"I'm just kinda tired, too," Shakya volunteered. "How 'bout you, Anaprada?"

"Actually, I'm good," she responded, sounding relieved, "I didn't know if I would get seasick or not, but so far, so good."

Motor-sailing along Oahu's coast in the late afternoon,

Shakya and his guitar occupied the cockpit, entertaining us with funny songs. Anuprada, too, laughed and encouraged him to sing another one.

"I'm going to prepare dinner," I announced. The earlier lethargy had lifted. "I'm leaving the hatch open so I can hear your songs." Laughing, I climbed below and strapped myself into the galley.

Spaghetti would be good tonight, I thought as I pulled the big pot out of its nest behind the counter. I wedged it in the sink as I used the foot pump to fill it halfway with water before placing it on the gimbaled propane stove, screwing the clamps tightly around it to keep it from jumping off. Lifting the bench under my berth, I propped it open while l found the pasta, a jar of sauce, and the tetra-pack of firm tofu for protein. The container of shake cheese was already in the basket of condiments behind the counter. I had a sourdough baguette in the food hammock to heat up in the oven, already wrapped in tinfoil. Once everything was warmed up, I dished up the plates, adding a handful of sprouts from my jar (instant salad), before handing them up to the cockpit.

"Anything else needed up here?" I asked, emerging from below and finding a seat in the cockpit.

"This is wonderful, Deb." Anuprada was impressed. "I can't believe you got all that done so fast and for so many of us, thank you."

"You're welcome. I'm happy to have everyone aboard for our maiden voyage. History in the making," I responded as I passed around napkins and extra shake cheese. It was a wonderful meal, together, with friends, a classic sunset dinner cruise off Waikiki. The boat was on an even keel, the winds exceptionally light and the motor purred.

"Anyone need more to drink? Remember to keep your cup full," I reminded them, "don't get dehydrated." Everyone had their own twelve-ounce lidded sippy cups, their name printed in large black letters with a Sharpie. The days of cases of individual plastic water bottles were not quite upon us.

"Yes, Mommy," Shakya teased me, laughing. "Thank you for taking good care of us."

The even keel was short lived. After dinner the sky gradually darkened, the wind started to come up and the motor was no longer necessary. By 2100 hours the wind came up for real, thirty knots, (thirty-five miles per hour) and Oscar, the autopilot, broke.

Sunday, May 31, 1992 (Day 3)

"What's going on?" I yelled out the hatch very early on Sunday morning. We were heeled over about thirty degrees and the wind speed indicator in the companionway by my shoulder was registering fifty knots, as fast as a car on the freeway. After being awakened by noise and the violent motion of the boat I'd stuck my head out the opening. The roaring wind instantly slapped my face, whipping my question away into the night. In the darkness I could make out faces, glowing red from the compass, tense with anxiety. And then I noticed our bow was almost into the wind.

While I was below trying to sleep, the boys had shortened sail by taking the main and jib sails down, leaving the fore and stay sails up. The course was set at 120 degrees on the compass with the bow into the wind. This was a difficult heading to keep with the head sails up and nothing to steady the ship aft, as difficult as controlling a seventeen-ton, fifty-foot trailer on the freeway with gusting fifty mile an hour crosswinds.

Tosh was hanging over the rail, retching as there was

nothing left in his stomach. My eyes found the outline of his harness, assuring myself his tether was securely attached to the boat. Anuprada appeared to be crying, Shakya trying to hold and comfort her through the stiff foul weather jackets. At the same time, he leaned his whole body into the wheel, struggling to hold course.

Realizing the sounds of the wind and the sea made conversation impossible, I quickly closed the hatch above me and made my way forward, to check on Gavin. He was blissfully unaware of the change in the weather, curled peacefully asleep in his bunk. Dressing as efficiently as possible in the dark and bracing myself from the rough motion, I noticed the time was 0035 hours. The awareness that my watch didn't officially start until 0100 barely registered as my mind began a process I would come to recognize and appreciate.

Slow motion took over. Not that I was moving in slow motion, but it felt like I was. Time somehow stretched out. There was suddenly plenty of it, enough to smooth my socks up my calves, and to properly fasten the Velcro cuffs of my heavy weather overalls around my ankles before stepping into my boots. Donning my jacket, there was a calm and quiet that filled my head despite the all-encompassing noise of the sea and wind. The powerful gusts were cold, whipping ocean spray off wave tops as if it was deluging salty rain. No one would have expected to need to use heavy weather pants and jackets in the summer in the Hawaiian Islands, yet here we were. Zipping up inner and outer zippers, I Velcroed the neck around the hood, and carefully sealed the wrists.

Opening the hatch, I hastily snapped my harness to the line before climbing out into the rage of wind, its ferocity determined to prevent me from making my way across the four feet to the wheel. Shakya and Anuprada quickly retreated down the hatch, fastening it securely behind them.

The screaming of the tempest in the rigging was deafening. Wedging myself behind the wheel as best I could, I held onto the spokes of the wheel, the wind and spray quickly whipping away any warmth left in my fingers. Scrunching my hands up inside my sleeves, I had a better grip on the wheel through the fabric of the jacket. The red glow of the compass allowed me to clearly see the heading. However, the wind would dictate our course tonight.

"Tosh," I yelled, trying to get his attention. He didn't seem to hear me or even notice I was calling his name. Panic threatened to take over. The wave *Elixir* was riding was a wall of water by my head. It was as close as extending my arm and getting wet, immersed in ocean water. *How is it that this wave doesn't crash on top of us, smashing the rig and sending us to the bottom of the sea?* I was sure we were moving backward, with no forward motion at all.

"Tosh," I yelled again, "we're moving backward. Tosh, what do I do?" Still no response from him. I started to rant to myself, anything to keep my brain from losing it, anything to keep my ability to tolerate the feeling of being at the mercy of the wind and the sea, the feeling that it would go on forever, no end in sight. "Is this the night we die? Is this how it is at sea? How does anyone survive this? How does anyone find their way in this pitch black? This is fucking crazy." I screamed into the wind, not caring what I said or who heard me because no one could.

My heart pounded. My stomach was about to force its way into my mouth and follow the words out into the chaos. My mind didn't seem to work. I was the navigator, and I had no idea where we were or where we were headed. Imagine driving in the pitch black without headlights, or walking blindfolded in a strange house. I was praying we didn't run into anything, a submerged container fallen off its ship, floating invisibly just beneath the surface, dense enough to bash in the side of *Elixir*.

Praying we didn't run into another ship, or even an island, there was nothing I could do but keep the helm into the wind as best I could until something changed, or my watch was over. If I let the bow fall off the wind, we would be capsized by the next wave as it hit us sideways. Except for an hour that Gavin came above decks and relieved me, I was on the helm for nearly four hours.

Things looked better as dawn brightened, the seas were calmer, and the wind had died down to ten knots. I could see now, where an hour before I couldn't even make out the bow of *Elixir* forty feet ahead of me.

As it started to get light, I coaxed Tosh up off the settee and onto the helm as I needed to go below and check the charts and see if there was a fix on the sat nav. The GPS system we have today was in its infancy, the Loran receiver only picked up satellite signals every few hours, and I prayed there would be one to give me a position I could work with. There wasn't.

Below, I attempted, unsuccessfully, to figure out where we were on the chart, and then got Shakya and Anuprada up to help raise the main and double reef it. This gave a more balanced helm as we continued to use the motor to keep us headed into the wind. Shakya fixed Oscar, the autopilot, also giving relief to whoever was on the wheel. After feeding everyone a breakfast of porridge and cleaning up the galley, I slept through the morning, knowing that at least whoever was on the wheel could see if land approached.

"How'd you sleep, Deb?" Shakya asked as I emerged from the hatch later that afternoon. The air was warm, tropical, the winds light, *Elixir* hardly heeled over.

"Good, but not long enough." I laughed, trying to keep it light. "What island is that?" I asked, noticing with relief the green of land to starboard.

"Not sure, after the storm last night, we weren't able to

keep to the course, we had to keep *Elixir* upright, so ... Yeah, well, we don't know where we are." Shakya admitted.

Why do I have these awful butterflies in my stomach? How did I ever think I could do this? Breathe, Deb, breathe.

"Okay, did you guys record the compass heading and hull speed every hour or so today?" I asked, keeping my voice matter of fact, despite my growing lack of confidence in my ability to figure this out.

"Sure thing, it's all in the log," Tosh mumbled from where he was still laying on the downhill settee.

"Hey, how are you feeling?" I asked, scooching him over a bit to settle on the bench beside him.

"I'm okay, haven't tossed my cookies for a couple of hours. It's been much calmer today," he answered, trying to be nonchalant, to minimize my concern as he took hold of my hand. Kissing him lightly on the cheek, I pulled myself upright and disappeared below, climbed into the nav station, and started making notes in my log. The compass headings and hull speed were recorded every few hours. Using the chart, the compass dividers and the parallel ruler as I had learned in my Coast Guard classes, I came up with a probable location.

"I think this is Molokai," I announced about twenty minutes later.

It was very pretty to be sailing off the shore but then, without warning, the winds picked up to thirty knots from the east down the channel. The seas were only five feet but close together.

"Yikes, we just get to relax a bit and then the wind and seas are hitting us again." Shakya lamented. "Are you guys sure you want to try to make it to Maui tonight? Isn't there a harbor near here we could go hide in for a bit? Take a time out?"

Wait a minute, don't we have to go to Maui? Isn't that the plan? Don't we just power on through, even though the condi-

tions are nasty? If this was the crossing, we couldn't just take a rest. Wow, slow down. What's going on here? Shakya may have a point. What's our hurry anyways? This is free time, right? And if it makes things easier, well, isn't it worth it? But will we ever even get to Maui? Will the conditions ever be better? Stop it, just relax a bit. Taking a few deep breaths, I responded.

"Molokai's Kaunakakai Harbor may be an option, it's close, I think, around that headland over there." After checking the chart below, I pointed out a landmark to steer toward.

In order to keep the wind in the sails, we were not able to steer straight to shore but made a zig-zagged course, reminiscent of mountain climbing days. On very steep inclines, the mountain top is such a short distance above, but so steep your feet cannot get a grip to walk straight up. Following a trail of switchbacks, walking miles in order to maintain a grade that you don't slip back down the mountain, you eventually make it to the top.

The ride was wet because of the narrow troughs, so wet and cold I needed my foulie (rain gear) jacket again even though it was not yet dark out. Oscar, once again, stopped working.

Finally making it into the very peaceful, small harbor at about 1800 hours, we anchored up. It was so quiet we could hear the birds singing, a contrast to the raging seas that had just thrown us about. While Tosh was over his acute sea sickness, all of us were traumatized from the extremes of sailing in the channels of the Hawaiian Islands, not to mention that we were actually lost for a good part of the day and previous night. This sailing business was a lot scarier than we had ever thought it could be.

And for one of us, it was impossible, actually paralyzing.

Chapter 31

Abandoned, Broken Gaff & End of Shakedown

"The sea never sleeps or stays the same. I must learn to sail under all conditions, even in impossible winds."

Hawaiian Islands
Monday, June 1, 1992 (Day 4)

"I'm flying home," Anuprada burst out. We were settled at anchor in a quiet bay on Molokai after a day and night of very rough sailing. Sitting in the cockpit together, the five of us were finishing up our dinner and turned to look at her. She had been quiet during dinner, not surprising after the last forty-eight hours.

"What?" I asked as I started collecting the dinner bowls. *Surely I had misunderstood. We were on a boat. How do you just decide to go home?*

"You heard me, Deb. I'm done with this. I can't take it. It's crazy." Her voice rose in pitch.

Putting the dishes back down beside me, I looked at her. She avoided my eyes.

"It was pretty scary out there, I admit," I began reasonably. *Hell, it was terrifying, but that doesn't mean we quit,* I thought to myself.

"You guys are crazy. You have no idea what you are doing," she interrupted as if I hadn't spoken.

What's going on with her? I wondered. *She is usually so calm and reasonable.*

"Hey, sweetie," Shakya, sliding over on the settee that was now blissfully level, put his arm protectively around her shoulders. "It's all good here. We're all safe, just a little wind is all."

"It's not safe. Everything is breaking and falling apart." She shrugged free of his arm, her face flushing.

"Well, not everything, Anuprada, just a few things, and they're all things that we can fix ..." He spoke calmly, reassuringly.

"This whole boat's gonna sink. I know it," she interrupted, pushing him away, ignoring his words. "I don't wanna die right now."

"Hey, Anuprada, we knew there would be some glitches, it is the shakedown cruise, for heaven's sake," I was suddenly impatient, my own voice rising. "For crying out loud, yeah, shit happened but it doesn't help get us through things if you get all blamey and jump ship. Let's talk about this."

"Whoa, Deb," Tosh interrupted. "Calm down, it's all good here."

"No, it isn't all good." *Oh no, stop it, shut your mouth.* Too late, I heard my voice continue. "We were all scared over these last days but no one else is having a meltdown. Do you think I liked watching Tosh puke his guts out?" *Shut it, Deb, just shut up.* "Do you think I felt like trying to find out where we were on the charts? Do you think I wanted to just get off and forget

the whole thing? Yeah, that's for sure. But it's not an option."
Oh my God, get a hold of yourself, it won't help if you are both hysterical.

"You guys are completely insane, all of you." She jerked her fingers toward each of us.

I took a deep breath and shut my mouth. As much as I wanted to let it rip and let it out, now was not the time. I had Tosh's warning look and his hand firmly squeezing my knee to prove it. His nickname for me was Volcano Lady, because I could just explode sometimes. But this situation was asking me to do it another way. I had to be under control. I looked over at her again. Refocused. She was not herself at all. It was like she couldn't hear what any of us were saying, and she just had a tape loop coming out of her mouth. *What's going on here? Surely the emergency room at the hospital must have had more intense situations than this?*

"I don't want any part of this, not even for another minute." She continued to gesture wildly; her eyes unfocused. *Was this hysteria? She must have treated people in shock, people who were panicking after car accidents, fires, gunshots?* I'd been too preoccupied with getting us safely into the harbor. Sure that feeding us all would calm everyone down, I had jumped right into preparing dinner. Any warning signs had gone unnoticed, overlooked.

"Hey now, Anuprada, calm down." Shakya tried again to reach her, to comfort and console her.

"I'm leaving right now, and don't try to stop me." She stood and unsteadily made her way to the companionway, disappearing down the ladder into the darkness of the cabin.

The rest of us looked at each other, not knowing what to say now that all of us confronted our own fears. The silence was odd after the constant noise of either wind or engine or both over the last three days and two nights.

"Sorry I lost it," I said into the space. "It's just been so intense. In a way, I feel the same way she does. Honestly, it's been fucking terrifying. And just for the record, I really had no idea where we were today." I paused for a bit before adding, "But I live here, so I can't run away." I laughed at myself.

"I get it," Tosh admitted. "Hell, I didn't know if I would pass out from vomiting last night, it was so violent. And I'm supposed to be the skipper."

"She was pretty terrified last night," Shakya admitted.

"How are you doing?" Tosh asked.

"I'm actually okay. Don't forget, I was in the navy, so I've been through a few gales in my time," he joked.

"I don't know why you guys are freaking out," Gavin joined in. "I thought it was a great ride today." He had his best contrary face on and shared a knowing laugh with Shakya, the laugh that allowed him to be separate and independent from his parents. Which was fine with me. He got along great with Shakya, who was like a favorite uncle.

"Yeah, well then you can take over as first mate for me, smart ass." Shakya roughed up Gavin's hair and shifted his gaze back to Tosh and me. "I better go below and try to get her to calm down and sleep aboard tonight."

"Yeah, you better get down there," Tosh agreed.

"And I hate to do this to you guys, but if she still wants to leave in the morning, I'll probably fly home with her. She's really not herself at all. I'm worried about her. She so wanted to be on this trip and was looking forward to it for the last year."

"I get it," Tosh reassured his friend, "get down there and take care of your wife. Maybe she'll be alright in the morning."

He quickly followed her below where, by the sounds of it, she was angrily stuffing things into her duffel bag. Their voices wafted up and out the hatch, the discord landing unbidden on our reluctant ears. His voice sounded calm and reassuring, hers more and more shrill and irrational.

Surrounded by the uncollected dinner dishes, Tosh, Gavin, and I sat in the cockpit, the sunset casting a reddish glow across the sky.

"Was that shock and hysteria?" I asked Tosh.

"Probably, although I'm surprised. She's always been so level-headed."

"Yeah, and she's been so supportive and enthusiastic about this shakedown cruise, especially over the last few months. I should be worried about her and hope she's okay, but man, all I can think about is how fucked we are if they leave," I responded.

"Mom, she's too uptight. This boat's not a good fit for her," Gavin said from across the cockpit.

"It's safer for all of us for her to leave if she's this upset," Tosh stated.

"I know the three of us can sail this boat, but you were so sick and incapacitated. I really don't want to continue without another strong man aboard." The thought of it brought back all the fear of the last few days, the distress evident in my voice.

"Don't worry, Deb. Maybe she'll be all right in the morning, and if she isn't the guys on Kauai said they'd fly over to help us out if we needed them. In the meantime, we're quite secure here in this bay for as long as we want. We may have an actual holiday for a few days, what do you think? Good idea after these last seventy-two hours?"

"Yeah, and maybe I'll see a sea turtle here." Gavin sounded excited about the possibility of swimming with the turtles, a long-time passion of his.

"Sea turtles? A holiday? How can you guys talk like this? We've been working on this boat for four long years, and we can't even sail it. I mean, Tosh, get real. You get really, really sick. How are we going to sail north? Honestly? Maybe we should rethink this? You know, sell the boat? Pack it in?" Tosh moved closer to me, his arm encircling my rigid shoulders. "No, it doesn't help. I'm really scared. I got lost for a day, and I don't know how to do this." I tried to push him away, tears spilling down my face. *Damn, why do I always cry when I get upset?*

"Deb, listen to me. We had a rough few days, it's true. But maybe Anuprada will feel better in the morning."

I listened to his soothing voice, letting it wash over me. His words felt better than my panic-filled negative ones. And voicing my doubts aloud had relieved some of the noise in my head. I couldn't hold it inside anymore, and hesitantly let myself cry on his shoulder. I let him hold me and reassure me. *There was way too much at stake to cave in now. I could do this, we could all do this. This is what following a dream is like. Super highs and super lows, no in between.* Slowly the fear and anger subsided, the emotions ebbing away as they leaked out my eyes and onto his shirt.

Gavin came over and snuggled up too. We were quiet as we heard the tumult gradually lessen in the cabin beneath us. Giving them a little more space alone, we watched the sky grow dark and the stars come out before finally going below for the night. Exhaustion and the rocking of the boat put us all to sleep, despite the looming possibility of losing our crew.

Tuesday, June 2 (Day 5)

Shakya had managed to dissuade her from going ashore that night but she was so shaken there was no way she would continue the cruise with us. They took a taxi to the airport early the next morning, just three days into the two-week inter-island cruise. Anuprada wouldn't look at us or say goodbye. She was like a wooden puppet, moving mechanically, without facial expression, the emotion from last night spent, leaving an empty shell of our friend. Shakya gave us each a bear hug and apologized again for bailing out on us.

"Hey, no worries, mate. It'll all work out. You just take care of her, and we'll see you back on Kauai," Tosh had reassured his friend.

"I can't believe they left," I said when Tosh returned from rowing them ashore. "They really did leave. What are we going to do now?" I could feel myself starting to panic again.

Tosh hugged me, acknowledging somehow without words the change in our situation, and the fact that I was struggling to stay calm.

Each of us, in our own way, spent the morning coming to terms with the extremes of wind and sea, as well as witnessing the breakdown of a friend and crew member. *Could that happen to me? To Tosh? To Gavin? How were we going to get back to Kauai, let alone cross the Pacific Ocean?*

My mind wouldn't stop. I tried reading like Tosh and Gavin, but the words on the pages didn't register. *How are we going to do an ocean crossing? How are we going to get back to Kauai? Should we sell the boat right now? Just stay in the islands and live aboard, illegally for another year? Or two? No, my mind screamed. No. This is all going to work out, you'll see. It had to.*

Giving up on my book, I looked around at the vivid green of the shore, the vibrant blue of the sky. The songs of shore birds filled my ears and the joy they expressed, as they chased each other in complete freedom high above the masts, resonated in my heart. The bay was calm, the small wavelets from the gentle trade winds made tiny slapping noises on the hull. By and by, I dove off the deck into the clear, warm water, welcoming the sight of the sandy bottom thirty feet below me. Coming up for air, Gavin landed beside me with a huge splash, his perfect cannonball even more effective off the bowsprit.

"Race you to the buoy, Mom," Gavin challenged.

Just like all those days after working in the boatyard, a swim washed away not just the sawdust but also the tension and worry about what we were attempting. Today the stakes were more immediate. Shakya and Anuprada were gone, and we were several days sail away from our home port, with broken boat parts waiting to be repaired. But slowly, as the water embraced me, I started to relax into our new circumstances: we were okay to stay at anchor here, more crew would arrive and we would carry on with our shakedown, somehow.

"So, how are we going to get back to Kauai?" I asked Tosh later, voicing out loud the question on all of our minds. "I mean, it's great to be playing in the water and hanging out aboard instead of working, but I can't really relax, can you?"

"Sort of, I'm fairly sure I can get Iraja and Richard to come meet us. At least they both said they would," Tosh reminded me before going below. Both experienced seamen, Iraja had crewed on several ocean crossings and Richard was a licensed delivery ship captain.

"I'm going ashore," Tosh announced a few minutes later. "Where are the laundry quarters?"

"In the basket above the nav table," I answered, looking up from my book, I could focus on the story now. "Making some phone calls?" I smiled. Tosh was exceptional at getting things handled. *Thank goodness, because I wouldn't know where to start finding new crew members right now.* The three of us could sail this boat, I knew that, but I sure didn't want to, not with Tosh's propensity to seasickness.

Friday, June 5 (Day 8)

"So glad you could make it," I said as I welcomed Iraja aboard a few days later. He was Tosh's height and coloring, his hair still black. His skin tanned dark from being at sea, his brown eyes covered with reflective glacier glasses complete with side shields, a cap pulled low over his brow, he looked like a sailor.

"I'm stoked to be able to sail this rig for a bit," he said as he casually dropped his small duffel bag down the companionway hatch.

"How was your flight?" I asked

"Oh fine, the usual." He plunked himself down in the cockpit, resting his feet up on the bench. "I haven't done any serious sailing on a schooner except in the harbor with you guys. Now we really get to see what this old girl is made of."

"Well, the channels are not the same as the harbor, that's for sure," I commented.

"These Hawaiian Island channels are wicked, as you found out. You guys sail here, you can sail anywhere. For real." Lifting his cap and smoothing his hair back before replacing it, he continued, "Ahh, this is the life. Hey, I'm sorry it didn't work out with Shakya and Anuprada."

"Yeah, that was a surprise. I didn't see that one coming from an emergency room nurse," Tosh responded as he finished tying up the dinghy alongside.

"It happens quite a bit in the crewing world, and generally with people you may not expect it from."

"Really? People sign up to crew across the ocean and have a nervous breakdown while they are out there?" I was incredulous.

"Oh yeah, it's the hardest thing to judge when choosing a crew. You just never know when it will happen and to whom. You guys were lucky it was just a small leg and those guys could get off the boat."

"I couldn't imagine having that happen on a crossing. I guess I just never thought about it," Tosh admitted.

"Count yourselves fortunate." As he spoke, he got up and made his way easily around the deck. He was so at home aboard, he didn't even need to hold on to anything. I watched as his gaze traveled up the mast, following the lines, his mind figuring out which ones went where. My shoulders relaxed and the tension in my belly dissipated, just a little. His familiarity with the boat and the sea were obvious, a contrast to our book learning and lack of experience.

The presence of an able seaman aboard did wonders for my peace of mind. Now I really could enjoy diving off the bow into the pristine sea. Boat work resumed; lifelines were assembled, and the stay sail was re-rigged without the clubfoot as it had broken during the wild ride in the channel on Sunday five days before.

On *Saturday (Day 9)*, we had an easy sail to Maui and anchored near Mala Wharf just north of Lahaina. The small anchorage was crowded, and the hook was not as secure as we would have liked, but miraculously, all was well through the night. We awoke on *Sunday (Day 10)*, to sea turtles feeding off to one side and just below the bow. The water was so clear, we could see the loops of anchor chain lying on the bottom, thirty feet below.

"It's way hotter here than on Kauai," Gavin moaned to me later as we walked to Lahaina through the touristy streets. "Mom, look! It's the Coasties off Kauai's cutter, the Point Harris."

"Hey, Gavin, how's the shakedown going?" one of the crew of the Coast Guard vessel asked, excited to see us.

"Well, aside from getting lost on the way over here, and our crew freaking out and flying home, it's all good," Gavin answered, enjoying the shocked looks on their faces.

"It wasn't your teaching, I promise." I laughed, trying to cover up how embarrassed I was about my inability to find my way around the islands. "Real life navigation is way trickier than I realized."

"It's all good experience," he assured me. "And the coast of North America is pretty hard to miss," he added with a wink. *Was he reading my mind?*

"See you back in Nawiliwili," Tosh promised.

————

Monday, June 8 (Day 11)

"What's going on?" I yelled over the wind, even though no one could hear me. It was sunny, with strong winds, twenty-five knots (thirty miles per hour). We'd weighed anchor and were sailing for Lanai. Tosh was frantically motioning me to come and take the wheel. He pointed aloft.

The foresail was flapping around, the gaff thrashing into the sail and mast twenty feet above the deck. It took me a few seconds to realize the gaff had snapped about two feet from the jaw,* where it rested against the mast. I could make out the jagged ends of wood where they had broken, like a giant matchstick, a matchstick twelve feet long and six inches in diameter.

"Take the wheel, keep her into the wind. We'll try to get the sail down," Tosh yelled in my ear as I reached the cockpit. Even though the fore boom was cinched tight, without a gaff holding the top of the sail the wind whipped it erratically, creating terrible smacking noises as the wooden spar splintered into the mast. *What else was going to break? Would the whole rig come down?*

As the sail slowly dropped, I held my breath and prayed the heavy spar wouldn't hit Tosh or Iraja. They were struggling to get it under control and keep their footing while *Elixir* bounced around in massive waves. It reminded me of trying to stand on a beach ball in a crowded swimming pool.

Meanwhile, I braced my weight against the wheel, straining to keep the bow into the wind, the spokes pressing into my hip through the life jacket. The intensity of the situation left no room to doubt my abilities. *Just focus and steer this boat.* Swallowing hard, I quickly wiped my sweaty palms on my shorts one at a time, hunched over, and tightened my grip on the wheel.

"I think that's got her," Iraja yelled after an interminable hour as he fell into the cockpit beside me, the foresail down and secure. "This is crazy. Let's run to Molokai again, and skip Lanai," he shouted over the roaring wind and crashing seas.

"No arguing with that," Tosh agreed.

Despite the change in course, the winds and seas grew worse.

"Deb, keep her nose in the wind. We'll try to get these sails reefed,*" Tosh screamed and gestured to me in the cockpit.

Finally reefed, *Elixir* heeled so far over I was standing on the seat back and still using all my body weight to hold the wheel on course. Way too much sail.

"Take 'em down," Iraja hollered.

And with just the stay sail, the smallest one, we were still doing six knots.

Exhausted but safe in Kaunakakai, we dropped the hook alongside *Escapade*, a boat we had met the week before. When they asked how the channel was, Tosh replied with an understated, "A little rough."

It was peaceful at anchor on Molokai, and a relief to have quiet and actually hear the birds again. Over the next few days, we repaired the fore gaff using the hand tools and epoxy onboard. Iraja flew home and Richard, the delivery boat captain, arrived to take his place. That night, auspiciously, the Southern Cross showed up in the night sky, a rare occurrence. In the northern latitudes, this constellation is close to the horizon and usually hidden by atmospheric haze.

Thursday, June 11 (Day 14)

"The weather radio has advisories in effect, eighteen-foot seas and thirty knot winds in the channel," I announced the next morning, concerned as we planned to head for Honolulu.

"I think we should go anyway," Richard, a seasoned sailor, said confidently.

It didn't take much convincing; the anchor came up and the boys were ready to go. Flying only half our sails, we averaged our hull speed and had an exceptional sail despite the earlier radio advisory. I felt more relaxed sailing, appreciating Richard, our experienced crew. My confidence in navigating got a boost, too, with accurate bearings utilizing the compass in the binoculars.

Honolulu, our final stop before returning to Kauai, was our last big city opportunity to stock up on supplies before the crossing. Grateful for the use of Richard's car, we filled a Costco cart and even found a blue vinyl bean bag chair. This addition to our cockpit allowed us to wedge ourselves in on long watches, no matter what the heel or how rough the seas.

After cruising for two weeks and spending the last two days in a concrete slip next to Waikiki, Guy, a friend from Kauai and another licensed captain, showed up to crew for the journey home. He, too, had been intimately involved with *Elixir*'s restoration and subsequent day sails out of Nawiliwili. For him it proved to be a rare opportunity and valuable experience to sail a schooner rig.

At midnight, *Saturday morning (Day 16)*, we left our peaceful mooring. Sailing down the leeward side of Oahu under the full moon, the crests of six-foot waves shone silver with reflected moonlight. Twenty knot winds kept the sails full, and the air filled with the watery swoosh of the hull moving through the swells. Bright moonlight, big ship traffic and hundreds of birds made the night as alive as day.

"Yahoo," Guy yelled as *Elixir* was suddenly slammed over with ferocious winds and seas, creating a wall of water beside us. "We're leaving the shelter of Oahu and are in for a ride," he whooped, excited as a cowboy who realizes his dream to ride that untamed bronco.

It was 0700 hours. And a wild ride it was. While we averaged about seven knots throughout the morning, the knot meter hit nine and a half several times as we careened down enormous wave fronts.

"Here she comes! Hang on tight!" Guy, on the helm, shouted as a huge wave crashed over the stern and filled the cockpit. We all held on as best we could but Tosh, incapacitated with seasickness, sloshed around, and struggled to hang onto his harness.

The winds and seas continued to build, faces of huge swells towering above us. *Damn, these waves are massive. How are we not swamped?* My mind quickly dissociated from the thoughts, focusing instead on my job to keep everyone fed and hydrated. Past time for lunch. I'd been waiting for smaller waves. That wasn't happening. *You need to go now.*

"Going below," I yelled, motioning to Gavin to slide the companionway closed after me. Quickly unbuckling my harness, I dropped through the hatch and it slid shut behind me but not before a shower of seawater poured down the ladder with me.

Blinking to clear my vision from sea water, my breath caught in my throat from the cold dowsing. And then I blinked and my breath caught again as I beheld the chaos before me: lockers were hanging open, wooden doors slamming back on their hinges with every breaker, their contents spilling onto the sole*. Everything was drenched. *Don't think about it. Get some food together and get back up on deck.* In spite of extensive research and effort to incorporate sea-worthy and watertight technologies, the ferocious turbulence of the inter-island passage had thwarted them all.

Grabbing the bum strap, I hastily fastened it around my hips, keeping a hand on the rail above the counter. One handed, I grabbed crackers, cheese, chips, juice boxes, nuts, and fruit, throwing it all in a bag. Climbing the ladder, I cracked the door and was rewarded with more cold seawater in the face. I promptly pulled it shut. Gavin slid the hatch back a moment later and pulled me up just before another wave filled the cockpit, the two four-inch drains back into the ocean unable to keep up. The bag of food landed on the cockpit floor, immediately brined, while I fumbled with wet cold fingers to latch my harness back onto the deck.

Afraid, the sea thunderous, there was no time or space to dwell on disaster scenarios or to allow myself to feel hysteria and panic. That would not help get us back to Kauai. I focused instead on gratitude for Guy and all his experience aboard with us. And sitting there in the cockpit, it truly was an adrenaline packed ride, one that would put an out-of-control roller coaster to shame. Guy's excitement and joy in guiding *Elixir* through the channel was almost infectious. Almost. It was a tremendous relief to arrive safely in Nawiliwili in the late afternoon and tie up, secure in our old slip.

This, the roughest of our inter-island passages, had slammed *Elixir* from every direction all day long. We suspected below decks was in havoc, but the total destruction that met us after we docked and went below was staggering.

The lockers had opened and dumped onto the sole, including those Corelle non-breakable dishes I had been so proud of. The dishes had smashed into tiny slivers and shards of glass spread throughout the cabin. I wanted to mutiny from exhaustion. After such a tough afternoon in heavy seas, and with Tosh sick, I had worried we wouldn't even make it home. I wanted a hot bath to get warm and get the salt off me, but no, there was yet more to do.

The settee cushions escaped their fiddles, detached from their Velcro and squirmed on the floor. Clothes lockers had exploded and mixed into broken glass in a wet, untidy mess. Unprecedented, before going below we had to don shoes and heavy gloves to prevent injury while we picked up everything.

Like so many of the last days, I had to do the next thing. There was no sense complaining or wishing it were different. That was a waste of valuable energy. I was learning the ways of the sea, and it was nothing like *Cruising World Magazine*.

Part Four

THE CROSSING

Chapter 32

Elixir's Last Bath & Leaving Kauai

"Being at sea offers a feeling of coming home, maybe because it's where all life comes from."

Nawiliwili Harbor, Kauai
June 19, 1992

"You are looking a little green there, Skipper." I couldn't help it. It was true. Hosing down the decks, I tried to keep my tone light, but I was dead serious, and seriously concerned.

It had been three days since our return from the dramatic shakedown cruise through the Hawaiian Islands, and Tosh still didn't feel like himself. He ignored me as he bobbed around in the dinghy alongside *Elixir*, washing the topsides, the motion triggering his ultra-sensitive inner ear and subsequent nausea.

Talk to me. Please, Tosh, this is terrifying. I am uncertain about even attempting this crossing and if you are going to be sick ... I can't do this thing without you. I really can't. I screamed inside; inside because the tension was already too high. I couldn't handle another fight, and one would surely ensue if I spoke my doubts aloud. The hose jerked my arm. *Crap, now what?* My stomach was in knots as I forced myself to carefully walk around the deck, trying to see what had snagged the hose. I resolutely untangled it from around the dorade, a vertical air shaft protruding above the deck, freeing up more length so I could continue *Elixir's* last bath.

This must be the most insane thing anyone has ever done. Am I ready to die? Is it okay if I go now? Why won't he talk to me? The mind continued its relentless torture, my stomach getting more and more uptight. *You can't hide behind endless tasks now, can you? Four years of hiding and now you must face it, it's done. The Elixir Project is complete.*

"Deb, hey, can you pass me the hose?"

Unwinding the hose from around the hatches, I passed it through the stanchions. Tosh still looked green around the gills, but determined to pretend he was fine and not willing to talk about it. I could tell from the thin line of his lips, pressed so tight that they disappeared, his face like a mask without a mouth.

As I stood there, waiting for him to finish rinsing, I couldn't help but notice the vibrant colors of the mountain behind the harbor, framed by the deep blue of the southern Pacific sky. *Maybe I could just stay here on the island. I mean, it is paradise, right?* I bit my tongue to keep from laying out all my doubts and fears on Tosh, expecting him to fix them and make everything better. *Well, it was his fault. I mean, this whole thing was his idea, right? I wouldn't have done this, not ever. Oh crap, stop it, stop it, stop it. But you don't even have any crew yet. You really can't sail without two more guys aboard, you really can't.*

"Here," he passed the nozzle up through the rails as I brought my mind back to the task.

In order to take advantage of optimum weather conditions, the trip north was best made in June and July. Our plan was to sail up to Hanalei Bay, anchor there, and sail away from the islands before the end of June. It was mid-June. If we were going north, we had to leave the harbor in the next few days. We had to commit.

Kauaian Waters
June 21, 1992

A few days later, Gavin shouted "All clear," as he released the last dock line from the bow, skipped down the slip and hopped aboard amidships, excited, playful, and filled with the naive optimism of youth. The adults aboard were quiet for a second or two as the reality of releasing *Elixir* from her berth of the last several years for a perilous ocean crossing slowly sunk in and registered.

"Yahoo," Tosh, our skipper, bellowed, exuberant as he stood at the wheel and slowly backed out of the tight space of the slip harbor. The crew joined in, exclaiming their unique versions of "Bon Voyage." Alex, our new crew member, Gavin, Tosh, and I were joined by four other sailing friends for the day. Behind us, more friends waved from the shore.

After stowing sail and hatch covers below, I made my way forward over the main cabin deck and released the sail ties before arriving at the shroud bars. I pulled out the belaying pins for the throats and peaks of the main and foresails. The heavy halyards made a hollow thump as they landed solidly on the deck, clear of snarls and ready to unwind as the sails were raised.

The puffy, dock bumpers, like giant white Cheetos, were

lifted aboard as I went, untying them from the rails for the last time, stowing them in their locker. *I wonder when and where we will be when I get these out again? I* pondered, or *even if we will ever use them again? Would this be the beginning of a new life aboard? Would it be the end, a final voyage? Stop it, you will jinx the whole thing.* Sailors are highly superstitious; I felt myself join their ranks. *Don't go there.*

Tosh shouting over the sound of the engine quickly brought me back from my morbid thoughts. "Tommy and Kenny, take the throat halyards. Gavin, show Alex how to do the peak at the main, and Cathy, you take the foresail peak."

Tosh had turned the boat around, and we were motoring out through the main harbor. The water was flat here, perfect for getting the sails up before we left the harbor mouth and slammed into the massive waves of the Pacific Ocean. It was a perfect Sunday afternoon, hot and sunny. We all wore life jackets over shorts, bare feet, and visored ball caps pulled tight and low over well secured black glacier glasses. Like the men in black without the suits.

"Alex and Cathy, tighten up those peaks. Gavin, make sure they are secure, and raise the forestaysail and the jib," Tosh shouted as he turned off the engine.

Instant silence washed over the boat. I felt the power of the sails as they filled and pulled *Elixir* forward and through the mouth of the harbor into the blue water. Michelle and I secured the sheets for the four lower sails, keeping an eye on the tell tales (tiny strings on the sail to show how the air flows) for optimum efficiency as we settled onto the first leg on a northerly course around the coast of Kauai to Hanalei Bay.

"Deb, zero out the knot log. This is it, the beginning of our crossing." He sounded excited, with none of the distress of the previous days evident in his voice or demeanor. He had taken his medicine and was wearing the sea bands on his wrists, another provision against seasickness we had read about.

Returning the knot log to zero on the companionway instrument panel, I headed below decks to the chart table. A navy-blue journal, the size of a school exercise book but with white spiral binding on the short side, awaited this moment. The front cover was decorated in large white letters spelling out *LOGBOOK*. Opening the pages, I entered the time, the weather, the sea and wind conditions, before moving onto the chart and penciling an X to mark the harbor, and the beginning of our long-anticipated crossing. As I entered the names of our crew, I paused on Alex, remembering our first meeting just a few days before.

"Dad, Deb, this is Alex," Nicole stood in the parking lot of the boatyard. "He is from South America, and he wants to do the crossing with you guys."

A young man, the same height as Nicole's five foot six inches, politely stepped forward, extending his hand. "Nice to meet you both." He had a pleasant voice, heavily accented.

"Have you ever sailed before?" Tosh asked in a conversational tone, kicking at the broken pavement with the toe of his running shoe, a hand on his hip.

"No, but I have always wanted to." His mustache fell below his jaw on either side, giving him a profoundly serious look.

"How long have you been on Kauai?" Tosh continued, his glance going between Alex's face and the hole in the sidewalk.

"Only a month. I have been traveling through the islands and want to head to the mainland."

I was fascinated by the way his mustache moved when he spoke.

"Well, I guess taking a month to sail there is one way to do it." Tosh chuckled. "You sure you want to go the slow way? I mean, you could fly, you know."

"Do you get seasick?" I asked, bluntly, interrupting.

"Not that I know of." There was definitely a twinkle in those dark eyes above the moving whiskers.

"Have you got bad weather gear?" I continued, going right to the practical basics.

"No, but I know Tommy, and he will lend me his."

"That's great." I paused. *How do you conduct an interview in a situation like this? I mean, a total stranger and we would be living in such close quarters.* I continued, "I don't mean to be rude, but I notice that you smoke and there can be no smoking on board, and we will be at sea for at least a month. Does that work for you?"

"Yes." As he nodded, his long dark hair slid forward, the sun-bleached blond ends covering his eye.

Tosh stopped messing around with the holey sidewalk and looked directly at Alex. "You can stop cold turkey like that?"

"I really want to do this."

After a pause, I jumped back into the conversation. "Wow, okay, well a couple other caveats while we're at it: The food will be vegetarian, no meat aboard, and no drugs, not even marijuana. If the Coast Guard finds any drugs aboard, they confiscate the ship. All clear?"

"Yes."

Tosh looked over at me, looking for a sign, yes or no. I raised an eyebrow, vexed. *I have no idea how to make a decision like this.* We were desperate.

Tosh reached over to shake his hand. "Okay then, be back here in two days. We leave for Hanalei Bay around noon."

"Thank you. See you Sunday." The mustache smiled. The

fact that the eyes did, too, was slightly reassuring. He climbed back into Nicole's car, and they drove away.

And now it was Sunday, Alex was aboard and we were underway. Yikes. At least he said he knew Tommy, a delivery skipper who often crewed with us. Improvements since the shakedown included new black melamine dishes, and extra Velcro to hold the cushions in place but no new latches on the lockers.

After checking the radio and writing in the log below, I went back on deck. I was surprised to see we were already about thirty miles off Alakukui Point just south of Kapa'a, the state park where we had conducted our early morning break-fast picnics. The winds out of the east ten to fifteen knots and two to four-foot seas matched the radio report I had just heard. Reassuring.

"Hey, look, dolphins." Gavin, who loved to sit up in the bow, motioned excitedly under the bowsprit, his head framed by the foresails.

"What a great beginning for your journey," Tommy yelled back to us in the cockpit as he made his way forward to peer over the rail. "Yup, they're here playing in the bow wave. They're good luck, you know."

By Kealia the winds became squirrelly and by mid-after-noon, as we passed Anahola, the wind died altogether, requiring the engine. I went below to make food and drinks. As I counted out the glasses and mixed a pitcher of Gatorade, I thought about the last two days since *Elixir*'s freshwater bath and the attending worry of not knowing if we would make the crossing or not.

Regardless of how insane it appeared, it seemed the only

option after all these years of preparation was to continue to move forward. So we spent a day getting extra-large foul weather gear for Shakya and buying the ham radio to supplement the VHS radio.

To help me relax, I spent time working on the photo albums I had meticulously kept over the course of the project and added the five new rolls of prints from the inter-island cruise. That was something that I knew how to do, something familiar, therapeutic, and relaxing in the midst of all the newness and uncertainty of embarking on a crossing.

Some shots captured the whitewater and extreme conditions we had experienced in the prior few weeks. Viewing the images helped my mind to assimilate the reality of what we were attempting and make the mental change from an internal vision of a life of sailing to the external actuality of being a sailor. This was really happening. I headed back up the companionway ladder, grateful for the ordinary, mundane task of feeding people.

"Who wants popcorn?" I yelled from the cockpit. I had used the new twelve-volt hot air popcorn maker for the first time. Munchies were a welcome distraction from the heat and almost still air as we sat around the cockpit together, reminiscing about our last four and a half years in the boat yard.

By early evening we had made it thirty-three nautical miles into Hanalei Bay and dropped anchor. After saying our goodbyes and rowing our well-wishing friends ashore, Tosh, Gavin, and I settled in for the night with Alex, our new crew member, feeling strange and unfamiliar inside and out.

Would Alex be okay at sea? Would Shakya be okay going against his wife's wishes and show up the next day? Would Tosh be okay?

Kauaian Waters
June 26, 1992 (Day 1)

It was 0530 hours and I was finishing my first dawn watch, curled up in the bean bag chair with my hands glued to the spokes on the wheel. The sky was still gray but lightening with winds and seas increasing to squalls. *Probably time to get the boys up here to reduce sail,* I thought to myself. *Just a few more minutes.*

I contemplated the last two days since leaving Nawiliwili Harbor. We had stayed moored in Hanalei Bay, swimming and listening to the weather radio, trying to decide when we should really and for keeps, raise anchor and sail away. Shakya had arrived and stowed his gear, Alex had his last smoke ashore, and last night, on Thursday, June 25, we'd finally raised the anchor and sailed away. It was 2200 hours, five of us aboard, the winds out of the east at twenty knots and the seas five feet. There was a small moon and many stars. The stars were amazing, especially the North Star, and on our heading, it was right between the forestays, truly setting a star guided course.

To preserve our night vision, no lights were used on deck and only red light was used below. The air was warm and the sounds of the wind over the sails and through the rigging was strong and steady, pushing us through the heavily phosphorescent sea. For the first time, upon using the head, I witnessed this phosphorescence in the toilet bowl, swirling around as I pumped the basin clear with fresh seawater.

Shakya wrote out a watch schedule and posted it in the navigation station. For safety, we had decided to have two people on deck for two and a half hour watches. Gavin, even though only fourteen, was taller and stronger than I and competent to stand watches and carry out his share of chores. Dish duty was Alex in the morning, Shakya for lunch, and Deb for dinner, with Gavin cooking breakfasts, and Deb cooking lunches and dinners.

Tosh was the skipper and would make all decisions about sail changes and use of the engine. He would be on deck to raise and lower sails and would walk out on the bowsprit for setting the flying jib, the jib and the stay sails. Shakya was our bosun and engineer and oversaw repairs and maintenance to the ship, the engine, and systems. I was the navigator, cook and radio operator. Alex and Gavin were deckhands.

My reverie was interrupted when the companionway hatch opened. Gavin's head appeared, quickly followed by the rest of him landing in the cockpit. He plunked himself down on the leeward bench, dressed in his sweatpants and shirtsleeves, his longish brown hair instantly blown back in the wind. He adjusted thick glasses on his young nose.

"Mom, I can't believe it," he sneezed.

"Bless you!" I yelled to make myself heard over the wind and sea. "Good morning to you, too, kiddo. Where's your harness?"

"Mom, you won't believe Alex," Gavin continued, coughing and ignoring my question.

"Uh huh, what's up with him?"

"Mom, he sprayed stuff under his arms for like ten minutes just now. It's totally toxic down there. I don't know how he can stand it," he continued, incredulous. "I can't stop sneezing."

"Well, toxic or not, go get your harness."

"Mom, I can't breathe down there, my nose is all stuffed up." It was true, he was completely congested. We generally used unscented products and no aerosols. Alex would learn.

"Ask the boys to pass it up to you," I directed, sensitivities to smells or not, if he got swept overboard it wouldn't matter if he was sneezing.

He opened the hatch and Shakya's arm immediately

extended a harness out the door. As Gavin quickly buckled it on and clipped himself to the boat, I could smell the offending deodorant as it passed my nose on its way out of the cabin.

"Pretty strong," I agreed. "Hey, get the boys up here. I think it's time to reduce sail. The wind's coming up."

Shakya, Tosh, and Alex all came up. I stayed on the wheel, keeping our bow into the wind while they double reefed the mainsail, and dropped the foresail leaving the jib up.

Tosh stayed on the wheel for the next watch while Gavin prepared a breakfast of hot oatmeal with brown sugar and milk. After eating my porridge and drinking a cup of hot Postum, I plotted our position on the nautical chart and filled in the ship's log. Throughout the rest of the second day and into the night, the heavy weather continued into gale force winds.

The third night was pitch black. I was on the helm for the predawn watch. Even if I screamed no one would hear me over the sound of the waves and the fierce wind; a wind so strong my slender body couldn't stand up without holding on to the boat. Tosh was asleep in the cockpit; three more crew were tied into their bunks below.

The compass glowed dim red in the blackness, preserving my night vision. It was the only thing my eyes discerned except the occasional foamy wave tops that glowed briefly with limey phosphorescence before being swept under the dark water of the next wave. My fingers, slick with rain and spray, encircled the spokes of the wheel as I adjusted our heading according to the pale numbers of the compass. I struggled to keep the needle on ooo, our northerly heading, but the violent pitching of the vessel made it almost impossible.

The end of June was supposed to be the ideal time to cross

the Pacific from Hawaii to Washington, a time when the conditions were the most stable. Yet here I was in forty-five knot winds: technically a gale and a nine on the Beaufort Wind Scale.

Harnessed to the boat, I clung to the wheel with my hands, to the decks with my bare toes, and to the compass heading with my eyes, but my mind rapidly started to spin out of control. Fear. Panic. Terror. *We'll be swamped, capsize and drown.*

The sea was immensely powerful, and *Elixir* was puny— fragile like a single piece of straw in an endless river. *The masts will break off like toothpicks, we'll tip over and sink.* I imagined myself sliding off the boat, the cold water seeping into my foul weather gear, the waves holding my head beneath the foaming sea, breathing in the salty water, gasping. My teeth clamped tight around a paper tongue. No saliva left. I tried licking salt-water off my lips but couldn't swallow.

What had I been thinking over the last five years of building this boat and deciding to sail it across the Pacific? How could I have ever thought it would be fun or exciting? How did I ever dare to presume I could learn to be at sea when conditions were less than ideal? Let alone in a gale?

Unable to find any relief from the deafening noise and violent motion of the storm, I tried to search inside myself for ways to navigate extreme distress and control my panic. All I found were images of me floating face down in the dark waves, alongside the corpses of my husband and son as we drifted among bits of a broken ship. And it was only our third night at sea; we'd only just begun our long ocean journey north.

What's that? My mind alerted me. *There's something on the rail.* I strained to see through the black night. *No, nothing.* Yet I sensed something there on the rail, despite the thrashing seas and the wail-scream in the rigging. Whatever it was, the beings

I intuited on the rail caught my attention, gradually pulling my focus away from my terror and thoughts of drowning. I had read books about people in life threatening situations, during which they experienced visions or heard voices that assisted them to survive untenable ordeals.

Angels? Could that be possible? Is this what is happening to me? Has my mind snapped from the intensity of my circumstances?

There seemed to be several of them, round and smushing together. A perception rather than an actual vision, they appeared to be joking with each other, laughing so hard they nearly fell off the rail. *I am definitely going off my rails.*

It was as if they were enjoying the ride, and at the same time assuring me that despite the enormity of the sea and the ferocity of the wind, the elements were merely frolicking. This communication was through a mixture of pictures, words, and feelings conveyed in a flash. *Frolicking? Really?* Wind at this speed rips branches off of trees and causes cars to veer off the road. The extremes of the Pacific Ocean proved larger, stronger and louder than any thunder and lightning I had ever experienced on the lake where I grew up in British Columbia.

And it worked. The angels on the rail, as I refer to my perception of them, succeeded in helping my mind get out of a tailspin of panic. Horribly uncomfortable and still terrified, I no longer felt paralyzed by fear, despite the awareness of our insanely precarious position in a small sailboat a thousand miles from any shore.

Chapter 33

Turn Back, Baths, Brownies & Bear Hugs

"After living a sheltered modern life, being on the open ocean in a small sailboat brings you face to face with life and death realities."

Pacific Ocean
June 28, 1992 (Day 3)

"I think we should go back," Shakya, our engineer, was propped up at the end of his berth in the main salon, naked except for his tighty-whities.

The heavy weather had afflicted us with seasickness. Gavin the least, the three men ill and vomiting. I was in the middle with moderate queasiness. Despite constant nausea, everyone had kept to their watch schedules and chores, but morale had crashed, following the vomit over the side of the rail and sinking to the bottom of the sea.

Today, at last, the sun was starting to come out and shafts of light, filled with golden dust motes, crossed the cabin, and landed on Shakya's exposed chest and rotund belly. Muggy and hot, his face was pale under unruly brown hair, damp and flat in the humidity. Three days' worth of beard shadowed his features. With black rimmed glasses askew on a prominent nose, his dark eyes were earnest. "I don't think I can take much more, honestly."

Our heavy weather gear, jackets, and pants were soaked through and despite hanging them throughout the cabin, nothing dried. The aft double bunk, where Tosh and I slept, was wet from the sea and rain coming in whenever we opened the companionway hatch. I now understood why some cruising boats had a canvas cover over the hatch. Water was everywhere, even on the navigation table, my chart so wet I couldn't draw on it anymore. It was the same with the ship's logbook, the pages soaked, the ink blurred and unreadable. Besides, even if I could have recorded on the wet paper, there was no way I could accurately plot our position after two whole days and a night of mayhem with the elements.

"You still feeling pretty sick?" I asked from where I was standing in the galley, a wide strap behind my bum to hold me in place as I prepared dinner. Despite the seasickness, all of us were hungry, another idiosyncrasy of being at sea.

"Yes, but I am not tossing my cookies like our skipper up there. He's still puking over the rail, and he has nothing left to throw up. I'm worried about him. He's seriously dehydrated, not an ideal situation," Shakya continued wryly.

"You're right," I quickly agreed. I was panicking inside and had been since my watch the night before but remembering Anuprada's highly visible and vocal melt down on our shake-down cruise, there was no way I was going to show it. I paused and glanced over at Alex.

He, too, was propped up at the end of his berth on the starboard salon seat, wearing only his underwear. Unlike his cabin mate though, Alex was a small, tidy man with fine features under dark Spanish eyes, the mustache present and neatly trimmed.

"How're you holding up?" I asked him.

"I am actually feeling a little better this afternoon." His accent did not detract from his well-spoken English. I didn't have to ask him if he was vomiting. In such tight quarters we all knew he'd been okay since last night.

Later, I took dinner to Tosh in the cockpit. It would go mostly untouched, but I had to try to get him to eat something. "What do you think, Tosh? Should we turn around? I mean, this is pretty extreme, you being this sick for three full days and nights. And the crossing will take a month ..." I let my voice trail off into the interminable wind.

"Honestly, I was thinking that strong astronaut medicine would work for me. I was hoping, anyway." He paused before continuing, "I didn't count on vomiting it up as soon as I swallowed it." He cracked a faint smile, thoughtful as he laid there on the settee in the cockpit, his face drained of color and his disappointment palpable beyond the few words exchanged. "But we better turn back. I don't see myself getting any better."

Shit, I thought to myself. *What a total mess. An entire dream felled by seasickness. Damn.* After a long time, I ventured a response out loud, the words terribly inadequate, "I am so sorry, Tosh. I know how much you've wanted to do this. And how hard you've tried. All the day sails to see if you would be less sick, the sea bands, the ginger tea, the astronaut medicine ..." After a few moments, I gathered up the dinner bowls to go below for our nightly radio broadcast.

Placing the dishes in the sink, I made the two steps to the navigation station and fell onto the seat in front of the chart table, grabbing the microphone on my way. I turned on the VHF radio and adjusted the dials to channel 75.

"This is Whiskey Hotel Six Charlie November Bravo aboard the fifty-foot schooner *Elixir*. We are at 26°12′ North, 160°21′ West, on a heading of 000 degrees north and three days out of Hanalei Bay on Kauai in the Hawaiian Islands. Do you read me? Over." I released my finger from the transmission key on the hand-held microphone and waited for a bit before repeating the message a second time. As I paused after my second transmission, I was startled by a static voice coming through the radio.

"*Elixir*, this is *Easy*. We are about five nautical miles north of you on the same heading. Where are you headed? Over."

"*Easy*, this is *Elixir*. We are headed north to Washington State and the Olympic Peninsula. How 'bout you? Over."

"*Elixir*, us too. Hey how did you make out in the gale the last thirty-six hours? Over."

"*Elixir* is doing fine, but her crew is in rough shape. And you? Over"

"There are just the two of us aboard, myself, Bob, and my wife Mary. And we're doing well. Fifteen years of blue water sailing has us both pretty used to being at sea. Tell me more about you and your crew. Over."

And I did. Including our decision to turn around and head back to Kauai. But, suddenly, the prognosis for our crossing was not so bleak. Bob, *Easy's* skipper, was quite matter of fact about the gales we had just sailed through. His on-board weather fax reported there would be easier winds and seas for the next few days. However, if we turned tail, we would be back into the heavy weather again, a pretty convincing argument to continue northward. He also confirmed what we had read; it takes about three days at sea to get over seasickness.

Even Tosh had no hesitation with this decision to continue north when he heard that turning back entailed returning to gale conditions. While I also agreed with everyone to continue our journey, I silently worried. Three or four days to return to Kauai with a sick skipper was a lot less than the twenty to thirty days it would take to make our way to the Olympic Peninsula.

Gradually, with the lighter air and calmer seas, everyone started to feel better, acclimating to the motion of the vessel. The only exception was our skipper, and while he had some better days, he never did get his sea legs.

It was agreed to buddy boat with *Easy*, including radio calls together every evening at eight thirty. They had experience and technology but were in their seventies. He was deaf, unable to hear the alarms on his equipment. She had just had bypass surgery and was unsteady on her feet, so she stayed below in the cabin. We had the manpower to keep twenty-four-hour watches and could alert them to adjust course when in danger of colliding with another ship but were neophytes at ocean crossings. The symbiotic partnership left both parties grateful.

Even though I had my Coast Guard training in navigation, real life sea conditions were proving considerably more challenging than school. Bob coached me on the practicalities of navigation and how we would keep track of our course, where we were in relation to each other's position, and our position in relation to the weather fronts he monitored on the weather fax; more accurate and detailed. By the fourth day the logbook and chart were dried out enough that I could once again write and record our watery route northward. Using a pencil now, though. I'd learned the hard way about ink and seawater.

Mid-morning the next day, I was kneading dough for the two loaves of whole wheat bread I baked every other day. Interrupting my task, I wiped my floury hands on the towel and opened the hatch. Alex was on the helm, dressed in red and white foul weather gear, his hood pulled up over a woolen toque and his eyes covered with wrap around black glacier glasses, like a Mount Everest climber. His gaze was off to the left, his posture relaxed into the bean bag chair.

"What's your heading, Alex?" I called out from the companionway.

Immediately, his glance returned to the compass and his hands adjusted the wheel. "o1o," he responded.

"ooo," I said, correcting him automatically. "Thanks, Alex." I had to hand it to him. He knew nothing about sailing and didn't know any of us prior to leaving Nawiliwili Harbor. It was gutsy of him to want to set out on a small sailboat with four other people. And not just on a day sail either, he came aboard straight into a blue water crossing.

Though quiet and pleasant, he had trouble keeping us on course during his watches. At first, I was incredulous that anyone could have difficulties with maintaining a compass course heading and was sure he would improve. He never did though, so we all kept sticking our heads out the hatch when he was on the helm to ask him his heading. A two- or three-hour watch, when the heading was not ooo, would get us off course by an exponential number of miles by the end of a day.

I returned to my task, immersing my hands in the warm dough. Shakya was on the port settee, again in his tighty-whities, with his guitar.

Oh, me father was the keeper of the Eddystone Light*
And he slept with a mermaid one fine night...

Gavin and I joined in the singing for the chorus, giggling at the silliness of the traditional English sea shanty.

Yo ho ho... the wind blows free
Oh for the life on the rolling sea...

I finished up the kneading and put towels over the dough and the whole bowl into the oven to keep it warm for a few hours. After cleaning the floury mess from the counters, I stuck my head out the hatch, "What's your heading again, Alex?" and returned to the dishes. Pumping salt water into one side of the deep double sink, I emptied the hot water from the kettle into it to make it warm and followed with a squirt of Joy dish soap, guaranteed to suds even in salt water. Gavin and Shakya were laughing louder than usual.

Oh, what has become of me children three?
... one was exhibited as a talking fish, the other was
served in a chafing dish...

"Hey, something's burning." Alarmed, I interrupted them. It wasn't the bread and the stove was off. "It smells like pot actually," I stuck my head around the mast so I could see them. "Shit. Where did that come from?" Gavin was holding a joint up for Shakya to take a toke while he played his guitar.

"Your son seems to have smuggled a stash aboard." Shakya chuckled.

"What? You guys all knew the rules before coming aboard."

I was instantly furious, and scared, too. I had assisted the Coast Guard in their training exercises in Nawiliwili over the last three years and if they found any kind of drugs aboard a vessel, even if just a roach, they took away the boat and could imprison the owners and crew. Oblivious, the boys kept laughing and singing.

Then the phosphorus flashed in her seaweed hair, I
looked again, but me mother wasn't there …

"Mom, it's okay, it's hardly anything, just dust really. Nicky's boyfriend gave it to me. We aren't even really stoned, Mom. It's so lame."

I was stunned and didn't know what to say. Obviously, there wasn't anything I could do about it now. "Do me a favor and smoke it all, will you? And make sure all the ashes and roaches and the bag and everything go overboard when you're done."

Yo ho ho … the wind blows free … the moral of the story
you'll find … fishes are for cookin', mermaids are for tales,
seaweed is for sushi and protecting is for whales …

June 29, 1992 (Day 4)

"Yay, I did it." While we were all good at ignoring whatever was going on in the head, the victory yell from our skipper, Tosh, in the boys' room got our attention and gave us permission to respond with "yay" and "good for you" and "finally." Having his first bowel movement in our four days at sea was a huge relief for him but also for the rest of us, as we were constantly concerned about his well-being. After lots of good-natured joking around, Shakya continued with his maintenance routine and added a quart of oil to the engine and confirmed the water levels were adequate. The new engine was doing well so far.

"It's a great day for a bath," Tosh announced after setting as much sail as possible and we were still barely moving three knots. "It will be too cold in the next day or two. We are pretty far north." He attached the bucket to a line and threw it overboard working hand over hand to bring it back aboard full of clear seawater. "Who's first?"

Gavin stripped down and sat on the cabin roof, wedging himself on the handhold to stop from sliding off. "Ahh," he squealed as the icy water cascaded over his head. I handed him the bottle of Joy dish soap. Squirting a liberal amount into his hands, he massaged it into his wet hair. Another bucket of sea water splashed over him as he soaped his whole body. A few more buckets rinsed him off. "You're next, Shakya. Get your big butt up here," Gavin joked, shivering as he toweled dry.

We all had a turn, and relaxed in the warm sunny air, our hair slowly drying in the light breeze.

"Hey, what are we doing with this garbage?" Alex asked later from the companionway. Having all had baths, it was time to do some housekeeping as well. "The wastebasket in the head is overflowing. Can we toss it overboard?"

"Yup, paper only," Tosh responded. "And of course any food garbage. But cans, glass and plastic all stay aboard until landfall."

Alex tipped the basket over the rail. "That's really weird," he commented as he watched the toilet paper slowly floating away, gradually sinking behind us.

Unlike on the land, there would be no tracks or trail of garbage to reveal our passing over this huge body of water called the Pacific Ocean. We would leave no trace.

June 30, 1992 (Day 5)

With the calmer seas, and easier ride, I baked brownies, a treat after enjoying a pasta dinner outside in the cockpit. "Great dinner once again, Deb. Thank you. Can we message Anuprada tonight? Let her know we are still alive?" Shakya was collecting the black melamine plates before heading below.

"Sure, let's do it now before our scheduled radio call with *Easy*." I followed him down the ladder, dropping more dishes in the deep galley sink beside the navigation station.

We patched into the phone service with the ham radio, but her line was busy. It was odd to hear the familiar 'Beep, beep, beep' of a busy signal after five days at sea.

"Just checking in with you, dear. We are all well." Shakya's message was short and sweet. He handed the microphone back to me. "I'm kinda glad she wasn't home. I don't think I could handle her worried questioning at this point." He chuckled. "Maybe she left me. She was pretty upset about my decision to do this."

As we started in on the pile of dishes, I asked, "Seriously, would she really leave you? Is it that bad?"

"I don't think so, but that experience in the channel during the shake-down cruise ..." He shook his head. "In the fifteen years we've been together, I actually never saw that side of her before."

"I was surprised when she lost it. I was looking forward to having a nurse aboard, as well as another woman. Hey, hurry up with the drying, there's no more room in the sink for these." I teased him as I piled the cleaned pots precariously on top of the rest of the dishes. It was calm enough that we could both stand in the galley; the bum strap hung idle on its hook at the end of the counter.

"Where do these bowls go again?"

I pointed to the bin behind the counter. "I want to thank you again for coming, Shakya. I know it put you in a difficult position with her." I was quiet as I pumped the dishwater out of the sink. "I appreciate your calm presence aboard, as well as your expertise."

"I wouldn't miss it. All the preparation over the last few years ... nope, there wouldn't be another opportunity like this one again." He was genuinely grateful and at home aboard, a solid, unpretentious wall of a man. A man I trusted with my life. His eyes met mine over the top of his heavy glasses, his chin down as he was taller than me. A surge of emotion washed up my body and spilled out my eyes. Quickly lowering my gaze, I wasn't quick enough. The dish towel went over his shoulder and his arms wrapped me up in a bear hug, my wet hands dripping on the galley floor.

Gavin's head appeared in the open hatch. "Hey, get back up here. The wind's coming up and it's time to reduce sail."

"Thanks," I mumbled into his white T-shirt, trying to quickly contain the tears, a miniscule reflection of the depth of fear and inexperience I held inside about what we were doing.

Letting me go, he made his way up the ladder, then turned to look down at me. "You are doing an amazing job, Deb. I honestly don't know how you keep it together." And he disappeared through the hatch.

Finishing up the dishes, I felt calmer, grateful for the moment of release and even more appreciative that Shakya was aboard and quietly aware of the enormity of what I internalized. With the boys doing the sail changes, I made my evening radio call to *Easy*. Bob updated me on the weather fax information and their position so I could chart accordingly.

"We have gone four-hundred-and-fifty nautical miles to date, just a little over a hundred nautical miles a day," I announced to the boys later.

"A hundred miles a day?" Shakya was incredulous. "We could bicycle faster than this."

The next day held light winds and seas until the evening when a squall hit with heavy gusts, forcing us to drop the sails. The jib fouled and all of us were freaked once again until we eventually got back on course by keeping the engine on all night.

The sea allows no complacency.

Chapter 34

Shakya in the Head, Waffles & Fish

"Anyone can sail in calm waters."

Pacific Ocean
July 1, 1992 (Day 6)

"Smells good over there. When is supper?" Alex asked, looking up from his book. His mustache had grown longer. Tosh was on watch, Gavin and Shakya keeping him company.

"An hour or so." I mixed up the coconut milk, peanut butter, and spices in the twelve-volt blender, working one-handed as I needed to hold on to the overhead bars. The bum strap holding me against the counter was not secure enough for the rough seas. The twelve-inch port was eye level and waves regularly washed across it; the rail buried in frothing white water.

We had been on a port tack, the boat leaning to the left, for six days and would stay on that tack until we reached the

Pacific high, the point in the middle of the ocean where currents of wind and water circled north around the coast of Asia and Japan, east along Alaska and then south along the coast of North America. Another wave washed over the port just a foot in front of my face. There were yellow boots visible through the water. I peered closer, looking up to see Shakya's foulie clad form standing wedged in the shrouds, the wire rigging that extended from the hull up to the top of the main mast.

"Hey, Alex, Shakya's been standing there for about half an hour."

"And he might be there another half hour," Alex chuckled.

"Why do you say that?" By now I knew the boys stood there to urinate downwind, but this was taking such a long time.

"It's kinda' rough out there, you know, scary to stand there with the water all washing over your boots and stuff ..." Alex was looking at me over his reading glasses like that would explain it. Seeing my blank expression, he continued, "Well, you know, it's hard to, you know, pee when you are scared ... you know ... scared of being washed overboard any minute ..."

I thought about it for a half second. *I didn't even like to sit in the cockpit on the lower side of a heel, let alone walk amidships and stand on a buried rail. Actually, no, I had never done that, and come to think of it, I wouldn't do that voluntarily.*

"Hmm, I get your point," I said aloud.

"And there is the other issue, too ... you know ..."

"Another issue?" I looked up from stirring the curry. It was starting to bubble. Shakya's boots were still in front of me. Unmoving. Craning my neck to peer upward again, one gloved hand was still gripping the wire shrouds.

"Well, ah, since we are getting more north, ah, well, you know, its uh, much colder ..." his voice trailed off.

I waited a bit, expecting the rest of the sentence. "And?"

"Well, you know, it shrinks in the cold ... and ah, you know, with ah, all the clothes on, ah, well ... well, it's kind of difficult ... I mean, we have to live in these clothes for a month, so ah, you know, you don't want to pee on them ..."

I started to laugh. I couldn't help it. Alex looked at me, stricken for a millisecond, and then he started to laugh, too.

"Well, I'll stop complaining about my trips to the head and getting bashed against the bulwarks ... and the pee sloshing out of the toilet bowl onto me when I don't flush fast enough," I conceded, never imagining before that moment that my plight as a female could actually be easier that what the boys were going through.

Later that night the weather was still turbulent, Shakya was in the head. *Elixir* lurched and we heard a scream, a real one.

"What's wrong? Are you okay in there?" Gavin looked at Alex, Alex looked at me, I looked at Gavin. Low moans were escaping through the louvers in the head door.

"Shakya, are you okay?" I yelled from the nav station where I had just finished my nightly radio call with Bob aboard *Easy*.

"Okay... I'm okay..." a strained voice answered.

We all looked at each other again, concerned, puzzled.

"What's going on?" I asked, persistent.

"Give me a minute..." He was panting, his voice pained.

We waited, silent except for the noises of *Elixir* slamming through the rough water and the winds howling around the rig.

"The toilet seat slid off the porcelain in that last wave," a long pause before he continued, still breathing heavily, "and ah, well, my balls got caught between the seat and the porcelain toilet bowl ... I'll just be sitting here a bit longer ..." He sighed heavily.

"Ah, man..." Gavin and Alex were squirming and quiet for

a moment before the laughter started ... the kind of laughter that made us all cry and our stomachs ache.

July 3, 1992 (Day 8)

My eyes slowly opened. *It was Friday, a week and a day,* I thought to myself. *I'm still here. We're actually doing this thing.* The sounds of the wind in the rig were steady, the hull slap smooth. The morning light was dim and dull, indicative of low overcast. We were not heeled over so far. The boys were on deck, Gavin still in his berth. I dressed quickly, expecting a rough wave to unbalance me, but there weren't any.

A giant stalk of bananas hung over the foot of Shakya's berth, the bottom row was yellow after more than eight days. A blue water sailing trick; the whole stalk is picked green, and the fruit slowly ripens from the bottom up, providing bananas for weeks. I was excited: flat seas and ripe bananas make perfect conditions for a waffle breakfast.

"Wow, smells amazing down there," Shakya stuck his head down the hatch fifteen minutes later, hungry and eager for breakfast, but he knew to let me be while I cooked.

"Here you go," I said, passing him a plate loaded with a perfect waffle decorated with sliced bananas and smothered in butter and syrup.

"What a treat," he responded, his eyes widening in surprise at this welcome addition to the menu.

"Yippee for the gentle ride today," I laughed. I enjoyed cooking when I wasn't worried the food would jump out of the pots onto the counters, the walls, and me. "We even get plates today." All three meals were usually eaten out of deep narrow bowls, to make sure the food didn't spill before making it into our mouths. Getting out the plates was like getting out the good china for a special occasion, or an honored guest. The galley smells woke Gavin, and he was into his foulies and out the hatch faster than I'd seen him move in awhile.

The radio crackled to life.

"*Elixir*, this is *Easy*, come in, over." Bob's radio voice filled the salon.

Dropping my licked clean plate in the sink, I slid onto the nav station bench and unhooked the microphone from the cabin side. Bob let us know, his grin practically leaking out of the radio, that the winds had shifted and it was time to turn right toward the mainland.

This turn was a crucial component of navigating a Pacific crossing. The winds circle around the Pacific in a clockwise direction. In the middle of these wind and ocean currents, the still air is known as the doldrums. To avoid being trapped without wind and forward momentum indefinitely, it is imperative to stay well out of this area by not turning east too soon. If you do, you die when your fuel, food and water run out, marooned in dead air.

"Did you hear that skipper?" I called out the hatch, excitement contagious. We'd been on the same course for eight days and nights. Turning east meant we were starting the second leg of our journey north and we were half-way there.

The following day was overcast and filled with sail changes and engine starts and stops. By late morning, we'd lost sight of *Easy*, and I wished we were back on our old course, with steady, consistent wind from the north.

"*Elixir*, come in. Over." It was Bob from *Easy* once again. And he told us that the new weather fax indicated the high was a lot further north than usual. We had turned too soon and needed to go back to our 000-course heading.

I took a deep breath and digested the new information. My wish had been granted.

"Roger that, *Easy*. By the way, we've lost sight of you with all the changes. We're at 45°25′ North and 146°13′ West. What's your position? Over." I kept my voice calm, forcing the panic into a vice grip on my pencil, as I recorded his location: eleven nautical miles west of us, interceptable on the new course heading. Hanging up the microphone, I quickly plotted our positions on the chart. Using the parallel rulers, I drew a line between the two locations, and walked the ruler over to the nearest compass rose.

"Our new heading is 020 northwest, and watch for *Easy*," I called across the cockpit after relaying the information that we had, indeed, turned too soon. I couldn't help but think of all the traditional sailors who had made this crossing and ended up in the doldrums. And that would have been us, without Bob and his weather fax, and our chance meeting across radio waves hundreds of miles out to sea.

The next day at dawn, Gavin's fishing lines were fully extended on both sides. *Oh, no, I may have to figure out how to cook fish after all.* Carefully uncurling myself from the bean bag chair, and untangling my tether from around the compass pedestal, I made my way to the hatch and called the boys up.

Checking aft again before I sat down, I couldn't see any

signs of a fish, just a colossal following wall of water. Miraculously, the crest never broke and cascaded into the dinghy where it hung from davits behind the transom.

"Really, Mom? Is there a fish on my line?" Gavin tugged on his gloves after emerging from the hatch, excitement animating his every move.

And there was a beautiful blue fish only five feet off the stern, still fighting to escape. Before I could register what was happening, Shakya swooped, there was a fish in the net and flying over the rail before landing with a heavy thud on the cockpit floor. It slapped, flipped, and jumped, flashing distressed silver while Shakya looked for a fish bat.

About fifteen pounds, the eyes were enormous and an iridescent blue, the clear gelatinous lids blinking in time with the gasping of its mouth as it slowly suffocated, the breathtaking blue iridescence disappearing into dull gray as it did.

Shakya knocked it unconscious with an oar. No sooner had it stopped flopping than Gavin started pulling in the second line. The fights between the bluefin tuna and the oar left the white cockpit splattered, like a can of red paint had fallen from the sky.

It was a lot of meat, and a welcome respite from our usual fare, but I told the boys that I didn't want to catch any more. They groaned, but after nonstop tuna three meals a day for a week, they got the point.

After the fish adventure, we lost sight of *Easy* again, but I fell into my berth in an exhausted torpor. In ten days, we had covered one-thousand-one-hundred and ten nautical miles.

"Hey, Deb, get up here," Shakya shouted down at me from the open hatch.

Cold rain hit my face, instantly waking me. The hatch slammed shut. Looking at my watch, the luminescent dial indicated one in the morning. The sea was rough, and loud. Pulling myself out of the lee cloth,* I grabbed the ladder and cracked the hatch open. More rain stung my face.

It was very dark, overcast and cold, the first quarter of the new moon stingy with her light. A red glow from the compass was all that illuminated Tosh and Shakya's fearful faces. Staring skyward, they ducked their heads to avoid a loose wire cable whipping around in the savage wind. It was flailing above the deck and lashing into the mainsail with ferocious cracks that sounded like thunder directly overhead.

"The running back stay broke," Tosh screamed toward me as he noticed the hatch open. "Hit the deck lights." The stays are cables that hold the masts in place. Unsupported in high winds and rough seas, the whole rig could come down.

The electric panel was at my elbow as I stood on the ladder, the switches labeled, deck lights in the top row. A quick sweep of my hand switched them all on, instantly illuminating the decks and sails as if on a stage.

Within thirty minutes, the boys had the broken ends captured and tied off. We were back on course, grateful for our traditional rig that allowed repairs with simple tools and line.

Speaking on the radio later that morning, Bob warned us of an approaching cold front and bad weather. By the afternoon, despite sunny blue skies, it was bone chilling cold with high winds and stinging spray.

Chapter 35

The Shakes, Knocked Out &
Jellyfish

"I learn from calm waters, as well as from stormy seas."

Pacific Ocean
July 7, 1992 (Day 12)

Okay. I was okay. I had completed my three-hour watch, a three-hour watch that felt like ten. It was midnight and I had three hours to sleep before I was back on deck again. Alex wasn't so good at keeping us on course during the night, so Tosh and I did the night watches. Almost two weeks, so far. Limited sleep was making me crazy. But not just limited sleep. The constant motion, noise and cold prevented even a moment of physical or mental repose.

Despite five years of preparation and reading sailing books, the reality of life at sea was vastly different than the romantic notion I had conjured up by reading *Cruising World Magazine.* Instead of relaxing in the cockpit with a gourmet meal and enjoying a spectacular sunset, I was hanging by my arms from overhead handholds, eating basic meals out of deep narrow bowls as fast as possible before they spilled, and glimpsing sunsets though sails and rigging while wedged uncomfortably between winches, seat backs and lines.

And tonight, the seas were particularly rough with screaming high winds and waves that battered the boat. Picture shaking a bottle with a cork floating inside. The cork was us. I was incredibly cold, everywhere. No chance of warming up, either. No heater, no hot shower, no dry warm bed.

Coming in off the helm, I tried to be quiet as I slipped off my harness, the big stainless carabiner (specialized shackle) clanged on the cabin sole before I could catch it. Struggling out of the foul weather gear, the Velcro fasteners on the neck and wrists rasped loudly. I stowed the boots in the aft locker and unsnapped the bib on the heavy overalls. After hanging the gear on the hook, I made my way past the sleeping crew to the head and a welcome pee break.

There is a red light in the head, making the porcelain toilet bowl look pink. I imagine for a moment that I am in a doll house with delicate feminine décor around me. Half a second and I am snapped back to reality as *Elixir* rolls with a wave and I am thrown against the bulkhead. Reaching for the handhold above the sink, I use one hand to undo my jeans and work my pants down, falling hard onto the cold toilet seat as another wave hits us. I brace my feet against the bulkhead and my hand against the sink, trying to relax enough to pee.

Done, I let go of the bulkhead to get some toilet paper. I try to do it fast, before another wave comes but don't quite make it. I have to let go of the paper and grab the bulkhead again. Okay, this time. Yup, paper in hand, a fast wipe and bam. Another wave. I drop the paper in the basket and once again brace my arm against the bulkhead. I stand quickly and turn to pump out the toilet bowl before another wave comes and sloshes the contents out. Whew. Quickly lowering the lid, I brace my feet well apart and work my pants back up with one hand. I wash in cold salt water, one hand at a time and decide it's too cold to wash my face. I'll stay dirty.

The cabin is icy, my breath visible as pinkish clouds until I reach up and click off the red light. Stretching up for the hand hold in the ceiling, I swing my way aft, falling into the berth with the next wave. Pulling the damp sleeping bag over me, I lay there, trying to calm my breathing, trying to relax, but my breath comes in and out, ragged and jerky. The lee cloths are tied with line up to the ceiling and separate the double berth that I share with Tosh. He was on deck now, Shakya on the helm. *He's so sick. Don't start thinking about that. Sleep.* Again, I try to calm focusing on my breath, in and out, in and out, slowly. *You are okay, everything is going to be okay.*

It was pitch black in the cabin now and full of motion. I couldn't see the storage hammocks swinging wildly, but the heavy foul weather jackets and overalls hanging off them whispered, rustling in the dark as they swung back and forth with every swell. Even above the cacophony of the elements in chaos outside, in the small respites from the rage of the wind, I could hear their zippers hit the cabin side from time to time. Alex, sleeping below the hammock, was snoring intermittently and that was barely noticeable above the ferocity playing on the other side of the cabin wall.

Elixir sliced and slammed through the rough seas, her wood hull creaking as she moved, alive and straining on her course. Then *bam. Crap. What was that?* I waited a few seconds and *Elixir* returned to her former rhythm. Every now and then a wave bigger than the others would smash into the hull with a loud crash. The larger wave and stronger force would shift the beat of the sea, setting my nerves even more on high alert. Like turbulence in an airplane, waiting for the wings to catch the security of steady air around them after hitting a downdraft.

Would this be the one? Would this wave be the one that knocks us down? That dismasts us? And then the previous motion would be restored. I took another breath, still feeling unnerved. I couldn't feel my toes because they were so cold. My body was tightly secured in the lee cloth, ensuring I didn't fall out onto the cabin wall, the lower side of the heel.

What was that other noise? A rhythmic humming that was getting very loud and high pitched? Generally noisy with the sound of the water whooshing past the hull and the winds tearing around the sails and over the rigging, my ears picked out a new noise, distinct above the rest.

It gave my mind something else to focus on. I ran through the troubleshooting list. *Where was it coming from?* Just to the left and behind my head, and below, yes also below. Well below. *As far back as the rudder?* Yes. *The propeller?* It was the propeller. I had never heard it so loud. We must be putting on some speed. Shakya had rigged the propeller to free wheel allowing it to go through the alternator and charge the batteries while under sail. *Well, our batteries would carry a full charge tomorrow by the sounds of things right now,* I thought to myself. *If I survive until tomorrow.* Back to the breathing, in and out, slowly. *Why did I ever agree to do this crossing? Don't go there, there is no going back. We must keep going forward until landfall.* Breathe. *Which may never happen.* Breathe. *And Tosh.* I was screaming inside. *Will he make it? He keeps throwing up. Nothing stays down. How long can he live like this? Breathe, Deb. Breathe. You have to go back out there in less than three hours.*

My body is suddenly shivering and shaking uncontrollably. *Relax, Deb. Relax. You will be okay.* But my body did not stop shaking. *Everything is shaking, the boat, the sea, the wind, my mind, my life.*

The stress of the last twelve days at sea was apparent. The body does not lie. But we did 161 nautical miles that day, one of our biggest.

July 8, 1992 (Day 13)

The following day, Tosh was on watch with Alex keeping him company. Gavin and Shakya sat on the settees in the salon. By now we all knew the words to his funny songs and were singing along, laughing uproariously.

> *"We had a chicken, no eggs would she lay,*
> *my wife said, 'honey, this isn't funny *...'"*

It was macaroni salad night on day thirteen of the crossing. The pasta was boiling in the pan, deep sided and screwed down tightly with restraints, the metal bars that wrapped around the outside of the pot to hold it on the stove. My body was also strapped snugly against the galley counter. On a starboard tack now, with the boat heeled over thirty-five degrees to the right, the twelve-inch porthole looked up at a pale sky, instead of down into the water. On the upside of the heel, it was a constant fight with gravity to keep my footing as I prepared the evening meal.

> *"One day a rooster came into our yard*
> *and caught that chicken right off her guard ..."*

Shakya sang on, verse after verse, sillier and sillier. "That smells good over there," he said in the middle of the song.

"Yeah, when's supper?" Gavin piped up.

"When it's done," I answered, feigning irritation. So much for training them not to bug me while I cooked. Mealtimes broke up the monotony of a long day cooped up in a small boat due to the cold, gray and wet weather at these northern latitudes. The boys sang for a while more and then went back to reading their fantasy books; Terry Brooks's *The Sword of Shannara* and Tolkien's *Lord of the Rings*.

I stuck my head out the hatch every once in a while, to check on Tosh. Badly compromised with seasickness, he was still keeping his watches and making sail changes.

Despite being another rocky day on the sea, morale was improving. Thank goodness for Shakya and his guitar. I had to admit that when he had come aboard in Hanalei Bay with his bags and guitar, I was annoyed. I mean, come on, five people with barely enough room for their gear, let alone a guitar. Not to mention it was valuable and would probably get bashed, wet, sat on, and moldy. But somehow it worked and after the initial three days of storms and intense seasickness, he played it every day. He sat on his bunk, sweatpants on now, a slight improvement over his usual tighty-whities. I was singing along with the words as I opened cans of beans, vegetables, and olives.

> *"... then came that rooster, into our yard, and caught that moo cow, right off of her guard..."*

Gavin and I joined in the chorus and laughed at the ridiculous words. I drained the cans into a sieve at the sink and dumped everything into a big stainless steel bowl that, like the pot, was clamped down on the stove with restraints. It was so bumpy that even with the wide strap tightened around my hips,

I still had to grab the overhead rails to keep my balance as I worked.

"We had an elephant, no tusks would she grow ..."

Shakya's tenor voice carried on the melody.

"Hey, wait a minute," Gavin shouted above the singing and noise from the stormy weather outside. "An elephant? Come on..."

Shakya laughed and sang simultaneously, undeterred, enjoying making up impossible new verses.

"... and the wife said, 'Honey, we're losing money...'"

That was all I heard. Abruptly airborne, I was thrown backward. The wave had flipped me out of the bum strap. My feet were flung up and over my head. Turned upside down, the ceiling of the cabin was a blur of white and mahogany across my vision, like a slow-motion scene in an action movie. Terrified, I realized I was being thrown like a stone from a sling shot across the cabin, straight into the wall, no longer restrained by the galley harness. There was no time to get my hands up to break my fall. There was a whoosh of air past my ears, just before my head smashed forcefully into the solid hardwood of the cabin. Everything went silent. And black.

Time disappeared. I don't know for how long. It could have been minutes, or it could have been hours. I gradually became aware of distant-sounding voices calling my name, over and over again. I could feel my legs and arms twisted painfully under me.

"Mom! Mom! Are you okay? *Mom, wake up!"*

Gavin's voice sounded far away as I came to on the starboard bunk, three sets of eyes hovering over me.

"Are you okay? Deb, say something. Oh, my God. Say something." Shakya slapped my cheeks.

"I'm fine. Don't worry. I'm okay." I struggled to sit up. My head hurt. So did the rest of me. "What happened? How long was I out?"

"You hit your head pretty hard." Shakya tried to sound calm, matter of fact, but his voice quavered with worry. "You've been out for a few minutes. Felt like forever."

"Mom, you should have heard it," Gavin interrupted with excitement. "It was the loudest smack I ever heard. Are you sure you aren't bleeding? It sounded like your head cracked open," he continued.

Shakya was checking my head, "Just a little cut, hardly any bleeding ..." He hesitated. "But you are growing a sizable bump already."

"I'm just fine. Just *fine*," I announced firmly. I forced myself to jump up off the bunk, pulling myself back over to the galley. *Shit,* I thought as I clipped myself back into the bum strap. *That was bad. What would happen if I really got injured?* With Tosh being seasick, I couldn't afford to have an injury or a concussion. Besides, there was no ambulance to call and who would do the radio, the navigation?

But my head was whacked, and I felt dizzy. *Don't let it show.* Intuitively, I knew under the joviality of the silly songs, we were all on edge and if anyone of us was injured, our thin veneer of normalcy would crack, morale would plummet, fear would take over. There could be no room for that. *Keep it together. You got this. You're* okay. *Nothing's broken.*

I checked the pasta; thankful the pot was still on the stove and the hot water hadn't dumped or scalded me or anyone else. *What a trip. We were two thousand miles from shore. Even the simplest things could be lethal at sea. Just one wave, one bump ... catastrophe.*

"Are you sure you are okay?" Shakya studied me closely, obviously concerned.

"Where is that rooster?" I asked. "I forget. What was I doing? Who am I? What's my name?" I joked and started to sing again, Shakya and Gavin joining in.

"Then came that rooster, into our yard..."

July 9, 1992 (Day 14)

"Where's *Easy*?" Shakya asked the next morning as he emerged from the companionway. We'd been motor sailing during the night with exceptionally light winds and almost flat seas. He scanned the cloudy skies to the horizon without success.

"Yeah, we have an ocean current of 0.6 knots moving south-southeast that swept us off course during the night," I replied from behind the wheel. "The current, plus *Easy* is a faster boat than us, left us behind." I laughed, trying to hide my discouragement.

"I noticed they get ahead of us quite a bit," Shakya observed.

"She has a lighter Marconi sail plan and can sail closer into the wind than our heavier schooner rig. Bob and I radioed this morning. Once we catch up, we'll stay in formation with them by keeping the sails up with the engine."

A few hours later, we noticed iridescent purple air bladders floating on the surface of the water, like large, exotically shaped soap bubbles. Their shimmering brilliance sparkled for as far as the eye could see.

"What do you think, Gavin?" I asked, passing binoculars his way.

"Jellyfish," he responded before he even looked through them.

"But so many of them, how can there be so many?" Shakya, from land-locked Arkansas, was shaking his head. "Shall we get a bucket and pull some up here for a closer look?"

"Ahh, I wouldn't do that if I were you," Gavin said while chuckling.

"Why not, Professor?" Shakya asked.

"I think they are Portuguese man-o-wars. Their tentacles hang down more than six feet. And they have a nasty sting," Gavin explained as he continued to scan the water through the binoculars.

It took us three days and nights to sail through this three-hundred-mile gathering of hydrozoa. Even though their shimmering colors were so beautiful, I couldn't stop myself from imagining a painful demise if I fell overboard and died, tangled up in thousands of their venomous tentacles. I only felt relief from these tortuous visions when I saw clear ocean water ahead.

On Saturday, July 11th, Day 16, three days after being knocked out, I had no further repercussions other than a lump on my head. We were finally able to turn east onto our final course to Cape Flattery. The busy shipping lanes were obvious, the horizon dotted with many ships of all sizes, colors, and shapes. Occasionally, we could identify them, their cargo, port of origin and destination. And sometimes, we even enjoyed radio contact. A Norwegian ship going to New Westminster, BC., had seen us and initiated a conversation on channel 75. I felt like a real mariner as we exchanged information about our ship, route, and weather adventures with a professional sailor on board such a behemoth of a ship.

"Deb, get up here," Shakya yelled down the hatch that afternoon. He was holding the binoculars out to me as I emerged and clipped my harness up.

"Holy crap, we're on a collision course with those two," I confirmed Shakya's alarm. "Their chances of spotting us are slim to none, those freighters are on autopilot with limited crew. Not to mention that a course change takes five miles to engage on those huge ships. Fall off course for now. Let me alert *Easy*."

I disappeared back down the hatch. Bob had reported that Mary Kay was not feeling well, her heart disease was acting up, and he was below decks with her most of the time. They were using their auto pilot, and we had agreed to keep watch for them.

"*Easy*, this is *Elixir*, come in. Over," I called over the radio.

"*Elixir*, this is *Easy*, over," Bob replied to my relief.

"There are two freighters at ten o'clock. Looks like a collision course. Suggest falling off to port until they are clear. Over," I relayed.

"Agreed. Will get up there right away. And thanks. *Easy* over," Bob acknowledged.

"How does she look?" I asked Shakya as he peered ahead through the binoculars at *Easy*.

"She's altered course. Do you think it's enough?" he asked.

"Will have to be. It's all we can do for now with the wind and the seas today. Fall off as much as you can without jibing," I suggested as I felt *Elixir* slow, then heard the sails start to luff as the wind fell out of them, the Dacron slack.

An hour later, both freighters crossed three hundred feet in front of our bow, their solid red broadsides looming twenty stories above us. It was a huge relief when they were past, and we could resume our course northward. And sobering to realize that even continuously announcing our presence and position on the radio, neither ship acknowledged our minuscule presence.

"In case we wondered why we keep watch," Shakya said aloud as we jounced through the choppy water of the ship's wake. "They wouldn't have noticed if they ran over us. We wouldn't even make a scratch on that huge hull." It was a while before the echoes of our bosun's sober words died away in our heads.

With ten-foot swells and light winds, our engine made certain we kept up with *Easy* into the next day. It was reassuring to keep close to our buddy boat, but it necessitated a careful eye on our fuel gages. There were eighty-three gallons of diesel left now and six-hundred-seventy-eight miles to go, too far to use the engine all the way.

Except for our concern over a seasick skipper, everyone was in good spirits, still singing songs and reading fantasy classics. Even the sun was optimistically trying to shine through the clouds, and dolphins frolicked everywhere around us. Two orcas appeared close by, probably following the pod of dolphins. As we slowly made our way across the endless Pacific Ocean, it amazed me how small the world can feel when, at the same time, it feels so immense.

"What's that noise?" Alex asked Tosh the next evening.

The engine was off but there was a rhythmic thumping from below. With every bump the hull shuddered, and our hearts collectively beat a little faster. *What now?*

"Sounds like the drive shaft," Tosh answered weakly from his bunk.

We'd been letting the propeller and drive shaft freewheel in order to keep a charge on our batteries.

"Yeah, I think we better tie it off from the alternator before it gets damaged," Shakya, the engineer, advised. "At this point, I think our batteries will be okay."

By noon on Thursday (*Day 21*), the gusty weather took its toll with our auto helm, and we broke another belt and the roll pin on Oscar. Shakya repaired it yet again, but we needed to continue steering by hand as there was too much stress on the rudder.

"Yeah, we broke another belt on our auto helm. That was our last one. Over." I was on my radio call with *Easy*. As usual, we each shared our mechanical challenges after ensuring all crew was safe and healthy on both ships.

"No worries, I have a couple over here. I can pass you one. Are you up for that? Over." Bob asked. This was a very tricky, and even dangerous, maneuver at sea. It would be difficult to get close enough to pass the belt over the water, and not bash into each other as both boats rolled with the substantial open ocean swells.

"Sure, let's give it a go. And thanks. See you in a bit. Over."

With the engine on, *Easy* was able to come in close despite the windy conditions. Bob passed us another belt by tying it to a line and tossing it across the water. The line fell short and disappeared into the sea. I could see Bob pulling the line back in, hand over hand. Both ships were bobbing haphazardly on the swells, the stability of forward momentum and the pressure of wind in the sails, absent for this maneuver. When *Easy* was in the trough of the swell, we could just see her mast, and she was only twenty feet away.

Again, Bob got his boat lined up on the top of the swell and quickly threw the line. It made it to us but was too far aft and again disappeared into the water. *This is nuts*, I thought. *Like playing ring toss at the fair during an earthquake.* But miraculously Shakya caught it on the third try. Before he let go of the line, I attached a waterproof bag of coveted Crystal Light, a powdered drink mix that makes drinking water from boat storage tanks more palatable.

I joked on the radio with *Easy* a few hours later. "Thanks so much, Bob. Shakya installed the belt and new pin. We'll see how long it holds up. Hey, I didn't realize what a big white beard you had. Over."

"Yeah, we've been talking on the radio all these weeks and had no idea what each other looked like. Your crew has some beards going on, too, but not as white as mine. Hey, thanks for the Crystal Light, we were all out of it. By the way, how's your skipper doing tonight? Over."

"The rougher sea conditions have made him feel worse. We're all praying he can hang on until landfall. Over." His question stabbed at the swelling balloon of anxiety lodged in my gut. If he didn't hang in there? An emergency radio call to the Coast Guard? If they could hear us. An emergency medivac? If they could find us ...

There was only two-hundred-forty miles left to go, maybe two days until landfall. Despite the amazing sunny skies, the ocean was ferocious. Below decks was in chaos from all the banging around in the immense twelve-foot swells. But that night we were able to keep our bow into the wind without the engine.

We had made it so far and I consoled myself with the surety that conditions couldn't possibly be any more formidable. However, the Pacific Ocean was not yet done with this tiny ship and her neophyte crew.

Chapter 36

Man Overboard & Land Ho

"The sea can be terrifying, especially the wind, rain, and storms that romantic stories fail to mention."

Pacific Ocean
July 18, 1992 (Day 23)

The next day dawned cold with the air full of sea spray. The light was flat white, and the wind screamed through the rigging. The sail on the foremast was triple reefed, and the gaff was lashed to the mast to make a small heavy weather foresail, barely enough to keep *Elixir* steady on her course even with the engine on full throttle. I was finishing my watch, the hatch opened a crack and Gavin handed me my breakfast, a small pile of hot porridge with tetra-pack milk in the bottom third of a deep plastic bowl.

I uncramped myself from behind the wheel where I was

wedged in a bean bag chair and crawled to the hatch. As I attempted to take my first spoonful of welcome warmth, a wave broke from above the cockpit and dumped a bathtub of icy sea water over my head. When *Elixir* righted herself and the cockpit drained, I calmly dumped the sea water out of my porridge bowl and continued to eat. I was tired. Beyond tired. My body completely overdosed on adrenaline, there was no more room for fear. I was maxed out, just getting through my watch, day after day. I didn't spend any more time on the stress of my situation. It was far more satisfying and exhilarating to focus on the part of my being that was watching the scene from outside myself.

The day was a fun day for the elements. The sun broke through the low ceiling and the tops of the waves were frothing, wind-whipped horizontally across the swells. The dolphins played, jumping out of waves nearly forty feet above me, re-entering the wave just above my head and coming out of the wave again just below *Elixir*'s bottom rail. Everything sparkled from the early sun's rays, the sea-foam laden air filled with rainbows. It was a glorious, alive and vastly exuberant morning.

I was struck with how ill-equipped *Elixir* and we as human beings were to be out in such strong roughhousing. It was far beyond the tolerance of such frail beings to survive, and I had dissociated from my petrified physical body. There was absolutely no doubt that only grace separated us from annihilation. While there was no malice in the gale that morning, its powerful playfulness was both awesome and terrifying.

I finished the cold salty porridge, warming up a little as the sun got higher in the sky. Gavin was next on watch. He crawled out of the hatch, fully covered in his yellow gear with the maroon harness already clipped onto the boat. He reached for my empty bowl and passed it down below. I held onto my adult sippy cup with its warm Postum. The lid kept the salt water out.

"Time for bed, Mom," he yelled across the three feet separating us.

"Sure thing," I yelled back as I slowly unwrapped myself from behind the wheel again. "Check out the rainbows." I nodded toward the sunrise, the gale blowing spray, hissing above us.

"Holy crap," Alex emerged from below, astounded at the seascape. I could tell he would love to take a video, but the camera would be destroyed. It was too rough and wet.

Leaving Tosh laying on the settee and Gavin at the helm, I made my way down the companionway, only unclasping my harness after I was well down the ladder. Alex was already back below. I slid the hatch closed over my head, trying in vain to keep the sea from finding its way inside and onto my bed.

Everything was wet. So, so wet, that sticky, scratchy kind of wet like you get at the beach after swimming in the ocean. I managed to get my gear off, my fingers stiff with cold. It was much warmer in the cabin. After a wash up I fell into my berth and zipped up the damp sleeping bag, the noises at sea a familiar ambiance. I was miraculously able to sleep after three hours outside in a gale.

I awoke suddenly. *Elixir* was laying completely on her side. *Oh, no,* I thought, my mind instantly on high alert. I waited for the ship to return to its original heel, but *oh my gosh, is this it? Is this a knock down?*

I waited and, not only did the boat stay down on her side, she keeled over even more. My stomach panicked and my brain flooded with familiar tape loops. *Okay, this really is it. Are we going down now? Deb, are you ready to die now, to transition to the next place?* And then just as suddenly, it was over, and the familiar motion of the sea was re-established. The exhaustion and familiarity of extreme adrenaline rushes could no longer keep me awake.

I awoke several hours later to the sounds of the guys talking. The sun was higher, and its beams danced through the ports filling the crowded cabin with warm light.

"Good morning," Shakya greeted me from his settee as I sat up and pulled myself out of the bunk. "You'll be happy to know the wind has died down, and the seas are more humane today."

"Thank God. It was insane this morning, absolutely insane." I thought about it for a moment, remembering my dawn watch "But, holy smokes, it was crazy beautiful, too. Did you see it? Did you go out in it?"

"Oh, yeah," he drawled in his Arkansas way.

The hatch was open. Fresh air poured into the cabin. I could see Alex outside on the helm, Gavin sprawled on the settee immersed in Tolkien. Tosh, laying limply on the other, appeared to be sleeping.

"How's the course?" I asked, my constant question especially with Alex on the helm. The most important question. The question that kept my mind on the task at hand instead of all the other voices that kept arguing in the back of my head.

"070," Alex responded as he quickly adjusted the wheel.

Ducking back below, I sat at the chart table, got my readings from the sat nav, 48°28' North, 128°32' West, and plotted our morning position on the chart.

"Hey guys, only a hundred-and-thirty-five nautical miles to go," I cheered. "Only twenty-four more hours, we should make landfall tomorrow."

"Really? You think tomorrow is the day?" Shakya asked, teasing.

"Well, tomorrow will tell the tale," Alex chimed in good naturedly, his dry sense of humor his way of fighting off adrenaline overload and physical exhaustion.

"Well, how was the morning?" I asked, sticking my head out the hatch. "I see the weather decided to mellow out."

"Oh, it was a pretty exciting morning," Gavin piped up from behind his book. "Tosh got washed overboard."

"*What?*" I yelled. *Holy shit.*

"Hey ... we agreed ... we weren't going ... to tell her," Tosh protested in a thin voice from where he reclined on the other settee.

"*Oh my gosh!* You weren't going to tell me?" I said, my body shaking violently.

"We had a rogue wave this morning, and we got knocked down," Gavin continued undeterred in his matter of fact, bare bones way.

Silence.

"*And?*" I prompted. *What was with these guys? Holy shit.*

"I pulled him back up," Gavin finished, as if that was the end of it.

"Okay, you guys, start from the beginning," I demanded.

"Well, we weren't going to tell you, because Tosh said you would get upset."

"Duh, pretty much," I said sarcastically, my anger setting in after my initial freak out.

"There ... was ... a rogue ... wave," Tosh clarified quietly, his speech slow and strange from weakness and his tongue sticking to his teeth because his mouth was so dry from weeks of vomiting.

"Yeah, this huge wave just knocked us over flat on our side, the spreaders were in the water, Mom." Gavin sounded excited, like this was just the coolest thing ever. "And all this water filled the cockpit and just washed him out."

"I was hanging ... by my harness ... and dangling ... over the rail," Tosh continued.

"Well, how did you get back in? Didn't you get soaked?"

"I think ... it was a double ... wave," Tosh persisted despite his weakness. "My feet ... were dangling ... ten feet ... above the water ... It was weird ... And then another wave ... came and picked me up ... and washed me ... back in the boat."

"I tried to pull him back into the boat, Mom, but he was too heavy. It was a good thing that wave came and just picked him up and threw him back in here."

"Yeah ... the sea ... spit me back out ... didn't want ... any seasick guys," he said, trying to make a joke to ease my distress and the tension of almost losing him.

"Why aren't you soaked through?"

"Funny thing ... is ... except ... around my face and ... a little around ... my neck ... this gear ... is waterproof ... Seriously ... Kinda unbelievable ... but true."

"So, the drawstring at the top of the high rubber boots actually kept the water out of your boots, too?"

"Uh ... huh."

"Wow," I shrugged on my harness over my sweater and climbed out of the companionway. I sat beside him where he rested on the settee and laid my head on his chest. With all his sea sickness and now almost overboard, I couldn't bear to think about it. I focused on breathing, with his jacket rough against my cheek and his hand resting weakly on my back.

"I'm ... okay ... it's ... okay," he whispered.

Later that day, my hand trembled as I held the straw upright in the juice box, pressing it to his mouth. Tosh weakly pushed my hand back, turning his head away from me. I was perched precariously on the edge of our berth, reaching over the lee cloths that held him where he'd been sleeping all day.

"Tosh, please," I pleaded. "You must drink something."

My heart raced. He'd been unresponsive most of the time, despite attempts to give him a cup of fluid every half hour. Tears ran down my cheeks, warm against the chilly north Pacific air of the cabin. Helpless and ready to give up, I felt exhausted. Panic just waited to take over, hysterics close behind and pressing at the edges of my control.

After three weeks at sea with constant sea sickness, Tosh, who had been in and out of delirium over the last week, was now completely disoriented, the signs of dehydration evident in his hollow cheekbones, obvious even under the thick, silver beard; his eyes sunken into purple depressions below his dark lashes. I struggled inside to get strong, one more time. I had to.

"Tosh," I said, louder, pulling on my anger to help me, finding my frustration and resentment at being in such a predicament, blaming him.

"You wanted to do this, you'll finish it. You don't get to skip out now," I hissed through clenched teeth, forcing his head toward me, and then pressing the straw between his cracked lips one more time.

Alex was on watch after supper. With Tosh incapacitated, the watch schedule had to change. Everyone was so exhausted, we also shortened the watches to every two hours. I sat at the nav station, charting in preparation for the nightly call with Bob aboard *Easy*. *Yes, after charting our position, it looked like we would make landfall tomorrow.*

But there was another call I could make first despite feeling completely wiped out. All I wanted to do was have a hot bath and sleep for a hundred years. After not talking to anyone except Bob aboard *Easy* for nearly a month, I wanted to call my parents to reassure them that we had survived. The only way to do that was through the VHS channel 70, a public radio where everyone could listen to the exchange. After turning on the radio, I pulled the microphone to my mouth and contacted the marine operator.

"Yes, can you please make a collect call to area code 604-352-6384 to Ron Monty?"

"Your name, please?"

"Debbie."

Through the static of the radio, I could hear the extraordinarily ordinary sound of a phone ringing.

"Hello?" Dad's voice, though sounding far away, was very clear.

"Will you accept a collect call from Debbie?"

"Yes," I can hear the excitement in his voice as he realizes it's me.

"You may go ahead, ma'am," the operator prompted.

"Hi, Dad," I said, suppressing my excitement for etiquette on public radio.

"Oh, thank God. Doreen," he called to Mom, "it's Debbie. Where are you, dear?"

"Just off the Straights of Juan de Fuca. We should make landfall tomorrow."

"Oh, that's good, dear." His response was as if I had just gone for a holiday, or a walk in the local park. I had risked my life for the last month, and I could tell from his voice that he had no idea of the extremes we had been through. In a flash of insight, I knew it would be impossible to portray to him or anyone else who hadn't done it, what it is like to be at sea for twenty-three days. I realized in that moment, hearing the sameness of my father's response, how irretrievably altered I felt deep inside, and to my very core.

July 19, 1992 (Day 24)

"Good morning, *Elixir*, this is *Easy*. Over." It was 0830 hours and the radio crackled to life for the scheduled morning call, our last one.

"*Elixir* here, good morning, you two. Over," I answered easily now after nearly a month at sea.

"Happy birthday to you, happy birthday to you, happy birthday, dear Gavin, happy birthday to you. Over." Bob and Mary Kay both sang over VHF channel 75, the whole world could hear it was Gavin's birthday. I handed him the microphone.

"Hey, thanks, you guys. Over."

"How old are you, kiddo? Over."

"Fifteen. Over."

"Your birthday *and* landfall today. Wow, what a great day. Over."

"Yeah, and when I went to make breakfast this morning, Alex had left a chocolate bar in the porridge pot last night. I thought all the chocolate was gone weeks ago. Over."

"Are you going to share it? Shall we stop by for a piece? Over."

"Sorry, it's all gone already. And I tried to share it, but they made me eat it all by myself. It wasn't a very big one. Here's Mom again." Gavin handed the microphone back to me.

"Yeah, pretty special. What does the weather fax say today? Over."

And Bob filled me in. After the rough weather of the last

few days, we had wind out of the southeast at five miles per hour and seas of one to two feet with overcast skies, a welcome respite after gale conditions. Tosh was only slightly better this morning with a bad headache and nausea. Despite this, he ate a little porridge and wasn't vomiting so far. I took advantage of calmer conditions and made a chocolate birthday cake. It warmed the cabin up and got us all salivating; the caramel-chocolate aroma assaulting our noses. When it was done, I presented it to Gavin.

"Happy fifteenth birthday, Gavinooski," I said with a wide smile, expressing the maternal joy I felt about the normalcy of baking a cake and my son turning fifteen, at the same time as relieved exhilaration about the momentous occasion of approaching landfall.

"Mom, what happened to the cake?" He was looking at it with a frown.

"Gimbaled stove or not, we were on a heel while it was baking. I'm pretty sure it'll taste the same." I laughed acknowledging the crooked cake. "You won't ever forget this birthday."

It was a slow day filled with underlying excitement. The binoculars were in constant use, each of us wanting to be the first to actually see land. What would land look like after so long of only seeing the sea? And what would it feel like after all we had been through?

Looking back at that night of the first gale just a few days out of Hanalei Bay, I remembered the angels on the rail, as I refer to my perception of them. They had succeeded in helping my mind get out of a tailspin of panic, and they'd nudged me into being a bystander able to observe the storm from another perspective, that of the elements playing. While no less uncomfortable, I was more surrendered to Nature's extremes now.

Experiencing the immense power of the sea and wind, alongside my own and our boat's fragility, exposed me to the miracle of my life on this earth. I knew beyond any shadow of a doubt that my continued existence the night of that first gale and throughout the crossing was the result of fate, or chance, or luck. In those three hours of that predawn watch, I sailed through a rite of passage with the sea, in particular, and with my life, in general. I came to know how insignificant a life can be in the larger scheme of things. At the same time, I also came to know a sense of my own unique place, a place in this life that is lined and cushioned with a Presence and Intention far greater than myself or my own narrow understanding of Existence.

———————

With the calm sea conditions of the day, it was pleasant motor-sailing. My body, accustomed to the exterior motion of the boat and the interior fluctuations in adrenaline as the weather changed, felt relaxed inside, natural. Was I worn down and seasoned to fear now? Would I need such intimacy with anxiety in my new life? What would this new life hold? A house on land? Away from the sea? Or would we keep living aboard for a while, in our beautifully finished nautical abode? Would the sea be different here in the north? Would I miss my tropical island?

My mind wandered, not to the past and the Ranch, not to if we would be able to finish *Elixir*, not to wondering if we would make it across an ocean. Instead, I felt intensely aware of sailing through a paradigm-changing portal into the next chapter of my life. I was wondering what that new life would hold.

"Hey! Dolphins!" Gavin yelled from the bow where he was reading, curled up against the windlass and the bulwark. Dropping his book, he quickly lowered himself over the rail into the dolphin net below the bowsprit. From here he could reach into the water and touch them as they surfed in the bow wave ahead of *Elixir*.

"Maybe we're close," I suggested. "It's fitting, since we had dolphins leaving Nawiliwili and Hanalei and in the middle of the Pacific and now here they are at the end ..." My voice trailed off as I noticed Shakya straightening up, more alert as he looked through the binoculars.

"Is that land?" He pointed toward the horizon where it was all hazy, but the haze appeared darker than in other areas.

"Let me see." Even Tosh was excited and reached over for the binoculars. "Hmm, I don't know ..."

And so it went until early afternoon. I had given up trying to see anything on that obscure horizon. *Oh, my gosh!* "Hey, guys, look ..."

In the distance, a dark and jagged silhouette slowly materialized out of the haze, solid and real. But for the low purr of the engine and the soft swish of the light air in the sails, it was quiet. No one spoke. It really was the headlands of Cape Flattery. There was an end to this voyage, this crossing, this epic journey.

Tosh, sitting next to me, patted the bench beside him. I scooted closer until my back was pressed tightly against him. His arms circled around me, holding me close, despite his headache and nausea.

"Do you believe it, Tosh? There's land there? Actually North America?" I asked quietly, snuggling closer, relaxing more. *The navigation really did work. We really did find our way across the Pacific.*

"Oh, yeah, I believe it." He chuckled. "It has been quite a

journey, sweetheart." His arms rested lightly on my shoulders. Reassuring. Even through the high overcast, the warmth from the sun penetrated my damp sweater, saturated with salt from weeks at sea. The wind was light, it too was warm and drying on my skin, carrying scents of earth, of trees, of the fishy mud of extensive tidal flats of the Pacific Northwest.

"How are you feeling?" My continual question during the last twenty-three days, it was the last time I would ask it.

"I'm good." His usual answer. Feebly squeezing my shoulders, he smiled a spent smile as he added, "Well, maybe just a little weak."

Alex, Shakya and Gavin were taking down the sails, tying them up, and getting the fenders out of the lazarette. When they had been stowed while leaving our slip in Nawiliwili Harbor, I had wondered if, when, and where would we get them out again.

Slowly motoring closer now, the headlands loomed larger, more and more solid though still shrouded in thin mist, spray from the massive Pacific swells crashing against the cliffs of the cape. After seeing no land for twenty-three days, it was like an apparition appearing ahead of us, not just a landmark, but another milestone hovering in the distance.

Another milestone just like waking up in Kauai with an old boat filled with cockroaches, to *Elixir* rebuilt and moving across the boatyard, just like suddenly rushing down the boat launch ramp and being afloat without leaks, just like raising anchor and finding ourselves on an ocean crossing. And, too, just like leaving the farm and arriving on the Ranch, just like Celebrations with a master, or Ranch leaders leaving in the night, just like losing a son and finding him again, just like all of those preceding milestones, we had arrived on the other side.

There is another shore. We can navigate across unknown waters and unchartered territories within ourselves, with skills we don't know we possess, with guidance we don't see or hear or believe in. Meditations, regressions, spiritual retreats, spinning globes and finding masters, following heart songs to angels on rails and in *Easy*'s radio messages, pulling more of my soul into the material world and more of the material world into my soul, guidance no longer separate from my material existence, but real and part of my very life.

Epilogue

"My journey isn't done because you can't see my ship any longer. I've simply turned in a new direction."

Cape Flattery, Washington
July 19, 1992

"Wow, we are getting close. Let's drop sail one last time, crew." Somehow Tosh was reviving himself. The sails came down. We headed for shore at five knots with the engine full throttle.

The harbor was in Neah Bay on the Makah Reservation on the Olympic Peninsula, approximately one hundred and sixty miles northwest of Seattle, Washington. As we drew closer, trees and buildings slowly materialized until we eventually reached the dock, our lines fully prepared to disembark. There were a few people standing there, watching with curiosity, our big old schooner with gear well lashed down, and a grizzled crew in layers of sodden clothes, beards filled out and disheveled hair. Yes, it was obvious we'd been out for a bit.

"Toss me your line," a dark-haired, mackinaw-jacketed man directed. We could hear his voice clearly across the ten feet that separated us from the dock. Despite the engine noise, it was quiet without the wind and the sea.

I threw him the line, the memory of how to toss it so it landed without tangling coming back to me after a month. He caught it with ease and gently guided *Elixir* alongside the wooden dock. Shakya and Gavin hopped ashore with the other two mooring lines while I arranged the puffy, white fenders over the rails. *Well, here we are— another dock, another continent, another life. Not a final voyage after all.*

"Where did you sail from?" Mackinaw man asked, soft spoken and curious as he helped us get the mooring lines adjusted and secure.

"Kauai."

"How long were you out?" he continued, a few of his buddies also standing alongside, listening.

"Twenty-three days."

"Not bad," he commented, obviously knowledgeable of ocean crossings and familiar with being the initial landfall. "Any gales?"

"A couple," Tosh answered, low key. "Oh, hi, Bob."

Bob, the skipper from our buddy boat, had walked down the dock from where *Easy* had tied up ahead of us.

"Welcome ashore, Skipper." Bob took Tosh's hand and shook it. "We meet on land at last. How are you holding up?"

"Ah, been better," Tosh replied, "but also been worse. Where's the Harbor Master here? Do you know?"

After collecting their wallets, the two tired skippers walked unsteadily together down the dock to the Harbor Master's

Office to arrange for a slip for a few nights. They returned within ten minutes with permission to stay where we were.

I readied the spring lines to finish mooring *Elixir* before stepping onto the dock. It felt too hard, a shock to my feet and legs after the soft moving decks I'd walked upon for the last month. And even on the dock I felt like I was still moving, the motion of the sea alive in my inner ear, making me walk as if I was drunk. We laughed at each other, watching how funny we looked trying to step normally. Not possible.

"We're going into town," Shakya announced, dwarfing Alex as he stood beside him. "We're going for some real food," Shakya continued. "We'll find a McDonald's or something, get a burger."

"And a smoke," Alex chimed in.

Wow, Alex had gone a whole twenty-three days without a cigarette, and now he was going to smoke again?

"Okay, see you in a bit," I said.

We found a motel within walking distance and booked rooms for everyone, including Bob and Mary Kay. My small backpack with toiletries and I headed straight for the shower. I don't know how long I stood in there, but I do recall that it took five separate applications of shampoo before my hair sudsed at all. What a luxury to feel my hair squeak again. The only clean outfit I owned was raw silk, for special occasions. I guess this qualified. As the air was chilly in Neah Bay, I pulled my filthy wool sweater on over it.

After going out to dinner together, we gathered back at our room and the crooked birthday cake was set alight with fifteen party candles. Happy birthday turned into happy landfall, and he's a jolly good fellow, and then Shakya broke into his funny songs one last time: *We Had Some Chickens* and *Keeper of the Eddie Stone Light*. Bob and Mary Kay had heard about these songs during our radio conversations, and they enjoyed a live performance that night. We all laughed until our sides ached.

"What are your plans now, Bob? Mary Kay?" Shakya asked.

"We'll be putting *Easy* up for sale," Mary Kay said. "Hard to do after living aboard her for fifteen years. But it's time. We're kinda getting on in years now. I've recovered from my heart surgery, but I'm not quite the same."

"Ah, but the adventure isn't over yet, Mary Kay," Bob chimed in, feeling the melancholy start to creep in. "We're going to buy a motorhome, a land yacht, and drive across the country. I don't think we are quite ready to stay put just yet, right, honey?" He reached for her hand and patted it reassuringly.

They were sweet, both with heads of thick white hair, their blue eyes sparkling out of their deeply tanned faces, bundled up in heavy wool sweaters, unused to the chill and damp of the northwest.

"What about you boys?" Mary Kay asked.

"We're heading into Seattle and to the airport in the morning," Alex answered. "I've just booked a flight back to South America in the afternoon."

"And I'm flying back to Kauai tomorrow night," Shakya said. "Anuprada is pretty eager to see me again."

"Did you talk with her this afternoon when you guys went to town?" I asked. "How is she?"

"She's okay, but she was pretty worried about me. We didn't get to call her as often as she would have liked."

"That would have been every day, all day," Gavin piped up.

"Well, tell her a huge thank you for sharing you with us. I know she didn't want you to come on the trip. Words can't convey how much we appreciated having you aboard. I don't know what we would have done without you," I told him, my throat constricting before I could say more.

"And say hi to Kauai and all the crew back there for us. You can tell them all the grisly details," Tosh joked.

"And you three?" Mary Kay asked pointedly.

"Well, we are meeting my mom and my sister and her family," I began, "including Gavin's three cousins, in Port Angeles in a few days. They will crew with us up through the San Juan Islands to Point Roberts."

"We'll leave the boat there for a month while we take a holiday back up to the Kootenays and rest up from this adventure before coming back down to the coast. We'll motor *Elixir* up into Canada and through the Gulf Islands when we get back. We're thinking of building a dental practice on Saltspring Island," Tosh continued.

"Is there a high school there?" Gavin asked.

"Oh, yes," Tosh answered. "Are you going?"

"Well, yeah," he answered. "It's mandatory, right?"

"Pretty much, kiddo, and just think, you won't be the only houle kid anymore."

As Bob and Mary Kay headed for the door, last farewells were made with Shakya and Alex. The rest of us would buddy boat over to Port Angeles in a few days before we finally parted ways.

The next day was another gloomy foggy one in Neah Bay but we went back to the boat, refreshed after a night's sleep ashore and hot showers.

We found the dock wheelbarrows and wheeled them down to where the boats were still happily resting in their slips after the long and arduous crossing.

"Hey, look at *Elixir*'s topsides," Gavin shouted.

"Holy smokes." I laughed. "It was a rough crossing."

"Being on a starboard tack most of the time, her topside paint is all peeling off on one side," Tosh explained.

"She looks pretty sad," I said, ever mindful of upkeep for the paint and varnish.

"Yup, but then so do we," Tosh said, jokingly referring to the fact that we were all about ten pounds lighter than when we left Kauai. Tosh had shaved off his beard, and his gaunt appearance was even more pronounced. He was as skinny as he was when he came home from India after having dengue fever more than ten years earlier.

Climbing back aboard after our night off was bittersweet. Good to be 'home' but all the tidying up and repairs stared us in the face. We were exhausted just thinking about it. First things first, we loaded up bedding, foulies, and all the clothes in the three big wheelbarrows and headed for the laundromat. It took us all day and six machines at once, but we got things washed and dried out, finally.

⸻

Straights of Juan de Fuca, Washington
July 21, 1992

"*Brahhh. Brahhh.*" The endless blaring of the foghorn was starting to get on my nerves. I could barely make out the bow of the boat, let alone where we were going. It was indescribably eerie.

Tosh was on the helm, the engine on the lowest setting. Gavin was on the fore deck, scanning ahead and below. There were just the three of us aboard now, an empty feeling after living with five for the previous month.

"Hey, Tosh, can I put out my lines? This is perfect salmon fishing here," Gavin declared, enthusiastically making his way aft to get his gear out of the locker.

We departed Neah Bay early, after two full days of getting *Elixir* tidied up. Yesterday had been productive, getting our supplies restocked and our ice box filled with fresh vegetables. Bob and Mary Kay, who left about the same time, were just ahead of us. We could not see them, not at all, but we heard the soft purr of their engine somewhere nearby in the thick fog.

And so began the next chapter of my life and a new adventure into another unknown. This time without resistance to someone else's plans and dreams, even my natural reticence quelled, absent. The reserve and apprehension of the seeker of my younger days had been replaced by quiet openness and confidence.

I had developed new abilities to trust in my inner navigation system, my own connection to the Divine, and my own capacity to chart and steer a new course through whatever waters I would find myself in next.

Rajneesh Backstory
POSTSCRIPT

The time of the *Elixir* Project was a time of spiritual digestion. I had much to assimilate after the adventures of the nine years before I arrived on Kauai.

I remember sitting on the deck, varnishing rail caps and cabin sides, the balmy trade winds caressing me while I pondered what my life was supposed to be about. I had given everything to be part of a spiritual commune and dedicated my life to achieving enlightenment, and yet I was in a boatyard in Hawaii. What was so spiritual about that? Amazing as it sounds, it was during these years and doing repetitive mindless labor that I could sense changes in myself, my being integrating all that had transpired, especially what had happened with Bhagwan.

He had betrayed us, His disciples, and me personally as one of them. I knew that to be a fact. Working in Sheela's house and being privy to her nightly visits with the Master and all that went on before and after these duty calls, destroyed my propensity to pretty things up. 'Looking at the bright side' or giving Him the 'benefit of the doubt' proved to be impossible considering what I knew.

I knew He had been told about everything that was going on in the community and that it had been His express desire for certain actions to be taken. During those moments, as He denied things and blamed others, I can still feel myself drowning in utter disbelief and righteous outrage. This was quickly followed by waves of powerlessness, unable to do anything about what He was saying to the media.

I had an overwhelming desire to stand up amongst thousands of others and scream that He lied. Tosh's hand on my arm and the sudden acute awareness of the armed Peace Force surrounding us stopped me. I felt desperately critical of myself, that I was a coward for not standing up for the truth despite the guns. While a lifetime of events had led up to this moment in time, it was this one powerful experience that shook my belief framework to its very foundation.

My belief was that a spiritual person, a holy leader, could not lie, could not blame others. And me, I had not stood up for the truth that I knew, making me a hypocrite and a coward. Definitely not who I thought I was. And if He was a charlatan, I had been deceived. That put me at fault for believing in Him. It made my decisions to place my desire for spiritual fulfillment first in this lifetime erroneous and sadly misguided.

Had I wasted my life? Were my values misplaced and should I have gone for the white picket fence life of pretense of security, instead? Really? Were the masses of society correct in going for the status quo? Was I the rash one for following my heart and wanting to know 'what the love was really?' Was I too idealistic as my father had warned me?

During this time with the boat, which felt like a spiritual vacuum, the natural beauty of Hawaii, the gentle climate and the warm seas were medicine for my broken soul. The *Elixir*

Project provided the mental and physical stabilization necessary for integration. I was finding my way through feelings of failure and self-loathing.

And what did I come to realize and embrace? Whether it was my youth in combination with idealism or not, I had believed what I thought was important and true and, of course, I was invincible. However, thinking that my spirituality would protect me from the nature of this material world was a mistake.

I came down off my high horse and realized that we eat, sleep, fornicate, defecate and then we die. I realized that everything is in a constant state of decay, or death. *Elixir* would look amazing and then three months later need to be refinished as the sun ate the varnish. No matter what the project, the boat, a house, a garden, a body, a mind—it all needs constant maintenance. Otherwise, it declines. This is the material plane and that is how it works here. Surrender.

I realized I had followed a spiritual master, and He had betrayed me in a way that I could not doubt. This gave me a push out of the nest and onto my own two feet. My reliance on a group was no longer appropriate for my growth. While I missed the 'Buddha-field' of the community, I needed to develop one inside myself. I needed to forge my sense of belonging in this world out of the failure of my previous desires to flee this world and create heaven on earth. I was forced to let go of a spiritual arrogance that persuaded me I was better than and beyond the rules of this place. Gratitude.

I realized the reason the masses don't follow the value system I have, is because it is hard. It is not for the faint of heart. Having crashed and burned a few times now, I still would not change my desire to know a deeper reality of what the love is, versus conforming to societal norms and values and a traditional material life bereft of any connection to the unseen, spiritual world.

I respect myself for my choices, and I respect others for theirs. My life is not a life I would wish on others. There is a price to pay, and for some reason I am willing to pay it. Not everyone is. And is it worth it? Yes, for me it is worth every tear and drop of sweat and blood. Is it a life different than the usual? Yes, and I am learning to be discerning and integrate into society where I can. And is that line between my value system and the value system of others black and white? No. I am discovering the places where they overlap and complement each other, and I know that things are never what they seem. Humility.

Afterword

We sailed through the San Juan Islands in the Pacific Northwest and settled on Saltspring Island, British Columbia, Canada. While living aboard, we built and worked in a dental practice there. *Elixir* entered the Wooden Boat Show in Victoria, B.C. and won Best Restoration in 1994. She was on the cover of *The Westcoast Mariner Magazine* in February 1996. We sold *Elixir* later that year to people in San Francisco, where she is currently working as a classic commercial charter vessel and sailing under the name *Aida*.

Anatomy of a Gaff-Rigged Schooner

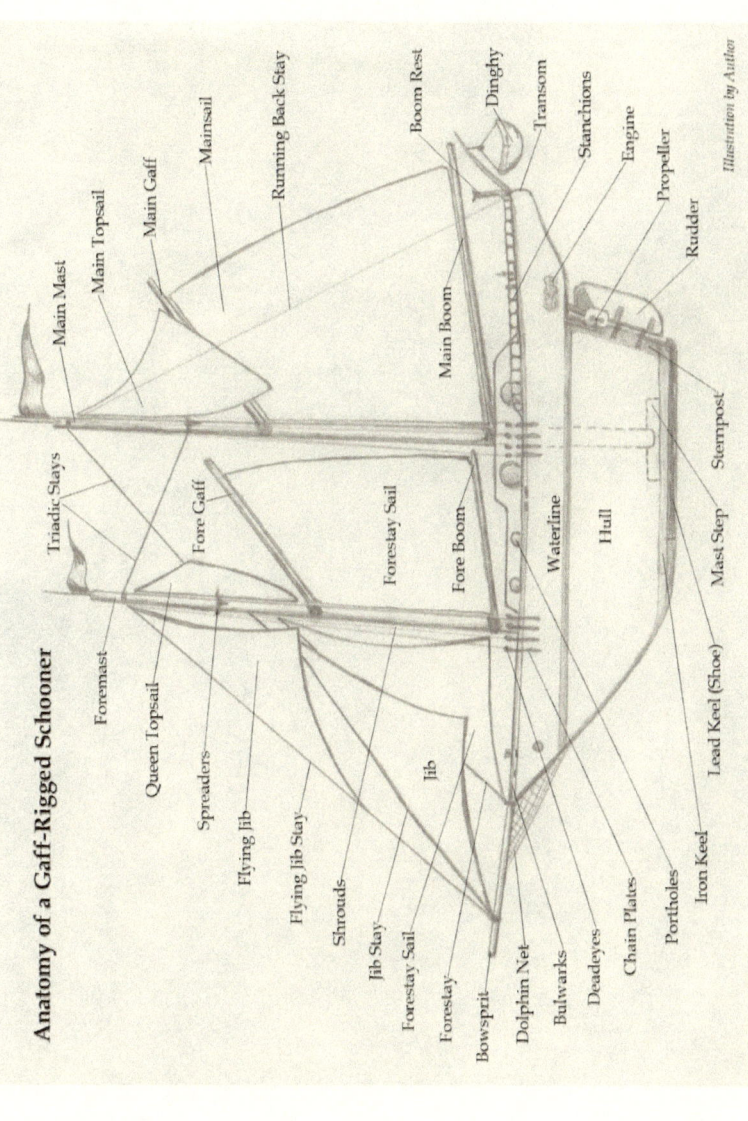

Main Mast
Main Topsail
Main Gaff
Mainsail
Running Back Stay
Boom Rest
Dinghy
Transom
Stanchions
Engine
Propeller
Rudder
Sternpost

Triadic Stays
Fore Gaff
Forestay Sail
Fore Boom
Main Boom
Waterline
Hull
Mast Step

Foremast
Queen Topsail
Spreaders
Flying Jib
Flying Jib Stay
Shrouds
Jib Stay
Forestay Sail
Forestay
Bowsprit
Dolphin Net
Bulwarks
Deadeyes
Chain Plates
Portholes
Iron Keel
Lead Keel (Shoe)

Jib

Illustration by Author

Glossary

AIDS: Despite not knowing a lot about the AIDS epidemic in the early 80s, Bhagwan was proactive with his disciples on the Ranch. We had protocols for preventing sexually transmitted diseases that included mandatory screening upon arriving at the Ranch and wearing an orange bead on your mala for the required two weeks until all tests had returned with negative results. Upon which time you went back to the medical center and restrung your mala minus the orange bead. This made it clear to all who were safe to interact with. When AIDS became known there were added rules, including always using a condom, wearing rubber gloves, and abstaining from oral and anal sex.

Beam shelf: The horizontal piece of wood running along the top inside edge of the planking, structural support as well as the beam the deck beams attach to.

Belaying pin: A solid metal or wooden device used

on traditionally rigged sailing vessels to secure lines of running rigging.

Blocks and tackle: Amplify the tension force in rope to lift heavy loads.

Boom gallows: Allows the boom to rest securely while at anchor. Refurbished with varnish and new leather, custom cut and attached with copper tacks.

Bulkheads: Upright wall within the hull for structural support as well as to separate the staterooms and head from the salon.

Cap rail: To bend it around the curve of the bulwarks, the caps were cut into three longitudinal strips. Initially, the middle section was pre-drilled, epoxied and fastened down with three inch silicone bronze screws. Then the outer and inner strips were sandwiched to the center strip using epoxy and temporarily held with C-clamps at twelve inch intervals. This particular job used a lot of clamps so we could only do a section of cap rail at a time. Our toolbox had twenty C-clamps and six bar clamps, all of which were utilized constantly over the years.

Chainplate: A metal plate used to fasten a shroud or stay to the hull of a sailboat. One end of the chain plate extends above the deck and holds the deadeye, which is connected to the shroud or stay, and the remainder of the chainplate normally has multiple holes that are bolted to the hull.

Deadeye: An item used in the standing and running rugging of traditional sailing ships. It is a smallish round thick wooden (usually lignum vitae) disc with one or more holes through it, perpendicular to the plane of the disc. Single and triple-hole deadeyes are most common.

Fiddles: Fiddles are small railings that keep things from sliding off shelves, counters and tables when the boat is underway.

Floors: Triangular pieces of wood that tie the frames together at the base of the hull. All thirty-five of them were completely replaced with showroom quality exotic wood and fastened with two twelve-inch galvanized drifts (metal threaded rods) and six galvanized frame bolts. Each floor was unique and scribed to match the curve of the hull.

Frame stringers: Are oriented parallel to the long axis of the hull and used in round hull shapes to add strength and stiffness.

Frames: Frames are ribs bolted or welded to the keel. Frames support the hull and give the ship its shape and strength. While some damaged components in the frames were completely replaced, often the rotten portion was excised and new wood inserted, epoxied, and clamped into position. All frame repairs were sistered with 3/4-inch marine plywood splints for additional strength. The replacement parts were faired using a long flexible fairing guide prior to painting and before refastening the planks in place.

Gaff jaw: A u-shaped piece of metal or wood that accommodates the pressure of the gaff on the mast, the jaw is between the mast and the stern end of the gaff. The gaff is the spar at the top of the main and foresails on a gaff-rigged vessel.

Gale: Winds of thirty-nine to fifty-four mph. Historically a strong gale is a nine on the Beaufort Wind Scale with a ten being a whole gale or a storm. Today the designations of seven, near gale, eight, and nine are the only categories used.

Guru: Spiritual Teacher.

Humaniversity: The name of the education center in the city of Rajneeshpuram. They offered courses in human development, meditation, and bodywork. Humaniversity is still operating today in various centers worldwide.

Leathering: Wire rigging was covered to preserve the wooden spars as well as protect the wire. The first step was to apply anhydrous lanolin to the sections of the wire that were to be covered. The second step was to parcel the wire with black cloth tape, from the bottom up with the lay of the wire. The third step was to serve the wire against the lay with a hardwood serving tool that Tosh had custom made. This meant wrapping eighth-inch black braided cotton twine firmly and consistently around the wire on top of the tape. The fourth step, leathering, was to wrap leather around the twine and stitch it firmly in place with a baseball stitch. The leather was ordered in bulk, strips measured, cut and hole-punched prior to placing on the rigging wire.

Lee cloth: A piece of canvas that acts like a safety net to keep a sailor in his or her bunk.

Mast collars or bands: Fit tightly around the mast and have eyes or lugs for attaching blocks.

Mast partner: The piece of wood where the mast goes through the deck on a keel stepped mast.

Mast Restoration: Upon arrival in Kauai, the masts were relocated to the boatyard and placed on well-padded sawhorses, up off the ground, in preparation for restoration. The remaining hardware and mast collars were removed and labeled. Multiple layers of peeling paint were sanded off to bare wood to assess where there was rot and separation. The masts were hollow spruce with long scarf joints that were mostly sound. Separated areas were repaired with new spruce wood and epoxy.

Mast steps: Solid chunks of yellow oak where the square end of the mast fits to rest on top of the keel. They were bolted into the floors beneath the cabin sole.

Peace Force: To incorporate Rajneeshpuram as a city, a city police force was required. In keeping with the overall philosophy of peace, it was agreed to have a police force, but it would be called the Peace Force. The officers were selected from the commune members and sent to Oregon's Police Academy for training. The professional training for police officers includes weapons training and certification from the state and is a requirement for all cities.

Reef: A way to make the sail smaller by folding the edge of the canvas or Dacron in on itself.

Running Rigging: The lines (ropes) on a sailing vessel that are used for raising, lowering, shaping, and controlling the sails, as opposed to the standing rigging, which supports the masts and bowsprit. Most of the lines were original with their ends re-spliced and finished. They were threaded using the bosun's chair after raising the masts.

Sail Restoration: As time presented itself, I would drag a sail onto the clean concrete of the driveway and scrub it on both sides with soap, Biz Bleach, and Whink Rust Stain Remover. After rinsing with the garden hose and drying in the sun, they looked and smelled redeemable. Oxidation on the head, tack and clew grommets was removed with a wire brush and Emory paper. Leather reinforcing was repaired or replaced, and bolt ropes were re-stitched by hand using a marlin spike to pull the stitches tight. Patches were sewn with a heavy-duty sewing machine where the sails were worn. Lastly, a new bag was sewn for each sail.

Sannyasin: A Sanskrit word that describes someone who has renounced material possessions and emotional ties. Their purpose is to perfect their understanding of the spiritual world and leads to final liberation from the cycle of death and rebirth. It is the final stage of spiritual practice where they can devote themselves wholly to the pursuit of the spiritual understanding that comes from meditation.

Shakedown: A trial journey undergone by a ship and its crew before being declared operational.

Sole: Cabin floor.

Spreaders: Spars on the mast of a sailboat that deflect the shrouds for more mast support.

Stem: The stem is the curved edge stretching from the keel below, up to the gunwale of the boat. It is part of the physical structure of a wooden boat or ship that gives it strength at the critical section of the structure, bringing together the port and starboard side planks of the hull.
Tosh had transferred the shape of the original stem onto a laminated block of rosewood using paper tracings. The scarfs, or grooves, where the planks attached were carved into the wood by hand with sharp chisels and the forward edge shaped with rasps and sanders. The outer stem was bolted through to the stem knee with 5/8ths-inch galvanized hex bolts coated in boatyard bedding compound.

Stepping the masts (Rigging): The masts were loaded with the standing rigging, first the shrouds, then the fore and aft stays. The back stays were a combination of wire, block and tackle, and line. The mast collars had chocks on them for the way the rigging could hang and there was only one way it could hang properly.

The wires and lines were arranged to come off the mast in the fairest configuration to prevent chafing between the rigging and sails. After rigging the mast head, the stays, shrouds and lines were carefully arranged and temporarily secured along the length of the mast to prevent snarling as the masts were hoisted with the crane.

Stern: This piece was scribed off the old stern timbers. The inner timber was reconditioned and through-bolted to new laminated outer pieces.

Sternpost: The upright post at the back of a wooden boat where the transoms are attached at the rearmost part of the stern.

Tacking: Sailing term for turning the bow of the vessel into and through the wind so the wind changes from one side of the vessel to the other.

End Notes

1. You Tube: Netflix India. Top 5 savage moments of Ma Anand Sheela / Wild Wild Country. June 26, 2019. Video. 0.57. https://www.youtube.com/watch?v=XbKDLqejBqY.

2. *Eddystone Light* (English folk song)
http://www.traditionalmusic.co.uk/sea-songs-shanties/me-father-was-the-keeper-of-the-eddystone-light.htm 12/9/17.

3. "Chickens" Sung by Harry Belafonte. Produced by Bob Bollard. Writers Charles Carl Carter & Fred Hellerman. RCA Release date 1960.

Acknowledgments

I kept notes and photos throughout the years of the boat project, but the idea for a book was nebulous until my neighbor, Pat Reed, met me on a beach one day and started asking questions. The opening, Gale, is the result of a paragraph I wrote that night in 2009. Thank you, Pat, for encouraging me to "just start anywhere."

By 2016, I had decided it would be a coffee table book of photos and had several chapters compiled. I attended a class with San Diego Writers Ink, the local writer's guild, on how to publish a book with Helen Chang. We met a few days later, and I showed her my draft. After listening patiently, she finally asked the defining question: is this a picture book? Or is there a story here? Taken aback, I had to answer that there was a story. She smiled, diagramed the Hero's Journey on a napkin, and referred me to Marni Freedman's memoir class. Thank you, Helen.

In memoir class, I learned even more about myself than I did about plot points, character arcs, and dialogue. Thank you, Marni, for being a dynamic teacher, for sharing your writing acumen, reading several drafts, and gently nudging me in the right direction.

Thank you, Tracy Jones, for all the years of coaching read and critique sessions, going over chapter after chapter, year after year. This book would not have been written without your insightful, and constant, inspiration.

Thank you to all my read and critique partners including Laura Engel, Kathleen McCabe, Franciene Lehmann, Jennifer Gasner, Stephanie Weaver, Katya McLane, Kenny Sucher, Suzi Gold, Lauren Cross, Saadia Esmail, and Leslie Ferguson. You gradually coaxed more of the story out of me, even the hard places where I would never have gone without your compassionate encouragement.

Thank you to Michele Goane for your beautiful photography and for holding my hand through website construction and the social media labyrinth.

Thank you to Holly Kammier and Jessica Therrien of Acorn Press for their confidence in this book and Nico and his team, for guiding me through the publishing process.

Thank you to my colleagues at Southwestern College for supporting me and answering polling questions about titles and cover designs, and the team at Coronado Dental Associates for being positive and encouraging throughout the years of writing in my after-work hours.

A huge thank you to my girlfriends and readers: Teddy Charles, Alison St John Inglis, Sami Longo-Disse. You were my sounding boards along the way and held my hand when I was sure I was falling.

To my family, you are an inseparable part of everything. Thank you to my sister, Colleen Smienk, and to my mom, Doreen Monty, for always believing in me during tumultuous times and throughout my writing journey. And to my brothers and sisters-in-law: Dean and Val Monty and Aaron and Lola Monty, the beach visits and phone calls remind me of all we share. Thank you, Dad, you taught me to keep, and value, a travel log during our family trips in a converted school bus.

Thank you, Nicole, for hanging in there with us throughout it all. I have always felt your passion for keeping us together and celebrating. Thank you, Gavin, for enjoying the ride almost every step of the way. Your unshakeable belief in yourself has been a source of pride, and inspiration to me. The almost daily pep talks gave me the momentum to leap off the cliff into publication. And thank you dear Tosh, for sharing your powerful visions and letting me tag along to share the adventures.

Lastly, I am grateful for this life and the opportunities I have had. I am grateful for finding the courage to jump into adventures despite resistance and fear. And I am grateful for all the people I was able to share precious moments of this journey with along the way.

About the Author

Deborah Rudell lives in San Diego where she is a college professor as well as part of a vibrant writing community focused on telling profound stories. She is a graduate of a Hay House Writers Conference and Marni Freedman's Memoir Certificate Program. An active member of San Diego Writers, Ink, and San Diego Memoir Association, she is published in their anthology, *Shaking the Tree Vol III*, after a competitive submission and selection process. This is Deborah Rudell's first book.

www.ingramcontent.com/pod-product-compliance
Lightning Source LLC
Chambersburg PA
CBHW021659120626
46545CB00004B/1314